Praise for *Social*

Marshall has long been my "go-to" guy for the most vexing questions in social media measurement. Social media analytics is one of the most important areas of our industry, with a growing number of vendors and tools. Marshall's knowledge of the players and the landscape is second to none.

—*Stephanie Agresta, EVP, Managing Director of Social Media, Weber Shandwick*

Marshall has a naturally curious mind that often unearths innovative solutions. He also has a way with words that explains how he did what he just did. It's a fascinating combination

—*Luke Brynley-Jones,* Our Social Times

You can't manage what you can't measure. Social media is a loosely defined category of interactive Web sites within the boundaries of netspace. Its numbers are legion, and the experts who say they can tell you what they are about are equally legion. Marshall Sponder stands apart from the crowd with this work. Marshall has managed to cut through the hype and provide a common-sense roadmap to understanding the potential of this genre. His case study approach, borne of real-world experience, provides the expert and the amateur alike with bibliography, tools, links, and examples to shortcut the path to bedrock successes. This is a reference work for anyone who wants to explore the potential of social networks. With the help of this book, you can measure what you need to manage.

—*W. Reid Cornwell, Ph.D., Chief Scientist, The Center for Internet Research*

It's not enough just to listen to or monitor online voices anymore. The challenge of separating the influential signals from noise in the cacophony of voices across social and online communities is too hard to do manually or with traditional monitoring tools. Sponder's book makes compelling arguments for why listening intelligence matters and why marketing forevermore is becoming a blur of science and art, with measurement, analytics, and marketing intelligence having an increasingly critical role within the CMO's suite and boardroom.

—*Gary Lee, CEO, mBLAST*

The gap between data and usable information in social media measurement is still quite wide. Many listening platforms and tools attempt to cover that distance, yet come up short. In *Social Media Analytics*, industry veteran analyst Marshall Sponder effectively bridges that gap and provides useful material to build the skills and understanding you need to extract value and measure the results of your programs.

—*Valeria Maltoni, Author,* Conversation Agent

Marshall is one of the world's top social media practitioners and thinkers. In this book he accomplishes the rare task of delivering practical advice on social media analytics without getting bogged down in theory. A tour de force!

—*Sebastian Wenzel, Webanalyticsbook.com*

Social media led to a real earthquake in my business, public relations. It also made millions of people start dealing with public communications without even knowing how to do it or what the rules are. And last, but not least, in social media now, when there are more questions than answers. And none of them has provided any answers except for Marshall Sponder. Read this book and keep it next to your desk or on the front page of your Kindle, and you will know the answers too.

—*Maxim Behar, CEO, M3 Communications Group, Inc.,*
a Hill & Knowlton Associate

Social media has mushroomed to encompass more than a billion people worldwide which leads to a very difficult and interesting question—how to measure market effectiveness (analytics) of this medium? Marshall has done an excellent job in describing the tools and metrics used by various real world companies to measure the analytics of social media. This book is a must read for a digital marketing professional who plans to maximize marketing ROI in social media space.

—*Dr. Ash Pahwa, CEO, A+ Web Services*

Social Media Analytics is a thoughtful exploration into the evolving landscape of multi-channel social marketing and how to gauge campaign effectiveness and ROI. As social media technologies become more of a pervasive part of consumer's lives, techniques presented in this book become invaluable in allowing electronic marketers to master this new medium.

—*Jared Freedman President, Code4Software & Code4Mobile*

Marshall's book helps you cut through the hype of social media to develop a step-by-step plan for identifying the right targets, the right tactics, and then collecting and interpreting the right data. He goes just beyond the normal monitoring recommendations into detail on collecting, understanding, and measuring the illusive ROI that has been missing from most social media books. Marshall uses his industry knowledge and practitioner experience to provide thought-provoking insights, vendor examples, case studies, and actionable advice for chasing the elusive social ROI.

—Bill Hunt, CEO, BackAzimuth Consulting;
Coauthor, Search Engine Marketing Inc.

Bouncing off boardroom walls across America is the mostly vacuous question, "What's the ROI of social media?" Marshall Sponder adds a necessary context to the question, mixes in a healthy dose of streetwise practicality, and delivers a thorough work to help executives answer the question they really meant to ask: How will we uncover, recognize, and utilize the value of emerging media? Though the ROI question seems intelligent, it hides a consuming fear of impending insignificance. Sponder's *Social Media Analytics* will help address the public question of return and give decision makers the peace of mind they seek before plunging into social media. I especially appreciate Marshall's focus on the value of real-life, human analysts and his unique exploration of the intersection of point-of-sale and social media (there's hidden treasure in those pages!).

—Trey Pennington, International Speaker

In *Social Media Analytics,* Marshall Sponder brilliantly describes the challenges, benefits, and thrill associated with understanding true customer behavior. By melding client case studies with actual data-driven tactics, Mr. Sponder provides the aspiring analytics expert with the tools necessary to be successful. He reviews successful activities at real companies, he interviews thought leaders who are truly in the trenches, and he provides a comprehensive outline of available resources and the analytical approaches they require. This book goes so far beyond the "I have 20,000 followers, I am successful" mind-set that is so common in social media today. Buy this book, and be prepared to leverage social media in a profitable, actionable, and credible manner.

—Kevin Hillstrom, President of MineThatData

Social analytics in 2011 remains a nascent capability, and this is reflected in my wholehearted endorsement of this book despite our different approaches to influence and ROI. Let's get this straight—there is no better independent authority on the tools and techniques of social analytics than Marshall Sponder, and ignoring this book is akin to ignoring your market.

—*Philip Sheldrake. Founding Partner, Meanwhile; Author,* The Business of Influence: Reframing Marketing and PR for the Digital Age, *April 2011*

Those working in social media, executives, agencies, consultants, take notice! Marshall Sponder has his finger on the pulse of the future of social media ... measurement and ROI. *Social Media Analytics* uses case studies, interviews, and multicultural campaigns to answer these questions: What's the value of a fan? What tools are needed to invest? How should influence and ROI be measured? A must read!

—*Dr. Ira Kaufman, Visiting Professor of Marketing, Lynchburg College and President of Entwine Digital*

Marshall Spenders' book, *Social Media Analytics,* is a must read for anyone who is tasked to make or support corporate decisions on product development, placement, marketing campaigns, public relations initiatives, or investor relation communication decisions, just to mention a few. This book gives meaningful insights, hands-on examples, well-researched information, and sources to the reader in a way that is easily understood and can be imminently and effectively applied. Marshall Sponder provides valuable insights and clearly communicates the meaning, value, and importance of social media analytics in today's corporate global environment and covers existing challenges such as commercializing/reacting to public opinion. This book is a must-have and an invaluable resource to anyone who needs to know!

—*Henri-Pierre Hirts, Interim Sr. Manager CEO, COO, and Consultant for Various International Companies*

Marshall takes the reader through the elusive question of how you can measure your social media marketing efforts. For those who are results-driven and -oriented, this is the book that will answer your questions on the ROI of social media.

—*Tamar Weinberg, social media strategist for www.techipedia.com and author of* The New Community Rules

SOCIAL MEDIA ANALYTICS

EFFECTIVE TOOLS FOR BUILDING, INTERPRETING, AND USING METRICS

MARSHALL SPONDER

New York   Chicago   San Francisco   Lisbon   London
Madrid   Mexico City   Milan   New Delhi   San Juan
Seoul   Singapore   Sydney   Toronto

1 2 3 4 5 6 7 8 9 0   LPI/LPI   1 9 8 7 6 5 4 3

ISBN   978-0-07-182449-1
MHID   0-07-182449-9

This publication is designed to provide accurate and authoritative information in regard to the subject matter covered. It is sold with the understanding that neither the author nor the publisher is engaged in rendering legal, accounting, or other professional service. If legal advice or other expert assistance is required, the services of a competent professional person should be sought.

—*From a Declaration of Principles Jointly Adopted*
by a Committee of the American Bar Association
and a Committee of Publishers and Association

McGraw-Hill Education books are available at special quantity discounts to use as premiums and sales promotions or for use in corporate training programs. To contact a representative, please visit the Contact Us pages at www.mhprofessional.com.

I dedicate this book to the emerging field of
Social Media Analytics and Social Media Metrics

CONTENTS

FOREWORD

I'm astonished at how much marketing has evolved in just the last 25 years.

We've lived in the era of "shout marketing," where effective marketing meant shouting ever louder on television or radio, in magazines and their ilk. Then the Web came along and brought with it "hyper relevant marketing." Now we could use delightful behavior signals (a search query, content on the page, and more) to show a highly relevant ad. Right under our feet, which are slowly giving way to "conversational marketing," where the ability to influence people is being powered by a brand's ability to participate in, and initiate, meaningful conversations with current and prospective customers.

It is tremendously exciting, and scary.

Partly because we live in a world of "and" and not in a world of "or." At least for now, you can't kill your entire TV budget, or your Bing budget, or your AOL display ads. It has to be TV and Bing and display ads, and now, Facebook and Twitter, and the next cool thing on the horizon. Partly because it is exceedingly hard to know what success looks like in the world of conversational marketing and how to measure it.

That is where Marshall's delightful book comes in.

In 12 breezy chapters, Marshall takes you from zero to ninety m.p.h. and covers every aspect of the social media space. Starting with identifying the watering holes your customers visit, taking action based on valuable content, the ins and outs of identifying the relevant data, and lovingly dissecting it all to separate the wheat from the chaff and to find the real gold. OK, I might be stretching the metaphor a bit, but I am sure you catch my drift.

You'll be a lot less scared of all the "social stuff" by the end of this book, and on behalf of your company, you'll craft an amazing social media strategy that will exponentially improve the value of your brand.

Allow me to close with a rule that I'd first postulated almost seven years ago. It's called the 10/90 rule. It states, simply, that if you would like to invest $100 in making smart decisions, then invest $10 in tools and invest $90 in smart brains.

We live in a world that is evolving and changing at an alarming rate (hurray!). We are surrounded by a raft of fantastic free tools and a number of very good paid tools. In the end, unlike in ancient times, having the most expensive tool will not determine your success, but having the right people in charge of your social analytics strategy will. People matter because they'll understand your business, they'll understand the ecosystem, they'll understand other people, and they'll think smart and move fast to ensure that the glory you deserve is delivered to you. So invest your budgets appropriately.

Good luck, and happy analytics!

Avinash Kaushik
Author: *Web Analytics 2.0* and
Web Analytics: An Hour a Day
Blog: http://www.kaushik.net/avinash

PREFACE

We are entering a world where technology and marketing converge. How our ideas are executed has become more important than what they are, and the medium has become the message. Perhaps nowhere is the latter more true than in the realm of social media analytics.

The technologies and methods put in place to communicate directly shape results, in terms of both cost and marketing effectiveness. In Chapter 8, Gary Angel, CTO of Semphonic, shared his view that the tools used drive the data we get from social media analytics and shape the results we are able to achieve. Make the wrong choice and the costs dramatically multiply, leading to failure or, at best, to partial success. Choose the right technologies and the work of sifting though social media is made much easier, more economical, useful, and enjoyable.

Despite all the information on what social media analytics is capable of, there is so much misinformation, fragmentation, and confusion within the marketplace today that it is very difficult to know how to choose the right platforms and how to set up the right processes to achieve our goals.

Another book needed to be written in order to make sense of it all.

Social Media Analytics is for anyone who seeks the right technologies to implement social listening and measurement programs. As a larger part of our lives have become ruled by social media, we need to know what these platforms are capable of and how to use them effectively to achieve our goals.

I wrote this book to share with my readers choices they should be aware of, but I stayed away from advising which platforms to pick (just as, during the first Gulf War, the coalition forces marched right up to Baghdad, and then stopped).

Technology shapes meaning, the medium becoming the message, and it reminds me of what Marshall McLuhan wrote 47 years ago in his famous book *Understanding Media: The Extensions of Man*. As a matter of fact, the first edition of McLuhan's *Understanding Media* was published by McGraw Hill, as is this book.

So many unpredictable things are happening in the world right now (what futurists would call "wild cards") that I think it's extremely hard to anticipate what is going to happen next, and this applies to the subject of the book.

As we grapple with communicating the effectiveness of social media, *Social Media Analytics* has become the medium through which relevant data and insights are being conveyed to decision makers and stakeholders. As with any medium, according to Marshall McLuhan, the message has changed, and the implications of that change are profound. The way we successfully communicate information about social media and business is through the artful use of the tools and platforms needed to monitor and measure the information, and the nature of the people who run those applications.

Information culled from online social listening data is crucial for many businesses and organizations both large and small, profit and nonprofit. As marketing and communications professionals use social media for outreach, customer relations, branding, and crisis management, the success of these efforts is being shaped by analysts who (hopefully) possess an understanding of the businesses they are monitoring.

I believe that analysts are the best suited of all to conceive, implement, and deliver this information to clients, stakeholders, and management. As you read this book, the reasons will become clear. This change in the messaging and deliverables is having a radical impact on the future of many fields, including public relations and marketing, which were hitherto dominated by content messaging, business development, ideas people, and spin. Social media analytics is now beginning to reach the boardroom. Agencies are increasingly refraining from reporting that which they too often do not understand, or from which they feel unable to get anything useful.

In February 2011, Paul Holmes, the originator of the Holmes Report and SABRE Awards, and I debated at the keynote presentation for the On the Top Conference in Davos, Switzerland. At this conference, Holmes said PR was going to take over marketing, and I was supposed to argue the reverse—that marketing would take over PR. Instead, I said that analytics would take over both.

As a result, somewhat convinced, Paul Holmes wrote a post at his blog (blog.holmesreport.com) titled, "Does Your Agency Need a Chief Analytics Officer?" Holmes agreed that PR people needed to understand analytics better, in order to make it a much more robust element in both their planning and their evaluation, and that, in two or three years from now, every public relations firm that wants to be taken seriously in the C-suite and/or to play a lead marketing role will have a chief analytics officer in its senior leadership ranks.

I think Holmes was right in what he said in Davos. When you finish reading this book, you will be much closer to knowing what your own position is and understanding how to make sense of the technology, methodology, and platform choices before us.

Marshall Sponder
Brooklyn, NY

ACKNOWLEDGMENTS

This book is too big to thank *any one person* for it's preparation, but I'd like to thank many people who helped me, usually found by browsing my Facebook and Skype friends (in no particular order, so as be fair to everyone) including my close friends, coworkers, and analytics subject area experts, including JoAnn Lefebvre, Leticia Colon, Cecilia Pineda Feret, Baraka Zahabian, Dean Landsman, Barry Flemming, Israel Mirsky, Stephanie Agresta, Rob Key, Stuart Levinson, Alexis Bizares, Mark Bennett, Philip Sheldrake, Giles Palmer, Luke Brynley-Jones, Murray Newlands, Simon McDermott, Gary Vaynerchuk, Loic Moisand, Michelle Chmielewski, Sebastian Wenzel, Dennis Mortensen, K. D. Paine, Lawrence Wintermeyer, Aleksander Stensby, Neil Scaife, Danny Dearlove, Elena Haliczer, Gianandrea Facchini, Valeria Maltoni, Gary Lee, Nathan Gilliatt, Drew Knapp, Richard Newton, Stuart Tracte, Trey Pennington, Jim Reynolds, Dennis Yu, Jennifer Needly, Gary Angel, Jim Sterne, Gail Gardner, Matthew Snodgrass, Bob Pearson, Jim Wiess, Paul Dyer, Jakub Hrabovsky, Kris Waldherr, Thomas Ross Miller, Alexa Scordato, Amber Naslund, Cory Hartlen, Amy Crehore, Avinash Kaushik, Bryan Eisenberg, Bill Hunt, Chase McMichael, Danielle Culmone Simon, Dani Horowitz, Charlie Oliver, Jeremy Merrin, Connie Bensen, David Meermen Scott, Dean Myers, Ingrid Saxon, Greg Verdino, Jayanth Vasudevan, Josh MacKey, Joseph Franklyn McElroy, Donna McElroy, Justin Kistner, Michael Demby, Paul Barron, Rebecca Lieb, Sara Holoubek, Stephanie Schwab, Valentina Atanasova, Warren Sukernek, Keith Woods-Holder, Sam Phillips, Sabrina Merchant, Drew Fortin, Eric Austrew, Karen Costa, Aaron C. Newman, Michael Hussey, Curtis Hogland, Pedro Leboy. Still, I probably left out a lot of people who helped me, and there's no way to acknowledge all of them, but I hope by to honor them all with the best book I could write.

I also want to give a special thanks to my agent, Dean Landsman, for helping me create strategies to tackle writing *Social Media Analytics* and keep me focused throughout this process, plus my editor at McGraw-Hill, Donya Dickerson, who believed in me enough to help make this book happen. Also, a heartly thanks to Julia Baxter at McGraw-Hill for helping to promote the book. Finally, special thanks to JoAnn Lefebvre of Shift2InBound Marketing for helping with my overall Web site messaging, and the city of Providence, where much of this book was written.

Last, but not least, I want thank my family, Ilona Grochalska and Adam Sponder, for bearing with me while I was creating this book.

chapter <u>1</u>

The Conundrum of Social Media: Where's the ROI?

The average social media campaign requires between three months and a year to show results.[1] What kind of numbers can be derived from social media to show if a campaign is successful? How much information is sufficient on which to base future strategy? These questions, among others, are those that users of social media want answered.

If Starbucks were to offer a $5 coupon to everyone on Twitter, it would likely get a great response—but how valuable would it be in the long run? Would such a campaign ultimately increase customer loyalty or drive long-term sales? When we need benchmarks to evaluate return on investment (ROI) effectiveness, marketing professionals first should determine the duration of a campaign and what milestones or standards they want to reach.

In 2004, vendors began developing and offering social media analytics platforms and providing data-crunching reports. As a matter of fact, the first recorded use of the term *social media* occurred in 2004, according to Merriam-

Webster's Online Dictionary. (More reporting and analytics platforms have been appearing, almost daily.) Although these platforms were expressions of data collection through a variety of lenses, at that time, no industrywide accepted standards and practices had emerged.

With so many advances rapidly taking place, including the promise of merging disparate data (including site analytics, search traffic, geolocal check-ins—à la Foursquare, Facebook Places, and Gowalla—along with customer data, such as e-mail and receipts), it appeared that market researchers and analysts would be better able to understand customer behavior stemming from social media, and businesses would be able to act on that behavior in real time or soon after, with actionable responses to the results of analytics.

Through my own research, I observed a 400 percent increase in searches on "social media" in search engines and in social media monitoring tools (such as Alterian Techrigy SM2[2]) took place in the third quarter of 2009. This increase in social media mentions may have been a direct result of Google's inclusion of Twitter and Facebook updates in search results. This news indicates a fuller and accelerated integration of search engines and social media for the foreseeable future.

In 2010, the social media analytics ROI discussion turned red hot. At the time of this writing, there were at least 8 books on the topic of social media ROI available on Amazon.com and 16 on social media analytics. What are known as social listening platforms are the collection and analysis of online mentions in Facebook and Twitter, geolocal check-ins, photo-sharing sites, blogs, message boards, forums, and online commentary from mainstream media produced by readers as well as music-sharing sites such as Last.fm and Pandora. However, there is still so much difference between the benefits and costs of social listening and information on what the platforms and tools actually can provide that there is clearly room for at least one more book—one that can provide an authoritative voice for the analyst and analytics.

Nobody has talked about the subject seriously and in sufficient depth to make enough of an impact. In the following pages, I share my own opinions regarding how analysts performing social listening tasks are regarded, how much time reports should take to create and develop, and additional costs associated with producing actionable data.

Many people have read my WebMetricsGuru.com blog over the past six years and can vouch for the fact that I know social media, search, and Web analytics quite well. It's gratifying that I'm considered by the industry to be a practitioner, a hands-on analyst, and an expert in the field. I am not a journalist or conference promoter; what I write about is the very work I'm involved in and have pondered over deeply for several years. Furthermore, if I have not been involved in something personally, I almost always know people who have been, and I've wrung the salt out of their wisdom at conferences, bars, and tweetups. I'm also close friends with many of the leaders in this field, many of whom have contributed to this book case studies and various insights you will encounter in the following pages. I'm fortunate to be in a position to see the social media metrics industry in a holistic way. As a result, I've created my own view based on personal experiences that I provide to the industry as a whole and to my readers in particular in this book.

Analytics Platforms and Their Users

The language of listening platforms has well surpassed the level of typical business users' normal vocabulary. By using arcane words that almost no one who runs a business is familiar with, the platform providers have implemented reporting and analytics that are failing to directly inform most businesses.

The disparity between vocabularies was created partly by design; using cutting-edge technology based on search engine crawling was an experiment, and companies mining Web data—getting their hands dirty, so to speak—were exploring how to gather information and what to do with it. Companies such as Collective Intellect and Brandwatch were pushing the edge of what was possible in 2004 to 2005, when the industry was first born.

The average business user, ageny owner, or stakeholder lacked (and still lacks) the understanding, patience, or sophistication to utilize these listening platforms effectively. As a result, these people hire analysts to access the platforms for them and to provide reporting data and dashboards. Dashboards are reports that give users a high-level snapshot of how their campaigns and business initiatives are performing online. Dashboards can be quickly viewed or shared. Now it seems as though analysts need to be experts on the businesses and industries they are monitoring in order to do effective listening by supplying the necessary context and perspective that are still too complex to program into a listening platform. This is similar to the way financial industry analysts or hedge fund managers need to understand the businesses they are reporting on, investing in, trading on, and profiting from in order to be effective as analysts.

However, the model of analyst as business expert is directly at odds with the current staffing practices at many types of agencies covering the spectrum of marketing, public relations, communications, and even large and medium lines of business that have not yet understood the best applications of the technologies being employed, or what they lack.

Using a group of interchangeable analysts, shifting them across reports, and thereby making analytics a "report factory" is an example of a common practice based on a fundamental misunderstanding of how effective listening and analytics work, and it is a poor way to perform actionable reporting or analysis. In this book I delve into why and how the current practice should be turned around by explaining how listening systems actually work.

All indications are that within the next couple of years, business models and listening platforms will mature, eventually converge, and then become integrated. This is yet another reason why it is the right time for a focused look at social media analytics.

The ROI Dilemma

Social listening platforms have recently begun to come up with ROI calculations and dashboards designed to meet the needs of business users who want this level of reporting. Without the ability to accurately measure social media, however, it's hard to see how accurate ROI calculations can be done well. While many people may be willing to settle for "good enough" measures and estimates of the value of a tweet or Facebook fan or friend, in the coming years businesses will desire more than "good enough" proxies for, doing calculations of ROI. They will want, and are even now asking for the hard numbers with all the data, much like a financial statement.

As you will read in later chapters, point of sale systems, commonly termed POS systems, will become ever more relied upon to capture social media transactions directly to cash registers. It makes perfect sense that the cash register be enabled for social media, especially because all the technology to make that happen is already here.

In the Apple store, there are no cash registers, and all transactions are done from iPhones and iPods with specially equipped POS system devices; we will be seeing more businesses moving over to mobile POS systems, and those systems will increasingly interface with social data, allowing for more accurate and actionable ROI reporting.

The social media listening platform Marketwire Sysomos created a program called Sysomos Audience, which is designed to match visitors to Web sites a business cares about (such as competitors or other interesting outlets) and then to score those data in the form of visitor value (in currency). This information can help business owners decide where to spend their marketing budgets and where to focus their social media outreach.

Sysomos Audience is an attempt to merge Web and social media data to produce superior ROI metrics—the kind that, up until now, we have not had in social media—and when available data are merged intelligently, patterns will emerge that would otherwise have remained invisible. Once all the necessary data are assembled and defined in a lexicon a business owner can relate to, the data become actionable.

Case Study: Lithium and Vistaprint

According to Erin Korogodsky, senior account manager at Lithium, a leading provider of social CRM and social listening: "The world's most innovative companies, such as AT&T, Barnes & Noble, Best Buy, Sephora, Univision, and HP, are using Lithium to engage their customers in breathtaking new ways. This company is increasing revenue, reducing expenses, and understanding and strengthening their brand's presence in the social Web. Most importantly, they're building a lasting competitive asset with their customers.

Lithium's social media monitoring platform is easy to configure, works in real time, and finds the best content from millions of social media sources. Lithium is helping hundreds of companies get a grasp on their presence in the social Web and what their customers are talking about, how often and how happy they are."

Customer Analytics Builds Stronger Customer Relationships

Just over two years ago, Vistaprint, the incredibly popular low-volume on-demand printing company, was facing the same issue as thousands of other companies: what does this social media explosion mean for us, and how do we harness it? After the classic starting point of a business magazine being thrown across the conference table accompanied by an edict to "work out this social media thing," the Vistaprint social team, headed by Jeff Esposito, has, in only over one year, gone from having a zero social footprint to owning a mature engagement process and a deep understanding of its social audience and how to turn that knowledge into measurable results.

Starting from scratch, Vistaprint defined what its social model would be, how best to engage its nine million customers, and how to quantify the dollar impact these actions would have on its business.

This activity is carried out using a version of Lithium's social media monitoring platform configured to track online mentions and conversations around Vistaprint business card products and services in order to measure all Twitter, Facebook, blog, and other social activity, giving Vistaprint a live window into the social Web. The insights are then combined with transaction data from Vistaprint's own e-commerce platform giving Jeff Esposito and the Vistaprint team unparalleled insight into the real monetary value of a tweet or other such user-generated social Web interaction and its direct financial value to Vistaprint.

Social Media Enablement Audit

Although social media ROI is hard to track and most businesses are just beginning to realize the level of investment in analytics required for the necessary tracking, the business climate and analytics platforms are maturing. One of the goals of this book is to map the landscape of the playing field for social media analytics and to help business owners and organizations decide how and what they should invest in. With the rapid increase of mobile technology and geolocation, much more data and the insights derived from them need to be collected, processed, and understood so a business owner can act on the information.

In August 2010, Facebook Places[3] appeared. This occurred shortly after Google Places was introduced under its new name. Both services are quickly evolving, with a goal to marry the details of local foot traffic with retail outlets and local events. To then add more information would likely lead to an ROI by providing businesses with real-time data on where their customers are and what they are doing. This is akin to how site analytics JavaScript tagging enabled similar information to be captured on Web sites. Now, more and more of the 600 million plus Facebook members are "checking in"—which is a way to let other members know where you are.

According to Hubspot's Kipp Bodnar, "If you are a marketer, Facebook Places demonstrates location-based social networks are transforming from a trend into a mainstream feature of social networking."[4]

Also, a new feature was added to Facebook allowing business owners to check in the same way users and customers do. This method will make it easier to show social media ROI because mobile devices, geolocation, quick response (QR) codes (a form of mobile bar code), and point of sale systems are rapidly becoming instrumented to keep track of social media outreach. When a customer checks into a location, the opportunity to engage with the customer directly increases satisfaction and loyalty; it also provides actionable information for social media analytics and can feed directly into ROI calculations that businesses often seek to measure.

The rapid increase in QR codes extends the concept of monitoring social media campaigns into the three-dimensional world, much as webpages have been monitored for several years using Web analytics from such platforms as Google Analytics, WebTrends, and Adobe Site Catalyst.

Havana Central

The New York City–based restaurant Havana Central[5] conducted a series of social media analytics projects in 2010 with Cecilia Pineda Feret, the community manager, who managed social media outreach for the restaurant chain. With the results, we collaborated with Compete.com to create a white paper and webinar on how to find ultraviolet data to show social media ROI as a result of community outreach and other marketing campaign initiatives that can be tracked all the way to the cash register.[6] "Ultraviolet," in this context, refers to data that are often not being tracked for business value and can be uncovered and made trackable (thereby adding business value to the data a business already has) by using an audit process I devised to identify and enable the missing analytics tracking.

An issue that sometimes arises in discussions regarding social media analytics is how to capture streams of rich data that usually exist in silos. In many cases the data necessary to determine outcomes or analyses come from separate, disparate sources or analytical tools. I also refer to this fragmentation of data, often necessary from a business perspective, but a road-block from the analytics perspective, as "ultraviolet activity."

As a result of this line of reasoning (*that all information can be tracked if we care enough to collect the data*), I created my Social Media Enablement Audit process and spreadsheets. This product allows any business, marketer, or analyst to customize an audit around business data sources (vertical) and campaigns (horizontal).

The Social Media Enablement Audit doesn't solve the problem of capturing missing data as much as it leads to solutions that can be put in place to capture pertinent data. Once the data are captured and put into a usable form, you can decide what to do with them. Better yet, this helps indicate which social media metrics or social media ROI formula to plug the data into. Without the right data no ROI formula will be of much help. That's why the measurement of social media ROI is not easily achieved.

One of the goals of the Social Media Enablement Audit is to help determine which data inputs are required to truly calculate ROI. When essential data are missing, such as a common key (a customer name or e-mail address), then what is collected is often unusable. I designed the audit as a productivity tool to assist both in acquiring information and in providing an ROI outcome for analysis of social media metrics.

In April 2010, the Altimeter Group and Web Analytics Demystified released a social marketing framework[7] to answer an industry challenge of business owners who could not measure social media ROI. They aligned some of the smartest minds in Web analytics—such as John Lovett (an ex-Forrester analyst) and Eric T. Peterson (an ex-Jupiter analyst), both of the Web Analytics Demystified firm—along with Altimeter founder Charlene Li's (another ex-Forrester analyst) and developed self-funded research for a social marketing analytics framework. They made a collective effort to examine the best ways to measure the rapidly changing social media marketing landscape.

While testing the social marketing framework on Havana Central (using Radian6 and Sysomos I found there was not enough guidance within the Altimeter framework to effectively apply the formulas to real marketing problems or test if the formulas were correct.[8] It also seemed that too much of the data necessary to populate formulas was missing or ultraviolet. There will have to be more solutions to measuring social media, and there will have to be more specific guidance for how to apply them in order to provide actionable insights.

Guidance for Social Media Analytics

Social media analytics is an emerging field, emanating from the boom of connectivity and interactive tools and sites associated with lifestyles and activities in the digital realm. Perhaps an established organization such as the Web Analytics Association (www.webanalyticsassocation.org) and the Internet Advertising Bureau (www.iab.net) is the right place for the formulation of guidance and standards for the practice of social media analytics: both widely represent industries for which social media analytics is crucial. The IAB, for instance, did wonders for online video monetization by coming up with the VAST (Video Advertising Standards Template) standard.[9]

Based on my experience as a board director at the Web Analytics Association from 2007 to 2009, I know firsthand that standards are necessary for the social media analytics field to mature to the point where it can interoperate with other business research disciplines. To that end, the UK-based IAB

Social Media Council has launched an initiative with a focus on standards drafting. Richard Pentin's "New Framework for Measuring Social Media Activity"[10] defines the four A's of social media measurement: awareness, appreciation, action, and advocacy. Pentin's paper proposes defining and measuring core key performance indicators by social media platform, marrying soft metrics with hard financials.

However, even in the absence of industrywide standards for social media measurement, there are other means available to attain more complete Web data, but they are vendor-specific. One supplier of such a service is Medallia, a company offering what it calls "360 degree analytics." Medallia reached out to me in mid 2010 to demonstrate its efforts in this respect. Medallia's solutions are more thorough than what Web analytics normally produces, providing several surveys along with deep dives, or custom analysis, that explore a site issue or problem closely in order to create a personalized customer-experience page for each visitor, along with real-time problem solving (for example, dealing with an irate customer).

Among the operational data Medallia handles are customer-relationship information such as call-resolution time, financial data such as purchase history, and Web analytics data such as data from later or earlier visits. Medallia alerts stakeholders immediately regarding unhappy customers and supplies customer-recovery workflows to help organizations address many at-risk relationships.

On yet another social media analytics front, metrics from Flash and Rich Media creative content have been among the most difficult to capture. Many sites employ animations or Flash movies driven by a programming language called ActionScript. ActionScript requires additional site analytics enablement by a creative-content developer working with the site analytics group, and for many reasons this is hard to coordinate and put into place.[11] For example, the Flash and Ajax elements of a Web site do not generate the page view information that most Web analytics platforms require in order to track visitor activities. In addition, although Flash content can be measured with additional scripting, it may be expensive to keep in sync with site analytics tracking, or there may be Flash elements of a site that were developed previously and the original programmer has moved on, making it unclear how to update these assets.

Another reason for Flash elements of a Web site being ultraviolet: site owners are often ignorant of tracking requirements and don't know what to do with the data when they collect them. Widespread adoption of the HTML 5 standard may solve some of these problems, but that is still a few years away. As a stopgap measure, in 2009 Google released a tracking specification for Ajax code[12] that allows any site to track Ajax pages by creating an additional static page for that content. Still, creating content that is fully trackable by analytics is a formidable challenge that few organizations have fully met.

The acquisition of Omniture and its family of tools by Adobe in September 2009 was yet another sign that social media may be easier to track in the future. This is due to the fact that site analytics are part of how to follow social media, and any ROI usually has a Web analytics component or input. Adobe's Creative Suite 5 (the latest update to Adobe Flash Development Suite) allows creators to add Flash tracking for Adobe Site Catalyst when creating Web sites with embedded Flash elements.[13] According to John Lovett in his blog at Web Analytics Demystified (www.webanalyticsdemystified.com):

"Say what you want about acquisitions and the slow moving integration process, but Creative Suite 5 debuted in April just six short months after the deal closed, with measurement hooks from Flash Pro and Dreamweaver into both Site Catalyst and Test & Target. They've also accomplished this remarkable feat using a visual interface allowing content editors and non power-users the ability to begin measuring their digital assets. This utilization of analytics places measurement at the operational level, yet by and large it's still within the marketing group."

While Site Analytics is only part of the data collection process used to gather social media data, it is often the most effective place to center all the information. It is becoming increasingly possible to track "pre-click" data of visitors immediately before they land on a specific Web site.

According to Dennis Mortensen, head of Visual Revenue LLC,[14] most of the data a Web analytics platform collects are "post-click." Getting at more motivational data is exciting because it's a window into the mind and intention of the visitor and could be linked to where she came from, especially if it was from a social media site such as Facebook, Twitter, or even a blog, forum, or message board.

Virtual Worlds

Another source for intriguing improvements in social media tracking and ROI resides in online virtual worlds. Many virtual worlds are social in nature, as in the case of the popular virtual world Second Life. A few years ago, virtual worlds were not considered part of social media, though many people view them as such now. Developments taking place in the past two years, such as HTTP-IN and LSL protocols, have led to much better analytics tracking that may be included as part of a social media ROI equation.[15] Using this programming, each object (say a jar or kiosk in a virtual world location) can have a unique Internet address, allowing it to be updated from a Web browser. Among the possibilities of using protocols such as HTTP-IN to communicate "between worlds" are:

- **Individuals:** Create your own virtual world that gets continuously updated with information from social media.
- **Health care:** Hospitals can have virtual rooms for patients that are updated with their medical history.
- **Marketing:** Corporations can make virtual rooms, and behind their firewalls customers can interact, via social media, without actually having to enter the virtual world location.
- **Analytics:** The ability to visualize information via analytics tools—such as Adobe Omniture Discover 2, Coremetrics, and Google Analytics—is rudimentary compared with the visualizations and rich graphic set of which virtual worlds are capable of providing.
- **Social media and public relations:** Visualization of social media data, social CRM, and social data-mining would make it much easier to set up campaigns for the likes of Coke, Pepsi, Dell, and the American Cancer Society in virtual worlds.

Consider Eric T. Peterson's response in late 2009 posted at the Web Analytics Demystified blog,[16] where he asked if "we" collectively are ready for the coming revolution in analytics tracking, where analytics is now getting a "seat at the corporate table" and integration of the many different tools that used to not be considered together now are: "Nobody is talking about Web analytics anymore; the entire focus has become one of systems integration, multichannel data analysis, and cross-channel analytics." He also added later that "Availability of third-generation Web analytics technologies will finally get digital measurement the seat at the table we've been fighting to get for years."

It is a simple leap to see that social media analytics can be added to the list of third-generation technologies and that ROI can be derived from this integration.

How Should We Measure Engagement?

Since 2006, I've tracked what people have been saying about engagement. Back then, click-through rates were not considered enough information to be fully actionable to a site or business owner (they still are not). It was also necessary to track from which channel the action was coming (ad campaign, industry, business), and even then, having one place to store all the data was cited as being necessary, although it still yet rarely happens.

In 2009, Radian6 founder Marcel Lebrun asserted that his program captured "engagement breadcrumbs," and many monitoring platforms were beginning to do the same thing.[17] Here's part of Lebrun's response to a WebMetricsGuru blog post on collecting video views:

We don't just index content, but we also crawl and index numerous social metrics about the content and continue to track these metrics dynamically as they change over time. These are all the "actions" or "digital breadcrumbs" that are left behind as people interact with the content and they tell you there is attention, activity, engagement, going on with the content. And yes, we allow the user to view content and trends, not just by number of articles, but by any of these metrics which can give you huge insights as you pointed out in your post.

Also, we don't just store the "latest counts" but keep the whole history so you can also see how the metrics changed over time for a specific piece of content or user. For example, if you see a video in the "river of news" with 130,000 views, but are wondering if the views (i.e. attention) is still accelerating vs. fading, just click on the metric you want (view count) and you can see a sparkline of the views over time revealing if the growth rate has flattened or increased. Try it with a tweet, for example, and we will show you the person's follower count as it has changed over time (which reveals interesting patterns too).

Information derived in this way is useful as businesses are becoming more social and wanting to know if their campaigns are having an effect. However, business users are beginning to demand more information from first- and second-generation listening platforms (such as Radian6, Sysomos MAP, and Alterian SM2) than what they were designed to provide. Case in point, most of the listening platforms still lack the ability to capture true context around social mentions (although Radian6's Insight Platform offers a solution by layering additional contextual information with online mentions, such as psychographics and demographics from affiliated vendors that collect such information).

Other platforms such as Crimson Hexagon and Glide Technologies integrate machine learning algorithms to capture context (often termed "metadata") around the online mentions they are aggregating, making the information more insightful and actionable. Although machine learning algorithms are becoming more sophisticated, they are still out of reach of most platforms monitoring and measuring social media today.

However, it is critical to the social media analytics evaluation process to understand what drives the information within an online stream of data being monitored with the aforementioned platforms. Collecting information about mentions or buzz about a product or service is no longer enough; time saved by collecting input such as video views by platforms still ends up leaving analysts and business users with more questions and frustrations around the meaning of the data for PR, communications, branding, and marketing and advertising professionals, who often figuratively pull their hair out trying to understand the meaning of the data for their businesses.

For example, in order to measure engagement more accurately, we need to know what a visitor wants to accomplish (often gathered using qualitative data from online questionnaires or surveys) when he visits a site and whether he has achieved his goals; social listening platforms rarely collect or gauge this type of information.

Solutions for Context Mining

A few solutions have come about to better capture the context in which information appears, particularly for a brand. The Digital Footprint Index, developed by the Zócalo Group (with DePaul University),[18] evaluates a brand's online presence in three dimensions: height, which represents the total volume of brand mentions; width, based on consumer engagement with online content; and depth, based on message saturation and sentiment. This index (in fact, a veritable scorecard) is one that is open for a variety of use cases and can be applied by social media analytics professionals in any number of use cases. Ogilvy's Conversation Impact[19] and Razorfish's Fluent[20] are composed of visualization of social activity on the Web.[21]

One benefit of the Digital Footprint Index is that it uses the metaphor of a three-dimensional view of social media mentions in much the same manner as people transverse the physical world, which helps to amplify the meanings within the information.

Summary

2011 moving into 2012 may well be the time frame when *social business* begins to replace *social media* as the term we use to define business using social channels such as Facebook, Twitter, and YouTube. Deeper and more meaningful marketing integrations and convergences using social data are becoming much more useful in a business or personal context.

chapter **2**

Targeting Your Customers: Using Data to Find Your Customer

Before the launch of an ad campaign, or any kind of marketing outreach, it is critical to identify the targeted group. Add to that the desired knowledge outcome and the underlying strategic or tactical factors of the campaign. To collect that information would seem to be a commonsense and fairly straightforward activity, but it's actually hard to accomplish.

Planning and project insight well in advance of launching a campaign are vital for collecting useful data. Data generated with information goals and project expectations in mind can add insight to the business issues behind the reports or results that will be generated. The most important point in this chapter is that research tools are all but useless unless they're used in context with the information needed for the project. Achieving this is part craft, part art, and part experimentation; it helps to determine beforehand whether all the information required is actually useful for the analysis.

It is first necessary to define the vocabulary needed to identify and track audience behavior, and then to determine how to acquire the information and research required for spreading the word.

Determining Audience

Demographic research allows business-to-business and business-to-consumer marketers to divvy up markets by size, age, income, education, ethnicity, zip code, and so forth.[1] Services such as DemographicsNow[2] offer a rich set of tools to find target audiences by attributes that are meaningful for marketing or advertising campaigns (depending on the pre-defined business goals). Knowledge of generational[3] characteristics helps uncover the motivations and underlying values of the audiences and how those motivations drive behavior.[4]

The U.S. Bureau of Labor Statistics[5] offers a trove of interesting data that are of potential use for audience research. InternetNews.com is a source for some of the latest research and surveys that might provide data of impact on marketing campaigns.[6] Nielsen's Claritas PRIZM platform[7] provides consumer behavior life-stage segmentation derived from highly processed U.S. census data. Experian offers geosegmentation data, as do HitWise[8] and ComScore Media Metrix.[9]

Two providers of such mashups are WeePlaces[10] and Twitter Demographics. These are among a variety of Internet research tools rapidly being created that were nearly impossible to envision even a few years ago, and they can provide very powerful insights, often for free, as is the case with Twitter Demographics.[11]

DoubleClick Ad Planner,[12] Google Insights for Search,[13] and Google Analytics can be used for audience research. The data from these tools come in handy: people self-identify their interests and motivations online, so the study of their click stream yields valuable insights. Offline behavior can be tracked using FourSquare and Facebook Places check-ins along with other geolocational data.

Microsoft provides free audience research tools such as Profile Matcher, [14] which generates a list of Microsoft Web sites sorted by demographics. Quantcast[15] provides information about audience demographics, but it is entirely Web site–based, and does not capture all the other social media information of interest to readers of this book.

Learning How to Reach People Where They Are

Determining your audience is only part of the game, however. There are several ways to effectively reach people where they are, and many of them are surprisingly inexpensive if accuracy is not critical.

■ Google Webmaster Tools shows how often impressions of site pages and keywords are displayed, as well as what position they are in once they are clicked.

■ Brandwatch, Radian6, and Sysomos sort online messages about a brand or a target subject via social media channels such as Twitter, Facebook, and MySpace.

■ Facebook Ads can be set up to target individuals who haven't filled out their profiles but have friends who have done so; Facebook learns what their friends like and serves a similar ad by algorithmic reasoning based on what the individual's friends like. Facebook Ads were also used to target gay Facebook members using a similar approach.

■ Using Facebook to identify members of a group or around a context (known as "profile targeting") can supply enough information to make a "neuro-targeted" ad in Facebook that will appear only to the individuals when they log in to Facebook.

- Targeting audience by location is performed by using FourSquare, Facebook, and other geolocation platforms and augmented reality browsers that serve ads and messages to those who use those services and track the results.

- Life-stage targeting is based on the idea of understanding what services people might need based on where they are in life, and placing information in their path that they may find valuable.

- Twitter Interest lists are based on whom users are following[16]; Google AdSense targets users based on interest information passed from Web browsers to AdSense-enabled sites.[17] No doubt Facebook targets by interest, and most other ad networks do as well.

Case Study: Telstra, Converseon, and Social Media Review

In 2010, the Australian telecommunications company Telstra Corporation Limited began its first foray into social network– and social media–based product release and review. In the lead-up to its exclusive launch of the HTC Desire, an Android-based smartphone, Telstra held a contest to select 25 "everyday" Australians to review the HTC Desire. Out of more than 2,000 applicants,[18] only 25 finalists were selected to receive a free, pre-public release of the HTC Desire phone, running on the Telstra Next G wireless network®. In exchange, the finalists were asked to write about their experiences on their blogs and share them via Twitter. The blog reviews were also aggregated on Telstra's Exchange blog (http://exchange.telstra.com.au/tag/htc-desire-social-review/) and identified on Twitter through a dedicated hashtag, #TelstraDesire. In short, Telstra surrendered its much-anticipated product to Australians from different backgrounds and from diverse parts of the country, in order to let them write about their actual user experiences—whether good or bad—with the phone and Telstra's Next G network.

This social media review campaign had immediate tactical value—it was designed to accomplish critical brand reputation management objectives—but it also had informational value. Telstra was able to evince unedited, unfiltered public reactions among a broad audience of market segments, as Australians publicly followed, commented on, linked to, and blogged and tweeted about the online diary entries written by the 25 social reviewers. By facilitating an Internet-mediated public event, Telstra realized a tremendously high return on investment, as it gained insight into the actual user experiences of, opinions about, and feelings toward Telstra.

After collaborating with Telstra to develop and implement the campaign, Converseon compiled, coded, analyzed, and reported on the set of social media data produced by Australians during the event. Telstra had Converseon conduct this research in order to decisively determine the effectiveness and reach of the campaign in addressing two key business challenges. First, although Telstra offered the best mobile phone coverage in Australia, brand associations with negative customer service were crowding out associations with superior service. Second, because of legal risks associated with comparative advertising under Australian law, Telstra chose not to make direct, explicit comparisons of its products with those of competitors, in marketing and advertising materials, making the first challenge that much more difficult to address.

The social review campaign, it was hoped, would provide an opportunity to circulate and promote a wholly different, positive set of brand associations, while simultaneously providing a place for direct comparisons with competitors' products to emerge organically in user-generated social media.

The social review campaign promised to build pre-product release brand and product awareness among a larger audience than is typically captured by consumer reviews in traditional tech media. It would therefore be everyday Australians themselves who would tell the story of the HTC Desire smartphone on the Telstra Next G wireless network.

Using Social Listening to Understand the Campaign

By analyzing the public archive of data generated during and by the review campaign, Converseon aimed to determine the degree to which the now complete campaign lived up to its intended design and effect. At the close of the event, Converseon identified and compiled all relevant social media content produced as part of the event—both content written by the 25 social reviewers and unprompted online talk in the form of Facebook posts, tweets, forum discussions, and blog comments written by members of the Australian public about the content produced by the original 25 bloggers. All records written by the social reviewers and a statistically significant sample of records from the general public were hand-coded by a team of human coders familiar with telecommunications concepts and terminology. Among other metrics, records were coded for voice (i.e., market segmentation), venue, topic, and sentiment. Finally, Converseon analyzed the data using its proprietary software, ultimately delivering a research report outlining key findings, actionable insights, and potential next steps for Telstra.

Results

The research revealed the social review campaign to be an unequivocal success. Positive brand associations were being articulated and circulating in Australian social media.

Some of the key points made were:

- Immediately following the announcement of the contest, traffic to the Telstra Exchange blog increased by well over 500 percent.
- The campaign generated more than 2,500 tweets, attributable to 360 different users totaling more than 19 million impressions.
- The campaign created relatively high levels of positive sentiment (32 percent positive, 22 percent negative, 46 percent neutral), as conversation participants enthusiastically discussed the campaign, the product, and Telstra's leadership in turning to social media for product review.
- The campaign drove consumers to the Telstra Facebook page, whose fan base increased by 10 percent over the course of the event.
- Numerous records were generated by both social reviewers and the general public in which Telstra fared positively in explicit brand comparisons of its network with those of competitors.

For Telstra, this research had important implications. It confirmed that the campaign had indeed achieved its intended objectives: positive brand associations were gaining momentum, and publicly circulated content was being created in which the superiority of the Telstra product to those of competitors was stated by word of mouth. But the research also had value moving forward: it established a permanent archive and benchmark against which subsequent campaigns and research could be compared, thereby making it possible to chart the ups and downs of Telstra's brand reputation and awareness over time.

Viral Marketing and Word-of-Mouth Tracking

One important way to reach people is through viral marketing. Joe Hall, a blogger at Marketing Pilgrim, points out that viral content must be interesting and original, and that one-off copies of other successful viral marketing efforts usually won't cut it.[19] A perfect example: the JK Wedding Entrance video makes viewers feel good, and as of this writing, it has been viewed more than 64 million times. It appears the video was created spontaneously, but for all we know, it may have been created by design by a smart viral marketing team paid to direct and amplify viewer responses early on to meet the initial thresholds needed in order to get front page listings on YouTube, where it would be seen by a much larger audience.

But even an inside job is hard to replicate, as we will see in more detail below in the BillShrink case study.

Dan Ackerman Greenberg, as documented on Tech-Crunch,[20] makes it clear how often videos that go viral are "planned." Greenberg spells out the guidelines for making a successful viral video:

1. The concept should be enticing and "shocking," use "fake headlines," and, as a last resort, "appeal to sex" (for instance, have an attractive woman in the video).

2. The video should get at least 50,000 views in the first 24 hours (this was true a few years ago; *in 2011, it may take far more than 50,000 views to get on the front page of YouTube*), often by reaching out to influential bloggers, paying them to post about the video and spread the link to other bloggers. (As a result of new FCC regulations enacted in 2009 and 2010, bloggers now must disclose such gifts.) Viral videos are then shared to a select e-mail list.
3. Viral traffic firms often have members with several "fake" YouTube accounts with which to post comments and engage debates in order to make the video seem more interesting than it really is.

It may not seem ethical to fabricate accounts to trump up popularity in social media, but it's important for the reader to understand that some marketers still utilize traffic-generating methods that make a thorough and accurate analysis far more complicated.

Tracking Viral Videos

There are several methods currently available for tracking viral videos. These include:

1. YouTube Insights[21] (observe the Links part of the report)
2. ViralHeat, which can track the spread of online content, including video[22]
3. Visible Measures and ViralTracker analytics platforms
4. TubeMogul, which tracks across multiple video platforms

Case Study: BlueGlass Interactive

BlueGlass Interactive is an Internet marketing company specializing in a wide variety of online marketing services. While other agencies may be truly proficient in one or two fields of online marketing, BlueGlass was formed with a unique vision to put together a team of top people in the field and social media gurus in order to be able to handle all industry services at the top level. With search engine optimization, social media marketing, online PR, conversion rate optimization, PPC, or a combination of those techniques, BlueGlass has helped businesses prosper online while keeping the overhead to a minimum, simply because the company does it all under one roof. Also, its viral marketing team is able to leverage all available application programming interfaces (APIs), along with Google Analytics, to provide in-depth analysis of the success of all viral campaigns. This includes votes on various platforms, inbound links, reblogs, and, depending on the platform, page views.

BillShrink is an Internet-based cost-saving tool that helps people figure out how they can save money on their mobile phone, credit card, and other bills by constantly tracking market changes. Its blog provides analyses on news and strives to provide data-based articles and infographics that not only offer information to its users but also have viral appeal in order to attract search traffic and inbound links to broaden the company's reach.

BlueGlass Interactive works with BillShrink to develop the viral content by providing data and other information to make it useful and interesting to the company's user base. The goals for this content are twofold: to inform the site's regular users and to attract attention elsewhere on the Internet, resulting in more traffic, better search results, and, eventually, more users. For this campaign, the goal for BillShrink was to gain attention for BlueGlass's ability to parse cell phone plans and help users find the best deals for their needs, and, to that end, improve search rankings for terms such as "compare cell phone plans" and "cell phone plans."

Details of Approach

Because one focus of BillShrink is helping its users compare cell phone plans and save money on them, it was decided to take a look at just how popular the iPhone was. The initial idea was to look and determine whether, despite its strong sales, the iPhone was leading the smartphone, into which category most Americans' cell phones fall (basic, BlackBerry, text-friendly phone with keys, or smartphone), what percentage of Americans own an iPhone, and how many Americans intend to purchase an iPhone in the next 12 months.

The resulting infographic was enormous and pulled in data from a large variety of sources; it put the iPhone fully in perspective: while the Apple product was huge among smartphone owners in the United States, iPhone owners were still the minority in the United States and an even smaller part of the world market.

BillShrink was kept in the loop and given several chances to see the infographic as it was developed. Infographics generally take a few weeks from inception to completion, and it was less than a month from the idea's approval to when it was posted on the BillShrink blog.

Conclusions

Given how much press the iPhone gets, the results were of great interest to many blogs and Web sites: the infographic hit the front page of Digg not only because of the number of hits on BillShrink, but also based on links from Mashable and IntoMobile.com.

The original success on Digg was accompanied by more than 1,000 shares on Facebook, hundreds of tweets, and popularity on

Reddit.com, StumbleUpon, Delicious, Mixx, and Kirtsy. All told, the infographic brought nearly 42,000 page views and more than 1,900 inbound links.

The two subsequent successes on Digg from the other two sites are harder to measure through analytics; the graphic was embedded with links back to the original BillShrink post, however, so at least some of the links and traffic trickled through back to BillShrink as well. The Mashable post received more than 3,100 tweets and 2,300 Facebook shares.

BillShrink's goal was to improve its ranking for the terms "compare cell phone plans" (where as of this writing it ranks at number two) and "cell phone plans" (where as of this writing it ranks at the top of the second page). Because of the huge success on social sites, the number of inbound links from highly reputable sources, including Mashable and the *Wall Street Journal* online, ensures that BillShrink will remain high in search results long after the residual effects of the social success fade.

The Integrasco Story

A specialist in social media analytics and frequent public speaker, Aleksander M. Stensby is a cofounder of Integrasco and a member of its advisory board. He holds a masters degree in computer science, specializing in pattern recognition and textual analysis. He runs the analytics team at Integrasco. (The author of this book is on their advisory board.)

Overview of Integrasco

Integrasco AS is a company in Norway, founded in 2004 with its main office in Grimstad, a city in the south of the country, near Agder University. The university is the source of the company's core R&D and has provided analytics team members' with their technical competence. Integrasco also has offices in London, Oslo, and Chengdu (China), with a workforce of 30 employees.

Integrasco operates in the social intelligence market, with services centered around providing social media monitoring and insight through analysis to help clients measure and manage how their companies are perceived in social media—and assist them in providing what is needed to build and maintain their reputations. Integrasco has more than 15 brands on its clients list. Most of these clients have purchased monthly tracking, monitoring, and analytical services from Integrasco.

How the Company Was Formed

In 2004, Integrasco was born out of Intermedium, a media-clip agency using search robots to trace trade papers on the Internet. Intermedium was gathering information about companies and their competitors, and sold the information to its clients. Jan Hansen (at the time a co-owner of Intermedium), Jaran Nilsen (a summer student intern), and Aleksander M. Stensby (also a student) together left Intermedium and founded Integrasco.

Upon starting up, Integrasco received some financial support from Norwegian venture funds. A year later, the company obtained its first big client, Sony Ericsson. With Sony Ericsson on board, Integrasco was up and running in 2005.

Integrasco started out as a self-service dashboard supplier, an approach that tended to be both cheap and simple. However, it soon became apparent that there was considerable demand from larger clients for more detailed analysis and reports. Starting in 2006, Integrasco recognized that its customers were having problems asking the right questions, writing the appropriate queries, and analyzing the resulting data. As a result, Integrasco decided to switch from being a dashboard provider to offering more comprehensive, detailed reports that were produced by highly trained analysts..

At this juncture, Integrasco's own internal analytics team suddenly became the biggest client for the technology being developed, because of its need to provide services to customers. Integrasco also had to fundamentally redesign its technology to meet the requirements of demanding brands for high-quality data sources and analytical services. In 2008, Integrasco established its office in Chengdu, with the primary objective of offering data management services for our source repository, which contains sanitized, soured, and index data from social media sources such as forums, discussion boards, blogs, microblogs (*mostly Twitter and Foursquare, which use 140-character messaging*), and other platforms.

In 2010 Integrasco took on a number of new clients in the U.K. and Europe, and dramatically scaled up its analytical business offerings—brand, product, and service tracking; early problem detection tracking; global product tracking; customer service tracking; CRM unstructured text and sentiment processing; and so on. The company is ready to continue its growth in Europe, but with an increasing focus on Asia.

Core Features and Strengths

Integrasco provides technology to track brand, product, and service buzz, sentiment, and lead influences across social media platforms. It crawls predefined forums, blogs, and various other social media sources that deliver continuous real-time data and ensures the quality of the scripts that filter and transform the information from unstructured to structured form. This part of the process is now mainly handled by the Chengdu office. Monitoring and analyzing social media conversations is not just about scraping Web pages like any other search engine; it is about organizing those conversations in a structure that allows us to slice and dice, drill down, and see the big picture of how these conversations are interconnected into one holistic view. Frankly, you just can't do that with most tools out there.

Without the technology and assistance from our automated algorithms, adjusted individually for each specific business vertical, it would be impossible to retrieve and analyze the enormous amounts of data that exist out there. This is where Integrasco's approach differs from Google's and other search engines', which follow every link on the Internet. Integrasco's search engine crawlers narrow down the amount of information so that only the specific information requested is retrieved.

Integrasco has spent a lot of time on ontology and categorizing in different languages, and has specialized in monitoring social media in a number of languages so that, for instance, a British company can find out what has been said about it in Japan, Russia, and South America. Integrasco's technology is language independent, and its analytical staff covers all major global markets.

What Makes Integrasco's Technology Different

When Integrasco was founded, it started out with the same technology that Intermedium had been using, but soon significantly upgraded and developed it, leading to a third generation of the technology by 2006 and 2007. Through advanced, learning-based algorithms, Integrasco now provides a near real-time flow of data, with 24/7 monitoring and alerts. Not having a dependence on third parties has always been very important for the company. Its end-to-end quality controls ensure that all its data are current, comprehensive, and appropriately documented as to source. Integrasco guarantees the data's quality.

Integrasco's systems, from the point the data is created to the point it is stored in a database and made searchable, are based on open-source frameworks, of which much is executing on the Java platform. Crawlers and data structures are tailored for social media, enabling Integrasco to collect data from all social media sources and store it with a high level of detailed metadata.

The vast amounts of information extracted from social media are stored in a relational database using MySQL, allowing Integrasco to match data by using common characteristics found within the data set, making the information more comprehensible. According to Aleksander Stansby, Integrasco has a unique data structure that provides seemingly endless possibilities when it comes to diving into the data and analyzing them for clients. This is where Integrasco's approach really differs from that of most other social media data-scraping endeavors, in the sense that Integrasco collects conversations and all the additional meta-information contained therein, not just Web page content. Integrasco uses Apache Lucene, a text search engine library written in Java, suitable for applications requiring full-text search, especially cross-platform; and Apache Solr, which allows for full-text search, hit highlighting, faceted search, dynamic clustering, database integration, and rich document handling (Word and PDF, for example).

Using data-mining and search engine technology, Integrasco's platform is able to structure and extract meaningful information from vast amounts of unstructured data. This is done by using pattern recognition, statistical modeling, and artificial intelligence (AI) techniques.

Integrasco's sentiment algorithms, for instance, are tailored and developed according to client needs. There are different algorithms designed for different categories. This is because Integrasco doesn't believe that shrink-wrapped solutions can produce the level of quality that its clients require. Users in social media express themselves differently when discussing different topics. The word *wicked*, for instance, is a positive term in the context of skateboards, but in terms of financial services, it has a completely different meaning. The algorithm is trained on sector- or industry-specific real data and evolves as new concepts occur. It is capable of breaking down each individual comment and accurately measuring sentiment in relation to both brands and products.

Integrasco has benchmarked the algorithm on an independent industry data set from Amazon reviews and has scored an accuracy rating of 90 percent. Human quality checks of sentiment are conducted by statistically sampling posts and manually assessing the sentiment on an ongoing basis.

To really get to the bottom of what is being summarized in large volumes of social media using sophisticated technology, highly experienced analysts who really understand both the tools and the business environment in which they operate are required. It is of key importance for analysts to understand clients and the industries they operate in. Integrasco analysts look at thousands of social media conversations to corroborate algorithmic outputs and distill them into actionable insights.

Integrasco's core competency consists of a mix of refined software and trend analysts with deep industry expertise. For example, if a brand name is fairly generic, like *Orange*, *Virgin*, or *Egg*, it is an enormous task to configure and exclude keywords mentioned within an irrelevant context. Without the ability to construct accurate and comprehensive taxonomies before embarking on exploration and then refine them over time, clients will be wasting their time and money, wading through conversational treacle while looking for the wrong needle in the wrong haystack. Clearly, getting this right from the beginning is critical. In addition, when dealing with sentiment analyses, nuances of the written word are difficult to detect. Sarcasm, for example, can be tricky to identify through any form of automated tool.

In many industries, there is highly complex terminology that requires genuinely deep understanding, not least because each industry has its own language and jargon. It is rare to find two brands with identical tracking needs, even if they are in the same market category. Accordingly, it is important to be capable of tailoring the offering to the client—what to track, where to track it, how to report it, how frequently to report it—and to provide the client with ready access.

Integrasco Social Media Monitoring Solutions and Services

Most software-only tools tend to be sold on a prefabricated, take-it-or-leave-it basis; it is unlikely that a "self-serve" solution will deliver what clients require to build and measure an accurate picture of what is going on with the brand, products, and services in their sectors, in social media.

Since Integrasco started as an early player in the development of social media technology, the company has had the chance to develop and refine its software tools, as well as to get experience on how to properly analyze certain industries. Finally, Integrasco has built up competence through experience, and the company is confident that it is delivering cutting-edge technology and analytical services well ahead of competitors.

Recruitment and Training

Integrasco has a policy of hiring young and talented students who are into the technology and have experience in using social media. The company needs open-minded people who are self-starters and who can undertake the challenge of mapping the social media universe—people who can see through all the noise of Internet data and sources and are able to keep updated on "the state of the art."

For example, Ole-Christoffer Granmo, an associate professor at Agder University, works at Integrasco with artificial learning systems and recruits talented students for the company. Addressing an international market, Integrasco understands the importance of hiring people with backgrounds from different universities, cultures, and languages, who are also willing to travel. Currently, Integrasco has Chinese, Asian, and South American graduates integrated into its European team.

Integrasco University is an internal training program that all new analysts attend in the first three months of their employment, consisting of formal training, on-the-job mentoring, and real work. Integrasco wants new employees to get real experience as soon as possible, so during the first training week, they are assigned to real-life client projects. During the program, analysts become acquainted with the technology, systems, and processes in the company. The purpose of the university is to get new hires on board and have them become productive as soon as possible.

Chapter Summary

We have barely scratched the surface of tracking Web and click-stream data. Both are challenging to effectively collect and derive meaning from, unlike Web analytics, point of sale, or internal house (database) data, which can be fully captured and understood using techniques such as regression analysis and data warehouses. (We will explore the uses of social data in Chapters 7 and 8.) Often panel data from providers such as Comscore or Nielsen are used to extrapolate behaviors, but the information gathered is strategic in nature.

Social data are also different from the information described above in that they are collected by queries that we pose to a collection system such as Integrasco's; the information derived is going to be only as complete or useful as the questions being asked (and posed for analysis to a collection system) along with analysts who can interpret the results and translate them into actionable insights a client can understand and use; that's a very tough job, and subject area expertise often is necessary for providing context to data culled from social media monitoring. It is possible to gather insight from even a partial understanding of where your visitors come from, how they react on a site, and where they go after they leave. When you can merge information being collected in context with a client's industry, actionable insights are born, which is what this book is all about.

In later chapters, we will explore how actionable data require a level of precision that most social data lack. Data are a commodity, and finding the meanings in data is a specialty, usually requiring costly premium solutions. With the right solutions in place, social data become an invaluable assset. We will also explore "self-serve" systems (e.g., Integrasco, Brandtology, Alterian SM2, Synthesio). No doubt in coming years the landscape for these systems will alter.

chapter <u>3</u>

Tracking International: Multicultural Social Media

It's not the author's intent to overly complicate international social media monitoring in this chapter, but the efforts to set up effective monitoring should not be oversimplified or trivialized.

There is clearly a need to know what the world is saying, especially when much of the world is composed of non-English-speaking people. In many cases, a system of writing other than our Latin-Roman alphabet is in use, and understanding those languages is one barrier. Another challenge is to crawl and cull the international data and provide language support for extended character sets that we cannot enter without keyboards that are specially adapted to Chinese, Japanese, Hindi, Sanskrit, and so on; even Romance languages such as French and Spanish can present some difficulties with scattered special typographical characters or with culling and processing data.

To successfully monitor social media internationally, it is critical to understand what we should track in each country or region, which in itself can present a challenge. There are

several platforms that can monitor social media internationally, but having a support staff, and the understandings that
come with it is often an additional service packaged along
with the monitoring platform.

By using a trained support staff, monitoring data are
"cleansed," categorized, and tagged in a manner supporting
both analysis and monitoring needs while making the information much easier to work with and more actionable. Without the support staff, international social media monitoring
is usually too difficult a nut to crack, unless you just want to
measure the volume of mentions.

As an example of just how challenging capturing and
understanding online activity is, consider the case of monitoring Chinese social media; the Chinese character set and
online channels where activities in China occur are shown in
Figure 3-1. Every country has its own set of channels where
activity occurs within the local cultural context, slang, and
syntax, making culling and understanding the international
online mentions spanning several regions and countries akin
to translating a modern Tower of Babel. The challenge of
social media monitoring is to act as a twenty-first-century
Rosetta stone, decoding the online chatter and revealing its
relevant meanings.

My awareness of how organizations monitor their reputation and campaigns internationally using social media
monitoring began in 2006 while reading Nathan Gilliatt's
"NetSavvy Marketer" blog. Through his blog, I had learned
about CIC, a Chinese social media analytics firm[1] that has
developed an extensive Chinese slang dictionary to monitor
Chinese online conversations. (This dictionary was necessary
in order to understand the deeper meanings around many of
those conversations.) Around that time, Sam Flemming, CEO

Figure 3-1 Social media in China

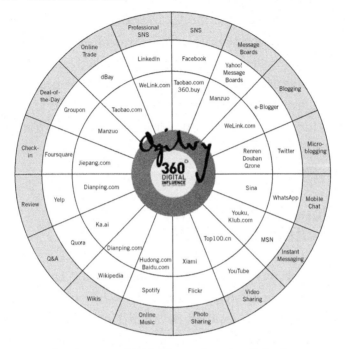

Source: Adapted from image provided by Thomas Crampton, Ogilvy Inc.

and founder of CIC, was interviewed by Nathan Gilliatt for the "Net Savvy Marketer" blog. According to Sam Flemming:

> *Chinese consumers are creative producers of slang, [and there are] 10–12 different ways to refer to "Bluetooth."* . . . *And there's the choice of technology. According to Technorati, the Chinese language represents 10 percent of blogs. The real action, though, is on message boards; that's where Chinese consumers share their opinions about companies, brands, and products. If you've seen online message boards, you get the idea, but add to your mental picture longer, blog-like articles and mainstream adoption. CIC Data tracks 4 million messages each month from automobile-related boards alone.*

But Chinese (in China and elsewhere) is just one of the many languages and locales in which products and brands are being discussed around the world at any given time. With so much content in various languages, businesses (and organizations and governments) will want or need to monitor conversations around certain topics, individuals, brands, products, and ideas, yet this level of online mention culling is extremely difficult to do well, and after reading this chapter, you will understand why.

Solutions That Perform Multicultural Monitoring

Some services handle international support and have their own dedicated internal staff, such as Attentio, Brandtology (which was just acquired by Media Monitors, Asia Pacific's leading online and social media intelligence company in February 2011), and Synthesio, to name a few of the handful of firms that have taken this challenge head on. Other monitoring companies, such as CIC, work with China exclusively.

The problem that emerges, though, is that no single platform offers a totally seamless solution for all countries and languages as well as a breakdown of how a company may want to visualize information; only a handful of firms have devoted the resources necessary to take on the task, even partially. Nor are common translation services the best fit for this kind of international monitoring (though you'd think they would be) because most such services focus on just providing document translation services, which is just a small part of what international monitoring encompasses.

For example, the technological challenges of crawling and culling international data are expensive and difficult to implement well. A strong technology focus and backend is required as more of the world engages in online social media while the tasks of monitoring, storing, and culling data increase exponentially.

In the preface, I mentioned that medium and message are interconnected as per Marshall McLuhan; the technology and infrastructure needed to perform international monitoring goes far beyond what simple document translation services have employed, making technology firms a better fit for international monitoring than those traditional translation services that are not technologically savvy.

It's likely that within the next two years, most of the platform vendors mentioned above will approach full international coverage.

- **SocialMetrix**[2] covers English, Spanish, and Portuguese, using semantic analysis and natural language processing.
- **Attentio** social media monitoring platform has analysts and software platforms to handle 17 languages, including Mandarin Chinese.
- **Brandtology** (http://www.brandtology.com) is able to monitor conversation and sentiment in 12 languages across most countries.
- **JamiQ** is a multilingual social media monitoring and measurement solution that provides the largest coverage of social media in Asia.

There are many methods available to assist with international and multilingual social media monitoring and tracking, especially if you want to do it yourself without hiring one of the platform providers mentioned previously. When monitoring internationally is something a business needs to do for small, one-off projects, yet the business cannot afford to hire companies like Brandtology, Synthesio, or Attentio to do it, self-serve platforms such as Radian6, Alterian SM2, Brandwatch, or Sysomos amply monitor multiple languages and regions for mentions of terms, although these platforms will not be able to decode the meanings within the culled data (where most of the value of international monitoring and online listening is).

I have used some of the DIY platforms below to monitor international chatter online and rated their features to show how they stack up against each other as of this writing.

Sysomos MAP (www.sysomos.com)

Languages covered: 22
Arabic, Chinese, Danish, Dutch, English, Estonian, Finnish, French, German, Greek, Hindi, Italian, Japanese, Korean, Norwegian, Polish, Portuguese, Russian, Spanish, Swedish, Thai, and Turkish
Countries: Most
Age: 10 to 75
Sex: Male and female

Radian6 (www.radian6.com)

Languages covered: 14
Chinese, Dutch, English, Finnish, French, German, Italian, Japanese, Korean, Norwegian, Portuguese, Russian, Spanish, and Swedish
Countries: Most
Age: Yes
Sex: Yes

(Note: In April 2011, the Radian6 Insights Platform was launched, adding several new capabilities to the platform, including Age/Sex/Location detection, which had not been previously available.)

According to the U.S. Census Bureau,[3] most minorities in the United States are concentrated in large cities, and this fact influences the quality of what is collected via social media (such as language and slang), in addition to the cultural context. The social media hubs for minorities may also be different, and monitoring solutions should take that into account. In fact, the same issues affecting online international monitoring and analysis also affect how well any online conversation is captured and understood. Among the challenges surrounding online monitoring are evaluating the meanings within content.

- Not every platform is able to evaluate emoticons, slang, nontraditional grammar, or SMS-like text (such as the kind we see on Twitter and Foursquare).
- Many communities have their own language and acronyms; it is challenging to adapt listening systems to understand the meanings for many of them (especially as online communities can form, grow, adapt, and change quickly, as seen in recent political developments in Iran, Egypt, and Libya, to name a few).

Challenges of Multilingual Social Media Monitoring

Most social media monitoring platforms are good at collecting data about what's being discussed with regard to a product or brand, but they often fail to handle variations in languages,

slang, regional idioms, misspellings, or nicknames for topics. This can make accurate online listening a difficult task,
as there are so many ways to say the same things (or the same
thing can mean something entirely different, depending on
the context).[4]

Disambiguation of Key Concepts and Phrases

Campbell-Ewald[5] came up with a guide for how to disambiguate linguistic problems that limit the accuracy and usefulness of social media monitoring. As an increasing number
of people use lesser-known variants of monitored phases, the
usefulness of the listening platform decreases rapidly because
the initial queries used to set up monitoring fail to capture
phrase variations or filter out noise in the data.

Why the Usefulness of Listening Platforms Is Decreasing

Some platforms like Integrasco (discussed in Chapter 2) are
able to build and run complex queries and taxonomies quickly
to capture a much fuller range of language and word variations. But most of the monitoring platforms mentioned in
this book fall short in the online listening department because
of limitations in their maximum query length (generally to a
few thousand characters per query).

When writing queries using Sysomos MAP, for example,
a maximum of 1,024 characters is allowed by the platform,
and any query over 700 characters displays a warning message
and slows down query execution. Brandwatch is able to handle 4,096 characters per query, which is long—usually enough
for most customers, but not for everyone.

I found that Radian6 has a limitation of 50 "do not include" words or phrases for each keyword grouping (set of queries) in a topic profile; this limit suffices for simple brand monitoring, but falls far short of the requirements for the larger industrial-strength monitoring tasks that many industries are increasingly requiring (such as pharmaceuticals; typically, I found more than 90 percent of online mentions are spam. As the query length gets longer and longer, at some point the listening platform is no longer able to filter out the noise and the value of monitoring rapidly decreases as the quality of the results degrades to the point where effective listening is no longer possible). An unsophisticated procurement process may easily result in the purchase of listening platforms without understanding their inherent limitations.

At the same time, most online listening platforms discussed in this book degrade in performance as the search queries get longer and longer (often necessary to filter out noise and catch slang and context), causing analysts and stakeholders to wait several minutes and sometimes hours for a query to display results. These delays are problematic, as most procurement decisions do not account for delays introduced by listening platforms inabilities to perform increasingly complex listening tasks well.

According to Campbell-Ewald:

■ **Linguistic variants** are the main reason keyword-based monitoring tools fail to capture all the conversations around a subject. Using **linguistic variant sets** (a set of alternative ways to say the same thing) is one way to disambiguate language variations and slang.[6]

■ **Regional variants** abound. Today's teenagers describe something amazing as "off the hook," while regional variants include "off the chain" (Detroit) and "off the heezy" (Brooklyn).

▪ **Intentional misspellings and variants** LOLCATS and 1337Speak (Elite Speak) are deliberate variants on written language used by select groups of individuals to communicate with one another. These variants are not currently understood by monitoring platforms.

▪ **Generational emoticons variants** Based on age, different emoticons may be used. For example, Baby Boomers rarely use emoticons, but Gen-X audiences use more emoticons than any other group. Gen-Y people tend to use emoticons more literally, often tying in faces to the emoticon.

▪ **Gender variants** Online identity is often open to question because people typically use pseudonyms when posting in forum threads, news, and blog comments.

Campbell-Ewald researchers found that influential members of a group are more likely to use slang words and terms than those outside the circle. (This fact can provide a hidden key to effective influencer analysis, but I have not seen any platform use it yet.) Once additional slang and linguistic variants are added to a set of keyword phrases used for monitoring, conversation volume increases by 50 percent or more.

Solutions to disambiguating key concepts and phrases in various languages being monitored include:

▪ Determining current search trends around a topic (Google Insights for Search, including Rising Search Terms; Google Adwords)

▪ Determining age and gender of author (Gender Genie, disambiguate emoticons, map to location and age)

■ Identifying online influencers, observing their linguistic patterns, and adding information to keyword-monitoring lists

Campbell-Ewald suggests utilizing the following tools to improve your keyword list by supplying free sources to disambiguate foreign language content:

■ **Urban Dictionary** (http://www.urbandictionary.com) to find linguistic variants and add or refine keyword queries in whichever social monitoring platform you decide to use. However, Urban Dictionary covers only the English and Spanish languages.
■ **Google Insights for Search** (http://www.google.com/insights/search) to add rising and breakout searches to keyword queries.
■ **Google Adwords** (http://adwords.google.com) to add keywords to your queries.
■ **Gender Genie** (http://www.bookblog.net/gender/genie.php) to obtain the probable sex of the person behind the online mention.
■ **Nicknames and Common Terms.** You can also ask your existing customers to provide nicknames and common terms that should be added to social media monitoring queries.

Example: Smirnoff Nightlife Exchange

To help demonstrate the difficulties of international social media monitoring, let's use a real-world example, the Smirnoff Nightlife Exchange. Smirnoff asked Facebook fans and followers in 14 international cities to swap their nightlife with one another. Fans posted suggestions to the Facebook pages around this campaign created by Smirnoff for each country.[7] Figure 3-2 shows an image from one of several videos around the campaign produced in fall 2010, featuring people in various cities celebrating the nightlife and culture of the other cities in the Smirnoff campaign.

The main purpose for discussing the Smirnoff project here is to demonstrate how online marketers encounter the same challenges as multinationals when running international and multilingual programs and campaigns. (Whether marketers choose to address these challenges with robust monitoring or not is the call of the agency that set up the campaign.) But multinational campaigns can also greatly enhance the brands that run them by providing invaluable intelligence, and we

Figure 3-2   Image from Smirnoff Nightlife Exchange project showing a club scene in Beirut, Lebanon

Source: YouTube, Smirnoff Nightlife Exchange Project

can expect to see a lot more of this kind of international monitoring in the years to come.

Brandtology

Brandtology is at the forefront of tracking international and multicultural social media. In late December 2010, I spoke with its founders, Alvin Chan and Kelly Choo. I also spoke with the company's media consultant, Jay Vasudevan, to get to the heart of what the company does.

Profile: Alvin Chan, Cofounder and Chief Technology Officer

Alvin Chan was a senior research scientist with Singapore's DSO National Laboratories, which provides leading-edge capabilities to the Singapore armed forces and contributes to the country's security. A specialist in the areas of information leakages, counterintelligence activities, and critical infrastructure protection, Chan analyzed emerging threats and identified technology to secure and enhance business processes. He graduated from the University of Aberdeen, Scotland, with a degree in electrical engineering and obtained his Ph.D. in engineering from the same school, specializing in the application of neural networks for information retrieval, software reverse engineering, and network-intrusion detection.

Profile: Kelly Choo, Cofounder and Business Development Director

Intrigued by the widespread influence of social media on society and organizations, Choo took a teaching-assistant role in the first Asian Facebook development course. Before that, he was involved in computing security in the Singapore armed forces. Studying at the Wharton School of the University of Pennsylvania, he worked as an IT consultant and was involved in launching two start-ups in the United States and was an advisor for a few more. Choo holds an honors degree in computing (specifically, e-commerce) with a minor in technopreneurship from the National University of Singapore. His role at Brandtology is to ensure that the company's products and services give customers and partners the greatest value possible, and to foster mutually beneficial partnerships with people and organizations globally. He has worked with brands such as Microsoft, Research in Motion (RIM), Hewlett-Packard, Procter & Gamble, and L'Oréal, along with various government ministries and a majority of global marketing, PR, digital, and research agencies.

Profile: Jay Vasudevan, Regional Social Media Consultant, Americas

Jay Vasudevan brings his passion for social media, Web technologies, and entrepreneurship to his experience in working with start-ups, transforming ideas into profitable products and services for multinational clients, as well as working with Brandtology. He studied management science and engineering at Stanford University and specialized in human-computer interaction, graduating with honors. Vasudevan also has a degree in engineering from the National University of Singapore and enjoys bringing about cross-cultural interactions between clients, partners, and other stakeholders in the United States and Asia. Vasudevan is also a friend of the author and the primary contact for Brandtology. It is due to his persistence and efforts that my interview with him took place in late December 2010. Excerpts derived from that interview follow.

The Methodology behind Brandtology

Kelly Choo describes the methodology that underlies Brand-tology: "We need to work closely with a client in order to understand where and how to monitor and crawl, as we cannot monitor everything; for monitoring channels, we decide where and what content to crawl and then we build custom crawlers. Normally, it takes us about 10 days of setup time; how far we crawl content depends on what information we are allowed to pull, and generally it can take from a few days up to two months to fully set up new crawlers, depending on the amount and complexity of the data.

"We do not build a customized dashboard for each client. It's all about how we extract all the necessary data. We constantly enhance our dashboards and extract all the information needed for clients, allowing us to enhance our analytics by allowing data to be viewed from different perspectives.

"Many businesses still do not understand the challenges around social media metrics; although the DNA of business may adapt to embrace effective listening and good analytics, this does take a while. We are constantly building and enhancing our library of crawlers when we go to a new market to make sure we have all the capability to gather all the information we need; currently our crawlers collect up to five million posts a day.

"We have a few companies that want to trade data with us, and we do get an occasional request to sell our data, although selling data is not our primary focus at this time. We have collected data that is very useful for research and have an internal self-help tool to look at social media data when needed."

Brandtology and Privacy Changes Affecting the Asian Market

Choo continues: "Privacy in Asia is not such a big issue as it is in the United States and United Kingdom, but South Koreans are quite adamant about their privacy rights. While we have the capacity to crawl most sites, we will not do so when privacy is an issue. We first make a determination whether there will be a privacy impact on us by harvesting the data on sites in question and then, should we find an issue, backing off from further crawling and monitoring of the site.

"Regarding forums, we noticed that in some Asian countries such as South Korea, our crawlers encountered Ajax and JavaScript code instead of pure HTML, producing errors in our databases. South Korea's forum issues were an especially tough nut to crack, but we figured out how to crawl these forums anyway, and we are quite proud of what we've done there.

"In China, anything goes in terms of how Web sites are designed, and there usually are no RSS [Rich Site Summary] feeds to crawl; as a result, you often have to start from scratch in order to find a way to crawl those sites and extract their data. Brandtology's second headquarters is in China; in fact, China is our fastest-growing market.

"We started international monitoring 18 months ago [in late June 2009] while working with a very large marketing agency group. When we won the RFP [request for proposal], we noted there were three or four different regions to cover, along with several different countries and languages. Upon researching other vendors in the space we realized no one covered everything. As a result we grew to become a global listening provider covering 90 percent of Internet conversations by country and language. In addition, we trained analysts native to the countries they work in, so they can integrate our technology and services there.

"There are countless numbers of times we've heard about solution providers claiming to have global coverage, but when we did our research we found it was not true."

Changes in Preparation for the Semantic Web

The Semantic Web is an evolving development of the World Wide Web where the meaning, or semantics, of information on a Web page is defined within the document metadata, making it possible for Web applications to behave more intelligently.

Kelly Choo comments on the impact of the Semantic Web on Brandtology: "It does not affect us very much because, unlike many of our competitors, we don't buy our data (from aggregators), and we control our own crawlers as well as how quickly and deeply sites are crawled. I don't say we are like Google in our ability to gather data from the Web; we have our own system to index sites and pages within a few minutes. In this sense, the semantic improvements occurring on the World Wide Web do not affect us that much because we do crawling and page extraction ourselves."

Deciding What to Crawl on the Web

Choo continues: "When we select a forum to crawl, we break it down by channel and location. For example, we will crawl a CNET forum for the term 'iPhone,' first creating a channel for it along with another channel for Android phones, and so on. Brandtology tracks everything happening within a forum, including how often members post and the influence of various members in that channel.

"In regard to SocialCRM, we're open to integrating SocialCRM whenever it makes business sense. However, sometimes we may be suffering from information overload, and we wonder if SocialCRM will overload people even more. We have clients with several different technologies in place and most of our clients have no dominant technology for us to integrate (SocialCRM) with. As a result, it is possible to have data integration through our dashboard, but the client still must integrate their own data themselves, through a third-party vendor or Brandtology development professional services."

Working with Machine Learning and Fuzzy Logic

Regarding machine learning and fuzzy logic, Choo says: "We are doing some machine learning with our social media dashboard aimed at helping our analysts deal with information overload. We have over 100 servers and are rapidly expanding our server farm by a couple of racks each quarter. In addition we have a team of 20 developers to build and maintain our crawlers.

"In terms of geolocation, we do not depend on domain names to classify the location of content. Instead, we classify a site's industry and country while the accuracy in our crawling is an undersold advantage and a point of differentiation from the data aggregators. As mentioned earlier, when aggregators say they crawl information by country they often don't; by looking at the API [application programming interface] we don't see that option."

How Information Brandtology Provides Is Actionable

"That," Choo indicates, "is the million-dollar question and the main reason why Brandtology is doing so well on the global stage. Before we developed our technology, we researched the industry and found we needed a global view of social media data and determine how to make it actionable.

"But we don't have 100 percent of the answer yet. What is actionable is totally subjective and everyone has his own idea of which insights are useful and which are not.

"For example, through using our platform, one of our clients, a very large global-software company, found their biggest issue was getting users motivated to move off of an old version of software to the newest version. Through employing our online listening we found a majority of people were comfortable with the old program and did not want to move up to newer software, adopting a 'wait and see' attitude. We brought this information to our clients' marketing department and asked how we could help them with convincing people to perform the upgrade.

"The brand ended up using banner ads successfully by addressing some of the most frequently asked questions users were asking about the upgrade, uncovered by our online listening using the Brandtology platform. As a result the ads' banner-clickthrough rates improved, encouraging people to upgrade their software."

What Data Brandtology Considers Actionable for a Client

Kelly Choo continues: "We always start by asking our clients what they are looking for and the KPIs they wish to measure. But there is no easy way to get past going through an iterative process to give people what they say they want to know about in order to find out what information to provide. Perhaps the DNA of business will change in 5 or 10 years to make it easier to do, but not now.

"In terms of working with clients to deliver actionable information, our analysts need to know what can or cannot be done while understanding the entire process of gathering actionable data from start (for example, crawling) to end. Just struggling with a tool or platform while trying to force it to deliver what you think it ought to provide will only set you on a path of 'manual labor' and potential burnout [an experience the author has witnessed far too many times lately]."

How Brandtology's Analytics Differ from the Rest

Choo describes how Brandtology's methods differ from its competitors': "A sample is chosen to represent the population as we cannot possibly monitor everyone online. For example, recently a census for Singapore found there were four million people living there but we could not knock on everyone's door to find out about them. Brandtology's analysts actively research in order to find the most influential channels and those are monitored on behalf of the client.

"To conclude, there are three things we will make sure we do well:

▪ **Technology:** Spending up to 20 percent of our revenue on R&D, new technology, and dashboard development.
▪ **Service quality:** Providing social media analysts paired with the platform. This is the key, marrying technology and trained professionals.
▪ **Process:** Ensuring our technology and trained professionals are coupled with a very good process that ensures high quality of our deliverables."

Further Challenges of International Monitoring

When a company is doing it all by itself, the challenges of running and online monitoring for an international campaign like the Smirnoff Nightlife Exchange project are considerable. Here are just a few of the challenges to be faced:

- Running, tracking, and understanding online content and conversation, such as the 14 international locations and languages in which Smirnoff ran its multilingual campaign.
- Tracking the intersection of online media with offline advertising has always been difficult, as offline data (such as attendance at an event) are usually not captured in analytics tracking via social media or Web analytics without deliberate enablement by using Web site tagging or campaign tracking and increasingly using QR codes tied to an event or campaign that can be scanned on location using smartphones.

Among the operational issues that a company needs to solve include:

- The need to know the culture, conventions, and slang of regions being monitored (often requiring people stationed "on the ground").
- Keeping track of branch or local office campaigns and operations.
- Poor sentiment analysis and geolocation capabilities within current listening platforms make sentiment analysis a manual process if accuracy and usefulness of the information is required.

Analyzing Chinese Online Chatter

Here are some examples of some of the difficulties with international monitoring in China:

▪ Analyzing Chinese-language media in the same manner as used for Western languages is ineffective; much like China, every other area of the world presents its own challenges.

▪ Chinese consumers are prolific producers of slang, such as the 10 to 12 different ways to refer to "Bluetooth" (the same slang challenges will present themselves in every region).

▪ Mobile phone terms in China are difficult to decipher.

▪ Linguistic variations and regional variants are problematic to track.

▪ Intentional misspellings and variants: younger audiences (especially Gen-Y) misspell more often than Gen-X and Baby Boomers. Acronyms are very common and accepted among younger users.

▪ Emoticon usage varies by generation, as mentioned earlier.

▪ Gender variants: gathering online gender identity is of questionable value due to the pseudonyms used in many forum threads, news, and blog comments by users.

We will examine international brand monitoring in greater depth with a case study.

Case Study: Synthesio and Accor

Accor runs hotels in 90 countries with more than 145,000 affiliates. With 4,100 hotels and close to 500,000 rooms, the group's brands offer various options to suit both business and leisure guests.

In 2008, Synthesio performed its first audit of the brand's reputation, a study that we will discuss in greater detail in a later chapter. Synthesio came to the conclusion, shown in Figure 3-3, about Accor Hotel brand reputation that a third of the online comments in review sites were made upon arrival at the hotel:

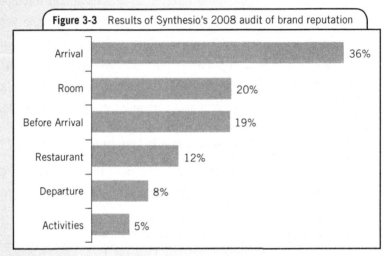

Figure 3-3 Results of Synthesio's 2008 audit of brand reputation

Source: Synthesio

Synthesio's findings also showed that 75 percent of comments published online were positive and customers were using review Web sites to give an objective comment on their stay. The brand decided to put into place an ongoing monitoring service to complement its regular customer satisfaction offline monitoring and raise brand awareness on social media using Synthesio's platform and services. Accor's goal was to monitor and evaluate more than 30 languages, including Arabic, Chinese, Russian, and Spanish, in both mainstream and social media for mentions and sentiment around Accor and competitor hotel properties around the world.

Synthesio created a global corporate marketing dashboard with all the information on brands, hotels, and competitors, along with 40 dashboards, one for each country where Accor has hotels, including competitors of Accor's hotel brands. Each Accor hotel also had its own dashboard with specific data for the hotel and nearby competitors.

Synthesio worked with the corporate marketing team to define a tool that analyzed Internet user satisfaction throughout all stages of a guest's stay and cross-analyzed the online listening data with other internal indicators of quality, such as online customer satisfaction surveys and field tests. As a result, Accor was able to take a closer look at customer satisfaction–related comments for both Accor's and competitors' hotels worldwide.

Metrics Derived from Social Media Listening

The tables following (Tables 3-1 and 3-2) display levels of customer satisfaction derived from Synthesio's social listening efforts.

Table 3-1   Customer Satisfaction of Accor Hotels*

Hotel	Before Arrival	Arrival	Food and Beverages	Activities	Leaving
Hotel A	100	100	100	0	0
Hotel B	97	84	85	57	67
Hotel C	100	100	100	0	100
Hotel D	83	82	0	0	0

*For sample purposes only. Actual data (including names of hotels) masked on request.
Source: Adapted from Synthesio Case Study of Accor Hotels

Table 3-2   Customer Satisfaction Index and Evolution over Time

Hotel	Rank May 10	Rank June 10	Average May 10	Average June 10	Trend
Hotel A	5	1	60	100	Up 40%
Hotel B	1	2	81	83	Up 2%
Hotel C	6	4	69	75	Up 75%
Hotel D	4	5	72	69	Up 3%

Source: Adapted from Synthesio Case Study of Accor Hotels

The numbers in Table 3-1 represent the percentage of satisfied customers of each of the four hotels (A, B, C, and D).

Challenges for Synthesio

Here are some of the challenges Synthesio had with monitoring social media for the Accor Hotel project:

- The main challenge was culling online mentions and making the data interoperable for a number of dashboards—it took Synthesio three months of R&D and setup to figure out how to extract the data needed to create the dashboards and reporting.
- Once the data were extracted, they needed to be segmented into 30 topics across eight languages; this required human coders, specifically natives of the countries where hotels were located. As a result, there were significant staffing and communications challenges to set up this project for Accor.

Results

Here are the results found:

- Overall online reputation was increased by 55 percent.
- New insights were gained, such as guests' room keys being demagnetized by smartphones; this would be difficult to collect without putting the listening process in place.
- Negative comments were immediately identified by the system Synthesio put in place, as well as to what they pertained and to which hotels the remarks were related. As a result, each hotelier was able to use interactions

within social media around the hotel chain to improve customer satisfaction and measure that improvement over time.

■ Accor can now get an overview of its online reputation in just a few clicks, instead of sifting through sites that are far different from one another.

Figure 3-4 is a graph charting the overall online sentiment (negative, neutral, or positive) for the Accor Hotel brand over an approximately two-year period.

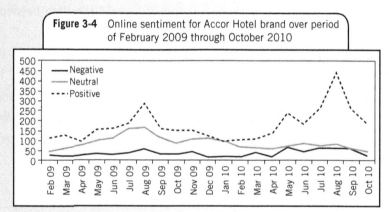

Figure 3-4 Online sentiment for Accor Hotel brand over period of February 2009 through October 2010

Source: Synthesio Case Study, Accor Hotels

Summary

International social media campaigns and sentiment tracking are extremely challenging to set up and perform well; few vendors possess all the resources needed to provide useful and actionable results. A combination of machine learning (a topic that was not covered in this chapter) and people who are conversant with the language and customs of each country/region may be required as these tasks become more widespread.

While translation services might initially sound like a good fit for online monitoring, most translation firms lack the technology underpinnings to create, utilize, or perform effective international monitoring and analysis. However, the author believes this is an opportunity for the right, technically savvy translation service to take on, or at least partner with, a listening platform to perform.

Finally, measurement campaigns within organizations require consensus and clear goals for how to categorize conversations, but the benefits of a well-set-up global monitoring program are usually worth the effort and expense.

chapter **4**

Online Social Intelligence: Extracting Signal from Noise

Online social intelligence is much more than a series of advanced artificial algorithms running on disparate computing platforms. These platforms cull, organize, classify, and act on online mentions that people generate. Still, online listening systems often fail to capture much of the "intelligence" within online mentions, such as underlying feelings, emotions, ideas, and themes. (This additional information is frequently termed "metadata," and it can be added to content using semantic markup language when it is created. However, listening systems are not able to add intelligence to information automatically, with a few exceptions such as Crimson Hexagon, which can assign tagging of content based on an algorithm.)

As a result, there is often more "noise" than "signal" in what is being monitored and collected by listening systems. By monitoring social media armed with the right information and queries, it is possible to create a social intelligence program from the world's biggest focus group—the activity data from posts, comments, and shares occurring on the World

Wide Web. However, most of that intelligence is created by humans who are reading and acting with the content, not by algorithms. In the future, automated algorithms that can act on data in a streamlined way will generate intelligence without human intervention, but that is largely not possible today.

In their Intention Web and Predictive Web writings,[1] Brian Solis and Jeremiah Owyang introduced a series of models to anticipate future demand, which was based on intelligence and insight extracted from online behavior. For example, businesses that have physical locations, such as retail, events, and packaged goods, can use online chatter around their locations to anticipate future activity, thereby allowing those businesses to better utilize the intelligence within social media.

Baynote is a company that leverages technological advances to create a "swarm intelligence" platform capable of adapting to user behavior in real time, using its UseRank engine. Baynote's secret sauce ingredient is the way the platform analyzes micro-behaviors to determine customer intent and content engagement. The company collects user data while observing subtle micro-behaviors (such as mouse movement, page scrolling, and text highlighting) as well as not-so-subtle behaviors (such as click path, conversions, dwell time, search terms used in external and onsite search engines, and terms in Web site links that customers click on).

It does not seem so far-fetched that a system could make intelligent decisions based on micro movements. Similarly, Google uses page loading time as a search engine ranking factor, as noted by Google blogger Matt Cutts.[2]

However, using micro signals can have unintended effects. Sometimes a site will not rank well in Google Search due to Google, not the site's creators. (For example, Google may make assumptions about a page or a site's content by examining its metadata and running it through several algorithms. While such operations are considered necessary due to the sheer volume of Web content and spam, the results are not always predictable, and in some cases the algorithms apply penalties to sites that did not make any content changes.) In other cases, algorithm changes may not be applied in uniform ways, leading site owners who are basing their SEO on search engine results to draw the wrong conclusions. In any case, making decisions using micro signals is just one way to gather online intelligence.

Increasing signal-to-noise ratio, according to Brian Solis,[3] is vital to improving social intelligence and social networking; noise is exponentially amplified when an increasing number of people use social media to create content and to exchange messages.

Improving Signal-to-Noise Ratio in Search Engines and Social Media Monitoring

Over 15 years ago, search engines began to simplify how people found information on the Web. Users began searching using one- or two-word queries and now have graduated to several-word queries (the Long Tail). While Google Page Rank worked great when it was rolled out in 1998, it has become less effective, despite frequent software updates and search patches from Google.[4]

Social media monitoring platforms started out as search engines and used keyword-based queries similar to Google's, but with more complex Boolean logic; the results, however, are only as good as the analyst who runs them.

Practically all monitoring platforms have some machine learning incorporated into their offerings, but only a few function mainly through artificial intelligence with human interaction. Glide Intelligence, for example, uses an analytics platform supercharged with Viterbi logic to analyze content for structure and context in order to derive key data points for sentiment, tone, relevance, and association.

A Viterbi logic decoder reads online content and compares it with a set of "probable" interpretations. The interpretation with the "least error" is selected and used. This logic is trainable within systems such as Glide Intelligence and Crimson Hexagon.

Another company using social intelligence to improve business results is ITA Software. Google began its acquisition of ITA in July 2010, and this was finalized in April 2011. ITA released Needlebase,[5] a system that merges multiple data sources into one consistent database that harvests structured data from Web sites and RSS feeds.[6] Marshall Kirkpatrick, who is not a programmer, quickly wrote about DIY applications using Needle and Needlebase at ReadWriteWeb, a leading industry blog about new Web technology.[7] Kirkpatrick called Needlebase part of his DIY Data Hackers Toolkit.[8] The way users can mash up data with Needle suggests a growing sophistication and intelligent application of data by anyone wishing to do so.

Google has been performing vector analysis on content since 2005, while SAS does something similar to LSI (Latent Semantic Indexing) with its text analytics platform; according to SAS's text analytics project manager Richard Foley.[9] However, Needlebase goes beyond vector analysis in mining data intelligence by creating its own database schema for each project. Needlebase surpasses LSI in its capabilities for extracting relevant information off the Web.

Why Did Google Acquire ITA Software?

My conjecture is that it comes down to 20100145902. That is, United States Patent Application 20100145902, which deals with the methods and systems to train models and extract information from data sources.[10] The application was filed in June 2010, and that led to the acquisition of ITA in the following month.

Needle is used internally at ITA for travel-data information extraction, but it turns out to be useful for many other purposes, including crawling the "dark web" of forms, which Google has difficulty doing (no doubt, with the ITA acquisition completed, Google's ability to crawl the dark web and extract information from it will improve).

Google's main goal was to make the world's information searchable, yet Google has indexed less than 1 percent of the world's content.[11] Needle provides a crucial link to the fruition of Google's goal, because most of the Web is still dark matter, as far as Google is concerned.[12]

Mobile Social Intelligence

Cyborg mapping applications[13] can gather real-time information about road conditions. Waze (a crowd-sourced mobile mapping application) and Trapster (a mobile speed trap and road-hazard mapping app) are crowd-sourced applications that collect real-time data from millions of people simultaneously posting updates from their mobile devices. Augmented reality browsers such as Layer also provide real-time information to users.

Another way of gathering intelligence using mobile devices is through the application of QR (quick response) codes to trigger an action.[14] Bit.ly automatically creates and tracks QR codes for any URL it shortens. The information provided by the bit.ly dashboard is still fairly rudimentary: detailed geolocation tracking shows only the country information. (However, many of the limitations on what bit.ly and other QR code providers have are tied back to the limitations of mobile devices and the networks they run on.)

RFID (radio frequency identification) chips provide tracking information[15] that can be used for social media tracking, among many other activities; in fact, states such as New York and Washington are starting to implement enhanced driver's licenses with unique ID numbers assigned via embedded RFID tags.

A technology that still needs to be developed is one connecting mobile information and decision-support systems to trigger actions based on real-time mobile data. Tying mobile data with social networks (such as a user profile on Facebook) offers the possibility of fully customizing a shopping experience.

Profile: Chase McMichael, CEO of InfiniGraph

Chase McMichael has over 15 years of senior-level product development and management experience in consumer messaging and marketing technologies, including social media, advertising software, and collaboration. At Unbound Technologies, Chase helped create the world's largest social marketing database by data mining Facebook; he also obtained U.S. Patent 6,941,339, received the 2008 Marketing Sherpa Viral Hall of Fame award, and deployed advanced social campaigns for *Vibe* magazine, BET, Ford, HP, HBO, and MTV.

At Oracle Corporation, McMichael managed the real-time collaboration presence and instant messaging services.

While working for Sprint, he created the enhanced messaging services (EMS) and instant messaging services. He served as vice president of product development, Internet services for Chase Manhattan Bank, where he was responsible for leading Internet and intranet application development and deployment. McMichael also developed a direct marketing and sales engine that leveraged user feedback and worked with several lines of business. He began his career in a research position at the Texas Center for Superconductivity and holds a B.S. from the University of Houston. He is inventor or coinventor on 13 U.S. patents and has written for many technical publications.

How InfiniGraph Can Crawl Deeper than Other Platforms

As InfiniGraph gets information from the Web, it also becomes more intelligent in how it selects and marks up data by monitoring the sharing activity of a brand's fans and friends of fans. The company's fundamental design is based on social intelligence and self-improving contextual data by social interaction (social rank), as well as improving interaction among a topic or interest affinity group (social density) to enable crowd-sourced social intelligence. Collective consumer integration around brands and content creates context, and that context requires massive levels of computation to organize it into actionable groupings.

How Changes in Online Privacy May Affect InfiniGraph

The company is not a cookie-based solution; however, its clients use cookies for ad targeting. The social intelligence platform utilizes the customers' API (on Facebook and Twitter) to determine their social graph and adheres to the TOS (terms of service) of those platform providers. As a result, changes in online privacy should not impact InfiniGraph as long as it continues to conform to TOS policies.

There is a large red herring here because of the ongoing privacy debate, which makes it very difficult to determine which laws will be put into place and to what extent privacy will be based on consumer control. As of now, to be accepted into a social media group, the consumer must release information to the group under its terms of service, while those that don't accept these terms should remove their accounts.

How the Information InfiniGraph Comes Up with Is Actionable

InfiniGraph is the first company to provide social aggregation, curation, and syndication of Web-based technology, allowing brands to engage audiences with real-time content and social relevance. Through the social intelligence platform, customers are able to trust and automatically publish this crowd-sourced relevant content based on collective interest categories, better known as affinities. InfiniGraph provides a brand with information about which of the content associated with the brand is most popular with its audiences, and makes this information available through a publishing platform and dashboard. The platform enables the use of distribution and tracking to self-improve content feeding into the social graph.

Because InfiniGraph social intelligence is able to find optimal trending content, the people who are creating interactions are part of the top 1 percent taking action on the social graph, and are also the ones that they want the brands to attract. To enhance the social interaction around a brand, the company also uses auto-follow on those people who are considered key influencers. All of these actions develop a real-time view of the health of the brand's RSS feed: its sense of what is trending currently. InfiniGraph employs artificial intelligence to create a predictive model of what is going to be hot in the near future around a brand's content.

What Sets InfiniGraph Apart?

Using keyword-based monitoring is very important, but for the brands that are looking for ongoing social engagement and activation in order to scale across all their social presences, with end-to-end feedback and self-optimization, there really is only one choice, and that is InfiniGraph.

If the brand or publisher is serious about social graph optimization and driving great social interaction based on social relevance, InfiniGraph will provide the scale and superior technology to fully automate the process. InfiniGraph provides brands with the intelligence to understand what their audiences want to consume, and that differentiates it from other publishing platforms that simply promote and distribute the content a publisher already has.

For brands using Facebook Ads, InfiniGraph provides the best trending "like/interest" reporting based on brands' social behavior, at the same time tracking influencers on the social graph. InfiniGraph is a social intelligence platform that is not based on online listening as much as it is based on relevant social interaction around the content of a specific brand. A brand is not required to create complex queries or advanced filters, nor does it have to think of which keywords to listen for. All this is done automatically, based on crowd-sourced social interactions; therefore the audience is the best source of what is relevant, providing ongoing intelligence back to the brand for activation, content automation, and social targeting.

InfiniGraph has over 2 billion brand affinities on more than 400 million people linked with 250,000 brands, including 1.5 million blogs. These are counted based on social relevance and ranked based on consumer interaction.

Details on the InfiniGraph Cloud Platform

Our social intelligence platform was designed specifically to run in the cloud and to bring up instances in real time in order to dynamically scale based on demand. This design was a year in the making, and now it runs on three cloud platforms. We do measurements based on demand processing. InfiniGraph does have an API for publishing and data access; however, this is available only for strategic partners.

What Issues Could Potentially Cause the Company's Downfall?

Not managing our branding or positioning of social intelligence, or not significantly pointing out the differences between our platform and other social listing and monitoring platforms would contribute to the company's downfall. Obtaining social relevance based on crowd-sourced social intelligence is highly disruptive in the social listing and monitoring business; InfiniGraph is able to identify tangible action and drive social measurable interaction, and that is greatly lacking in social listing and monitoring products, which is one of our key differentiation points.

The next two years will be a major washout for those platforms that fail to deliver results to the brands desiring to drive relevant action and reduce the cost of managing the social presence. Those platforms that are going beyond social listing and monitoring and passive analytics to aggressive sourcing of social interaction will be the winners.

Summary

The study and application of extracting signal from noise is continuously evolving. In the coming years, more "machine learning" algorithms will be added to many of the monitoring platforms, and they will begin to recognize and process sarcasm, irony, and emoticons as well as adding demographic, psychographic, and geolocational information that is now typically missing.

In fact, Radian6 offers much of this information on social mentions for an additional fee through its Insights Platform. No doubt other vendors will quickly follow suit, and the next few years will bring some amazing advances in online listening capabilities.

Finally, the features of the listening platforms we use today offer little more than an aggregation and tagging of online mentions; they are quickly becoming commodities, as customers will want much more of the online social intelligence that is currently missing from most platforms today.

chapter **5**

Friends, Fans, and Followers: Determining Their Worth

According to Augie Ray of Forrester Research, the value of Facebook fans and Twitter followers begins at $0.00.[1] He argues that their worth is created once a brand does something to engage them; accumulating fans and followers is just the first step. Others disagree, of course. In June 2010, the analytics company Syncapse released a study saying a Facebook fan was worth $136.38.[2] This figure was measured through a precise formula; however, the true value of any fan is a variable, according to the Syncapse study,[3] as we will discuss throughout this chapter.

What Is the Value of a Fan?

Not all fans are created equal. Some are extremely engaged with the brand they are enamored of, while others simply sign up on a brand's social media page and never participate again. Therefore, the monetary value of the brand's fans varies dramatically. Best-case scenarios take into account intensely social fans, while the worst-case presume totally inactive users. The most valuable fan in the survey was one of McDonald's, who presented an annual value to the organization of $508.16. This would be a loyal visitor to its locations, frequently referring others to and participating actively in its Facebook community. The average McDonald's fan netted the company a value of $259.82.

The value of each fan is calculated using the following five measures:

- Spending
- Loyalty
- Recommendations
- Earned media value
- Cost offset of fan acquisition

As used here, the term *spending* does not refer to how much the customer spends but instead is tied to the ability to visualize product spending and how this has an impact on the brand's presence. *Loyalty* here is defined as the ability to understand the available means to influence and promote brand loyalty within a target audience. *Recommendations* refers to the propensity to recommend a brand or product, or the probability that word-of-mouth recommendations will lead to sales. *Earned media value* is defined as the efficiencies of earned reach and frequency via the Facebook platform, and the *cost of fan acquisition* is considered to be the efficiency with which a brand's fans entice others to participate and drive organic membership to its fan page. The danger with calculations like this one is the tendency to make incomplete assessments of fan value, calculating certain positive aspects of activity and not others, such as brand detractors.

Vitrue Facebook Fan Value

In April 2010, Vitrue introduced a Facebook fan value calculation[4] of $3.60 by examining Facebook data from its clients' Web sites with a combined base of 41 million fans. Vitrue was able to apply a few formulas that defined the value of fans from its own perspective. In this study, the company found most fans yielded an extra impression per visit versus nonfans, based on all the Web analytics data it had in its client base. Vitrue determined that, on average, a fan base of one million translates into at least $3.6 million in equivalent media over a year. The company also found all fans are not created equal: its study found wildly divergent impression-to-fan ratios. Some marketers generated just 0.44 impression per fan, while another saw 3.6 impressions per fan. Using Vitrue's calculation, Starbucks' 6.5 million fan base, acquired in part with several big ad buys, is worth $23.4 million annually.

These differences in methodology explain how Syncapse came up with a different Facebook fan value than Vitrue did. While it is easy to get caught up in the calculations, there are generally no universally workable solutions for determining fan value. We must pick a method of calculation and then stick to it so data will be consistent over time.

Case Study: BuzzDetector and Associazione Canili Lazio

BuzzDetector is an Italian social media monitoring platform and consultancy founded in 2007. It collaborates with clients to help them use Web 2.0 technologies and social media to engage people in conversations that drive actions and sales, and build brands. The company's goal is to create valuable insight from the conversations their clients engage in with customers, prospects, and influencers.

Associazione Canili Lazio (ACL) is a nonprofit charitable association headquartered in Italy and devoted to rescuing abandoned dogs as well as promoting social change and fair treatment of animals; the organization is 100 percent funded by donations and charity. ACL has been exploring new ways of marketing in order to develop its fund-raising activity and to become more visible online within the crowded sea of charities.

BuzzDetector worked with ACL to analyze the form of communication used by other associations, spot weaknesses and strengths, and test the results on its Facebook page to see if it generates awareness and advocacy.

Methodology

First, BuzzDetector helped ACL set up a Facebook account to test the value of its page contents and different forms of narration, and to verify if and how the Facebook-paid advertising would perform for ACL. A Facebook banner ad that targeted 18-year-old Italians was run for six days, with a total investment of $70; it delivered 811 clicks, with a click-through rate of 0.4 percent, making the cost of each click 9 cents.

Through its proprietary platform, BuzzDetector entered into the analysis of posts, comments, likes on blogs, forums, and social networks. We scanned through the Facebook content to identify context, select a relevant number of keywords, display word clouds of the results, and relevant Web sites metrics such as page views, bounce rate, and so on. The initial goal of the campaign was examining how visitors moved from consideration, actively participating and advocating ACL through clicking on the "like" button or the "share" button while on the ACL fan page.

ACL's Campaign Results

The campaign helped drive awareness in the minds of donors and increased the number of Facebook fans for the brand. ACL ended up with the following numbers at the end of December 2010:

- Fans: 16,481
- Monthly active users: 13,344
- Weekly active users: 10,111 (week ending December 25, 2010)

Monitoring ACL's social media and competitors proved to be crucial in creating a totally new environment for the association's activity. Meanwhile, paid advertising failed to contribute in a significant way, and that surprised us. The banner ad alone, even with a stable level of clicks, did not end up delivering any new fans, and no one seemed to be clicking on the banner ad.

As a result of running this campaign, ACL launched an online store for merchandising, producing a 2011 calendar with pictures sent by fans (more than 3,000 entries), and launching fund-raising and live broadcast for special events. The association also learned to tell the same story, with different nuances, on the various social media channels it communicated through so as to be more in tune with a larger share of its audience. ACL created a remarkable base of a very active community, members of which were ready to participate in discussion, to share thoughts, and to engage in fund-raising.

Knowing How Much a Facebook Fan Is Worth

One way to understand how much your company is worth is to ask your customers. If a business uses e-mail marketing, it can employ questionnaires. If the business is larger, and it is important enough to know the value of building a presence on Facebook or evaluating the fandom already present, then the course of action might better be served by a survey company like Hotspex in order to get a fair, objective evaluation of how customers behave toward a brand. Of course, there are several ways to find out what your fans are worth.

Using the two numbers for fan value presented above yielded widely different results when applied to the marketing of the Havana Central restaurant chain:

Syncapse calculation = 1,811 fans × $136.38 = $246,984.00
Virtue calculation = 1,811 fans × $3.60 = $6,519.60

The differences in the value of a Facebook fan are directly related to which formula is being used to calculate it. Since standards do not exist for how to approach value on the Web, various claims are being made for return on investment based on the value of fans. The example above should make clear how dependent ROI is on the method of calculation used.

Of course, the value of fans can also be measured by how they behave. InfiniGraph enables distribution and tracking of content via the social graph (activity of fans and friends of fans of the top 1 percent who are taking action, and people on Facebook the brand wants to attract). InfiniGraph has produced technology to measure end-to-end engagement of fans. The result of its work with *Complex Magazine* (see Chapter 7) was, based on brand affinity, *Complex Magazine* was able to increase its proprietary Web site referral traffic by 30 percent, Twitter followers by 25 percent, and Facebook fans by 30 percent over a short period (one to two months).

Complex Magazine curated content based on fans' and their friends' (friends of fans) sharing activity on Facebook. InfiniGraph allows that curation (for instance, a community manager can decide on which content to publish, based on sharing or engagement activity among fans and friends of fans) and views the value of fans by what they *do*, which is more sophisticated than simply calculating how much they are likely to spend (as the other methods presented use).

The Dunbar Number

Another way to assess the value of individual fans and how many fans a page should have is by using formulas based on the Dunbar Number. Dennis Yu, a marketing expert with Blitz-Local (a Facebook marketing and analytics agency), came up with a threshold number of 3,000 fans per location using internal data collected from many clients. The number, named after researcher Robin Dunbar, is the maximum number of relationships a person can maintain; on average, Dunbar found that the average person maintains about 150 close friendships.

Keeping with this line of thinking, it may take a certain number of fans per brand location—say 3,000—to build truly worthwhile results through Facebook, according to Yu's data. Havana Central would need to have collected 9,000 fans (3,000 per location, assuming each location had its own fan page; there is only one page for all three locations today). If the Dunbar Number is accurate, attaining it would be a best practice for location-based brands, such as restaurants and hotel chains.

Havana Central's potential audience in New York City could be as much as one million people (anyone who would want to eat a Cuban meal), using the Dunbar calculation, a Facebook fan base of 3,000 would equal a potential Dunbar reach of 390,000 potential customers. In order to reach one million customers, all three of Havana Central's locations would need at least 3,000 fans each (or 1.17 million potential customers).

But it's also true that the more fans you have, the greater the chance of overlap among them, and the unduplicated audience decreases. When you have over 500,000 fans, then your factor of reach versus actual fans may be only low double digits. While decreased reach may appear bad, in reality, it is actually very good. It means each time you show the ad, it's going to increase the number of people whose endorsements are listed on screen below the ad. To put it in laypeople's terms, "awesomeness" on Facebook equals the ability to maximize peer pressure; if enough of your friends like and endorse a brand, so will you. Working with Facebook allows a brand to fully leverage peer pressure, perhaps better than any other form of audience communication.

Without enough Facebook fans, the critical threshold of transformation will not be reached. No business will have a strong enough impact on its own to make the effort to acquire fans worth the effort and cost. Yu mentions in an AllFacebook.com article[5] that Facebook ads can be targeted in very specific ways to help generate the number of "best" fans needed to make those critical threshold numbers.

Value of a Twitter Follower

The value of a Twitter follower was reported by TechCrunch to be less than one cent, according to the popular tech blog

Marketing Pilgrim. Others think a Twitter follower is worth closer to $3 per month,[6] but the actual value varies, depending on the Twitter campaign being run. Yet another valuation pegs Twitter followers as being worth from 17 to 20 cents each.[7] The blog Webucator has a reference to Twitter follower value, defined as the "#followers/#followees."[8] Author and blogger Beth Kanter thinks the value of a Twitter follower is 24 cents.[9] From my point of view, Twitter followers have no value beyond what we assign based on the calculations being applied.

Twitter Users Are More Engaged with Brands Than Facebook Fans Are

According to a study by ExactTarget and CoTweet, Twitter followers are most interested in getting information about a brand or future updates on a brand product.[10] Twitter followers are also more likely to purchase or recommend a brand than e-mail subscribers or Facebook fans.[11] Meanwhile, Facebook fans are motivated more strongly by discounts and promotions than by any other factor. Given these findings, it is tempting to think that form follows function, that the medium profoundly affects the message. As users interact with information differently on each platform, their interests, behavior, and motivations vary.

Value of Sharing on Facebook Versus Twitter

In 2009, the value of a Facebook friend was determined to be 37 cents; that figure was based on a famous Burger King campaign.[12] One way to approach measuring the value of Facebook fans based on a campaign is to determine how many Facebook fans were gained during a campaign and divide it by the increased sales (hopefully) resulting from the campaign after it is completed. Here's a formula I came up with that is based on that idea, which is more complex than it looks, because you first need to determine the increase in sales (which means you need a baseline sales number to begin with).

$$\frac{\text{(No. of FB friends at project end)} - \text{(No. of FB friends at project start)}}{\text{Increase in sales over baseline from project start to project end}}$$

It seems almost pointless to define the value of a tweet, considering the greater amounts of spam that are common on Twitter, yet there are several attempts. Two of them follow:

- BlogCalculator[13] offers users a calculation of the value of its blog by using weighting factors such as unique blog design, global audience, unique visitors per month, blog income, domain age, and blog posts per month.
- Toyota placed a value on tweeting for a particular campaign instead of trying to figure out what an individual tweet is worth. A brand can determine the value of a particular metric for a campaign or promotion, such as the one on the Toyotathonshareathon.com site.

While we're discussing the value of Facebook fans and Twitter followers to some extent, it is also worthwhile to take a look at the value of creating content on blogs.

Value of a Blog Post

Amber Naslund maintains a blog titled "Brass Tack Thinking,"[14] along with her work at Radian6. She has devoted serious thought and used reasonable methodologies to measure the ROI of a particular blog post she did in 2010.[15] Many of her calculations can be automated and possibly run from a monitoring platform such as Radian6.

Among the measures Naslund used are:

- Bit.ly links (linking to the blog post)
- Blog visitors for the 24-hour period of the post
- Percentage of blog visits attributable to the post
- Comments, bookmarks, Facebook shares, likes, and votes on the post
- Traffic sources to the post (direct, Twitter, RSS, Google, etc.)
- Number of retweets of the post
- Potential reach of the post content (usually a calculated number of followers each Twitter user has, multiplied by the number of the user's retweets of the post)
- E-mail inquiries as a result of the post (within same 24 hours)
- Referrals to Radian6 (company site)

Based on the data that monitoring platforms such as Radian6 can capture out of the box, about 85 percent of what Naslund mentions can be tracked by Radian6 using built-in automation. In fact, using Radian6's Engagement Console Extension application, any user could potentialy set up their own automation in this fashion. An automated ROI dashboard for content could evolve out of the calculations now conducted manually by Naslund. The missing piece today has been e-mail integration into Radian6. However, with the announcement of the Radian6 Insights Platform in April 2011, many different providers now have the capability to overlay their data onto Radian6, and that may eventually include e-mail databases. In addition, with the Salesforce acquisition of Radian6 in late March 2011, Radian6 is becoming a place where all social media data merge with other analytics.

Case Study: Beachbody and Radian6

Each January people make resolutions to start the New Year off on the right foot, achieve their goals, and make plans for a successful year. A healthy, balanced lifestyle—with a renewed focus on losing weight, getting in shape, and becoming fit—is often at the top of the list. That's exactly what makes it a busy time for *Beachbody*, a company that started almost 12 years ago, specializing in DVD home-fitness programs featuring online support, fitness gear, and supplements. Among the bestselling programs are P90X, 10 Minute Trainer, Turbo Jam, and Slim in 6, brands that may be familiar through TV infomercials.

Beachbody

Beachbody's owner, Carl Daikeler, recognized early on the potential of infomercials to sell fitness. When he was just 24 years old, he helped build the first infomercial network in the United States, viewed by 50 percent of all TV households in the country. In the mid-1990s, he helped build an affiliate network of more than 100 radio and TV stations to promote fitness products. Now social media figures into the business plan, and Beachbody looks to measure just how fit the social Web really is. Daikeler has a *blog* in which he discusses business ideas and customer success stories; it's one of the many features in the community and support section of the Web site.

Beachbody is active on Facebook, Twitter, YouTube, and Flickr, as are many of its trainers and several product brands. While these are new initiatives, the number of Facebook fans for the P90X brand has reached more than 275,000. There's also a blogger outreach program in which fitness and *mommy bloggers* are offered a free fitness program and asked to blog honestly about the experience.

Social media is part of Beachbody's strategy to proactively connect with customers and passively gauge its online reputation. Beachbody monitors mentions and conversations on the social Web for most of its product brands. In fact, before it was anybody's job to listen, a motivated employee was monitoring and took the initiative to alert the company's customer service VP as to what was being said. That employee now has the only job in the company with "social media" in the title: Pierre Abraham is the social media specialist for Beachbody, and at that earliest point he was listening for disgruntled customers. Now he uses Radian6 to sort through and prioritize over 40,000 mentions per month (and they're all positive, he says).

Most mentions are about P90X, a favorite among celebrities such as actors *Demi Moore and Ashton Kutcher*, singer *Sheryl Crow*, and professional athletes including Philadelphia Eagles' football kicker *David Akers*. Akers started using P90X to regain his strength after a disappointing 2007 season.

Listening Creates Opportunity

Beachbody isn't responding to just actors and actresses; Abraham is always on the lookout for influencers, too. So when the CTO of networking systems giant Cisco, Padmasree Warrior, mentioned on Twitter that she suspected Santa would give her P90X for Christmas instead of chocolates, Abraham quickly saw that she had more than a million followers. He jumped at the opportunity to respond with a word of encouragement. Warrior jovially reciprocated the connection from @beachbody, creating the opportunity for her approximately 1.4 million followers to see the P90X brand, experience the personal outreach, hear the message, and learn that Beachbody is listening.

Radian6

Radian6 provides organizations with a platform to help them monitor and engage in conversations across the social Web. This platform tracks mentions across hundreds of millions of sites and sources, including blogs, forums, comments, photo-, and video-sharing sites, the full Twitter Firehose, and the public Facebook API. Real-time results are automatically pushed to an interactive dashboard that ensures no posts are missed. Clients explore their data via in-depth metrics, filtering, and segmentation tools that find meaningful results in ways that suit their business. The Radian6 Engagement Console allows an enterprise to manage its social media efforts from one window.

Businesses, not-for-profits, and governments use Radian6 to explore sentiment, find influencers, and benchmark their results within their industry or sector. In addition to listening and measuring, Radian6 allows comments to be tagged and assigned for follow-up, making it a powerful component of sales, customer service, and market research. The majority of Fortune 100 companies use Radian6.

The Radian6 platform enabled Abraham to track the above-mentioned connections over time and measure the success of word of mouth on the Web, whether that was following a rise in mentions after launching a new ad campaign or product, or seeing if a new contest builds attention and excitement. One of the strengths in which Abraham sees great value is the ability to save data so he can graph and analyze trends. It has allowed Beachbody to create relationships with its customers, celebrate their success stories, and uncover influencers. He also enjoys the convenience of having one platform to easily track 10 brands across the social Web instead of using several tools, then aggregating the results manually.

Beachbody is in the early phases of using social media, but it's already informing and shaping the company's business strategy.

What the Future Holds: Integration

Vendors are now in a pivotal position to achieve an integration of social media metrics and analytics that, while they're still imperfect, is sufficient to tell a company how it's doing in the social media realm (often considered the Holy Grail of marketing).

The caveat, or gotcha, is that the metric(s) may still not be truly useful or accurate, because consensus is lacking from standards bodies such as IAB, WAA, and CIPR. An intermediate step is needed where analysts step forward and suggest what the final set of metrics ought to be. When working from the business goal out, a convention is needed that shows which data are needed to track ROI information. A few larger, more "instrumented" and data-driven companies are already putting a lot of effort, money, and man hours into this, it is clearly possible, and it is probably on the near horizon.

Radian6, Sysomos, Brandwatch, and Integrasco provide integrations for clients by industry and business type. Much of the ultraviolet data I have written about in my Compete. com paper on Spectrum Analytics[16] is beginning to become visible in dashboards built into the monitoring platforms (with drill-downs, as needed).

My Scribd paper gave examples of the dashboard integrations for Havana Central, the restaurant chain based in New York City, by showing how to integrate Opentable.com, SeamlessWeb.com, Google Analytics, CRM, POS systems cash register income generated from social media, mobile check-ins, QR codes, and RFID/geofencing/mobile geolocation.

Summary

By 2012, the ability of business to integrate, use, and synthesize social listening platforms, capabilities will intersect with the mostly underused capabilities that have been developing. A new era of convergence is dawning in which social listening and analytics will be married to business intelligence. The integration of social listening and business analytics is already taking place through the Radian6 Insights Platform and the Radian6 Engagement Console Extension Gallery (similar to an app store, allowing programmers to add their own routines or programs to Radian6 for message processing).

As we move into 2012, a fuller convergence of listening systems, Web search, Web analytics, social CRM, and internal house data (including e-mail lists) appears very doable, whereas a few years ago, it was much harder to see how that would happen. And as listening platforms continue to mature, analysts will have more control over the role and use of analytics in corporations, perhaps moving into a more pivotal role.

chapter **6**

Influence:
Finding It and Measuring It

This chapter discusses various theories about influence and how to measure it. Influence is so deep a subject that it is impossible to express everything there is to say about it in a single chapter. Furthermore, as a social media topic, influence is evolving quickly, and anything contained in this book will surely need to be updated almost as soon as it is published. But such a book would not be complete without a chapter discussing influencer identification and influencer measurement. This is an interesting wrinkle in the world of analytics, especially around social media, where the number of voices can be difficult to monitor and where it is even harder to determine the significance of each.

According to Gary Lee, CEO of mBLAST.com (you will read more about him later in this chapter), measuring influence is not new and has been discussed for over 100 years.

In a 1898 article "L'opinion et la conversation," later reprinted in his book, L'opinion et la foule, Gabriel Tarde wrote that conversa-

tions among people were what really allowed the media (aka newspapers) to survive. He wrote "if no one conversed, the newspapers would appear to no avail . . . because they would exercise no profound influence on any minds. They would be like a string vibrating without a sounding board.[1]

Tarde felt strongly that only conversations among people about things they read in the media can complete the full cycle of "news," as individuals read information, talk about it with others, and sway public opinion. Tarde's was the first identified academic study of how people influence others. To go back even further, we could point to the book of Exodus in the Bible, where Moses was instructed to convey messages to the Israelites, who were wandering in the desert for 40 years; according to Lee, this may be the first published account of using an "influencer" to spread news.

Here is a more recent, though not quite current, example of the power of social influence. In 1944, sociologist Paul Lazarsfeld[2] published his seminal book, *The People's Choice*, which examined the 1940 presidential election and the factors that shaped voter behavior and action in a county in Ohio. Until this study, the media was viewed as a magic bullet, able to *directly* sway the mass population very effectively. (In fact, during the Second World War, this theory was put to work in various propaganda efforts.) In contrast, however, *The People's Choice* discussed a two-step flow of information from the media to the masses.

In Lazarsfeld's theory, "opinion leaders" were directly involved in the dissemination of information and distribution of that information to the masses. These opinion leaders read what the media said and then repeated it via conversations with their followers—not unlike what occurs in social media today.

This discovery of the two-step model was considered revolutionary by many sociologists at the time and set off a flurry of academic and economic studies to try to learn more about these opinion leaders. Publishers and marketing professionals in particular had a keen interest in learning who these people were, as they realized that identifying and therefore influencing them could translate into actual economic benefits.

In case you still think this is all new, it's not. In his book *The Influentials*, Gabriel Weimann, a professor of communications at Haifa University, states that over 3,900 studies on influentials, opinion leaders, and personal influence have been conducted over the years.

What Is Influence?

When a social media influencer makes a recommendation or asks his readers to do something, the resulting action is similar to the force of gravity in the sense that we attempt to find a way to measure the effects and velocity of the influencer's recommendation or request, establishing the amount of influence present.

But in order to measure influence, we need a benchmark to measure against; and, as of today, definitions and benchmarks for influence are undefined. According to Mike Arauz, a senior strategist at the firm Undercurrent, located in New York, "The most successful influencers [are those] who have found a way to channel their popularity and reputation into collective action. Perhaps they have a tribe of readers who buys every one of their books when they come out, like Seth Godin. Maybe they've used Twitter to inspire evangelists and get loyal customers, like Zappos."[3]

How influential has Chris Brogan, a well-known author, been in plugging Steve Robbins's 2010 book *Get-It-Done*

Guy's 9 Steps to Work Less and Do More?[4] Rather than specu-
late on Brogan's impact, let's take a look at what data we
would need to have in order to measure Brogan's influence.
See Figure 6-1.

Here are some possible measurements of how much Brogan
influenced the sales of Robbins's book:

1. Measure the influence of Brogan's post http://www.chris
    brogan.com/work-less-do-more/
2. Measure the influence of YouTube video http://www
    .youtube.com/watch?v=8LlinpfUBCM&feature=player
    _embedded using YouTube Insights (turned off in this
    case; too bad!)
3. Measure the incidence of Brogan's name with Robbins's
    over time

Figure 6-1 Sysomos Map retweet of Chris Brogan's promotion
of Stever Robbins's book

Source: YouTube.

4. Set up a specific landing page or code tying Brogan's plug to a visit and possible sale of Robbins's book

5. Set up BeenCounter (beencounter.com), Tealium (tealium .com), or a similar browser-history checker that records every visit to any Robbins page that was "exposed" to a Brogan page (you need an entire list of any sites and pages associated with Brogan)

6. Look for overlaps in searches between "Chris Brogan" and "Steven Robbins"

These measurements reveal a correlation between Brogan and mentions about Robbins and his book (see Figure 6-2). But unless extensive analytics were set up beforehand, it would be very difficult, perhaps impossible, to measure with full accuracy the degree of influence Chris Brogan had on the

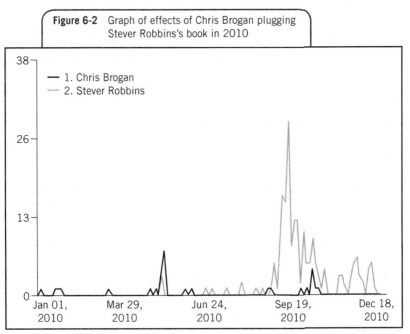

Figure 6-2   Graph of effects of Chris Brogan plugging Steven Robbins's book in 2010

Source: Sysomos.

sales of Steve Robbins's book. (He is sometimes known as "steve robbins," which is, by the way, an example of "linguistic variations" as discussed in Chapter 3.)

I made the case to prove influence and social media ROI exists (in that the data exist) but is "ultraviolet" (not viewable or traceable because we lack the right information to track it).[5] In order to track social media ROI (and, by proxy, influence), the first step is to enable the right measurement tracking and next include all the lacking information until all the ultraviolet data are visible and able to be tracked.[6]

My fundamental belief is that influence and social media ROI can be fully tracked, but the right formulas and the data to populate the formulas have not been developed or standardized to the extent they are useful to business.

Can Data Serve as a Proxy for Influence?

It is tempting to define influence as a combination of digital signals that are currently measureable (for example, number of retweets, number of lists, number of likes, and number of friends and/or shares), but the right combination of metrics still does not necessarily yield reliable influence scoring. However, MBlast's Influence platform threatens to improve and disrupt the current ways to measure influence online.[7] This is potentially a good thing, as disruptions often bring improvement. See Figure 6-3.

Peter Shankman, a well-known Internet celebrity, uses Klout Scores in order to decide who to invite to his parties.[8] Now owned by AOL, the Internet newspaper *Huffington Post* uses Klout Scores and the Adaptive Semantics platform to define the influence of its readers.[9]

The presence of Klout along with newer semantic platforms such as Adaptive Semantics bring influence mapping

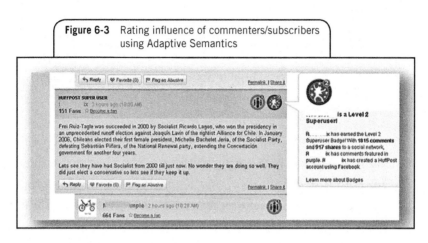

Figure 6-3 Rating influence of commenters/subscribers using Adaptive Semantics

Source: Huffington Post

up to a higher level. Still, it remains unknown if these signals truly refer back to influence as it is generally understood. And most of all, people want to know and use lists—in this case, lists of influentials. An influencer list is a collection of online accounts of individuals considered important to groups of people specializing in a particular subject or service.

Influence has a number of components that can be calculated independently, while scores can be weighted and an overall influencer rating can be assigned based on those calculations, yet the quality of the results remains questionable.[10]

Measures for Influence

There are several ideas about what creates the influence we are trying to measure and how far back in time one should go to determine it. Authority Score (Sysomos), Peek Score (PeekYou), and countless other rank sites are using measures such as page rank, compete visits (when available), Alexa rank, back links, and updates (posting frequency) because the information is openly available via APIs.

Proxies for influence continue to be disappointing, however, because they are not topical, up-to-date, or accurate enough. Plus, a person's indirect influence on a subject or situation is not directly measurable with any online platforms currently on the market.

Even worse, there is a fundamental mismatch between outputs of social monitoring platforms (a series of sites ranked for authority or influence) and usable lists of individuals that marketers are interested in; it takes a considerable amount of work to filter and translate any monitoring output into one. However, the m-PACT and TRAACKR Influence platforms do address this issue by providing lists of influencers (instead of lists of Web sites) with relevant and up-to-date contact information and a short biography of each influencer.

Monitoring Platforms Used to Find Influencers

Here are some examples of monitoring platforms that are being used to find influencers:

Radian6

We've talked about this company in other contexts so far, but its technology can also be used to track influence. Radian6 has an influence-reporting feature called the Influencer widget that can provide a list of on-topic influencers for blogs, message boards, and mainstream media, video, photo-sharing, and micro-blogging sites such as Twitter. Influence ranking is affected by how sliders are set up in the Influencer EQ dashboard in its topic profile configuration, as shown in Figure 6-4.

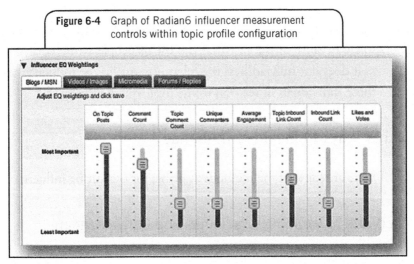

Figure 6-4 Graph of Radian6 influencer measurement controls within topic profile configuration

Source: Radian6.com

Sysomos

By identifying blog influencers (sorted by authority), Sysomos MAP can produce several thousand sites that could potentially be influential. The author ran informal tests and found that the ratio of signal-to-noise is about 35:65, but the results are filtered to a state-and-city level in some cases. The typical times it takes to generate and sort a list is about 8 to 16 hours, and the list will need to be further vetted for contact information, names, and so on (an additional 8 to 16 hours).

Alterian SM2

Alterian SM2 produces a list of top authors it can use as an influencer list, but top authors are simply a list of top contributors to whatever data SM2 collected in a profile. Alterian can produce a list of content authors, but it is unlikely that the list will be useful solely because of the fact that the list of people wrote content, as it does not fully address the relevance, quality, or influence of those individuals in relation to the topic query or subject.

Other Ways to Measure Influence

Here are some of the methods available for measuring influence:

Web Site or Web Page Backlinks and Categorization

Individuals may be influential on a particular subject or set of subjects by following a trail of Web links (or what are commonly called "backlinks") referring to Web pages authored by individuals, businesses, or organizations. This was the original premise of Google's PageRank, named after Larry Page's algorithm that worked out a credible way to derive a Web page's "rank" by the quality of other Web pages linking to it.

Web Directories

Lists such as Yahoo! Directories are considered by search engines to have a high degree of accuracy (signal) with a low degree of noise (spam and/or false sites in a category) because they are maintained by humans. The fundamental reason to register a Web site for a directory, besides driving traffic to it, is to inform search engines of categorical definitions (for example, Architects/houses/house plans).

As a by-product of the original search engine categorizations, what I categorize as first-generation social media monitoring platforms (founded between 2005 and 2008), running similar sets of algorithms as search engines (social monitoring platforms are often based on search-engine technology and are search engines in every sense of the word) often share the same categorizations and found influencer sites and authors.

Profile: Gary Lee, CEO of mBLAST

Gary Lee has over 25 years of experience in high-tech marketing development and executive management in various global telecom and high-tech companies, including Nortel, Sprint, and General DataComm. He has served as CEO at FlexLight Networks and as president and chief operating officer at Home Wireless Networks. These two companies established business operations in North America, Europe, China, and Israel, and were backed by close to $100 million in investments from Lucent, Telenor, Groupo Carso, BT, Accel Partners, and St. Paul Venture Capital, among others. In both start-ups, Lee took the companies from concept to market launch and revenue.

He also was the North American CEO of global PR and marketing services agency Mi liberty, working with wireless and telecommunications companies around the globe for both business-to-business and business-to-consumer markets. He earned a BA in computer science from Furman University and an MBA from Belmont University's Massey School of Business.

Introduction to m-PACT and mBLAST

According to Gary Lee, "m-PACT is a new influence measurement platform that is shaking up the waters with a free offering (as of May 2011); m-PACT PRO includes full Boolean queries and integrations with databases containing hundreds of thousands of media contacts, publications, blogs, and editorial calendar opportunities. We frequently use m-PACT

PRO and I have endorsed the platform (a quote of mine is on the mBLAST home page where the free version of m-PACT can be accessed).

"mBLAST is made up of marketers, PR experts, and influencers. We understand what marketers need from influencers, how influencers need to interact with marketers, and how to make it all happen effectively and efficiently.

"We're experienced professionals with strong depth in leading-edge technologies, organizational leadership, and start-up management and exit success. In combination, the mBLAST leadership has directly led more than a half-dozen firms and been involved with more than 100 start-ups in the high-tech arena. This experience is powering mBLAST to a leadership position in media and marketing relationship management."

How m-PACT Works

Gary continues, "We do far more than just derive data for our clients; for example, we follow articles, blogs, and tweets. We also provide a layer of intelligence on top to actually allow clients to see who are the most important voices in all those articles, blogs, and tweets, and then provide information for clients to contact the authors for additional engagement. Further, we identify opportunities where clients may be able to influence these influencers through their future actions.

"Sorting through the media used to be easy. Smart marketers knew the media professionals and influencers in their field and regularly courted these people to sway their own influence over them—something we call 'influencing the influencer.' In the present day, however, there are now thousands of voices that must be listened to and evaluated to determine which have influence and authority. (This is a relatively new development, given the creation of social media tools, blogs, and other 'self-publishing' tools.)

"And that's why, in a world where social and online media has forever changed how information is shared 24/7/364— 364 because everyone should take at least one day off a year to actually do something other than be connected to everyone else electronically. It's a lot harder now to measure who the influencers are. In fact, to those in the media and to those software providers touting influencer identification as the next, big, new thing . . . it's not.

"Instead, it's something smart marketing professionals have known about forever and have long been taking advantage of in their marketing efforts. Intelligent marketing professionals have always identified voices in the media and conversation streams that influence their market. It's a two-step process, where marketing professionals look first to identify those in the traditional world of journalism and analysts who are widely followed and whose opinions matters. Then the marketers look at the second layer, where highly influential people take the work of these media professionals and apply it in their own messages to influence others.

"This is the role traditionally played by smart PR and communications professionals: to identify who those influencers are and to work to engage with them. Again, it's not anything new. But something *has* changed, and that is the sheer volume of voices that one needs to listen to in order to determine who the real influencers are."

What Makes m-PACT Different

Gary Lee continues, "We deploy influencer identification and influencer mapping using a very sophisticated set of algorithms to measure influence. We start with a topics-based approach that is sensible for the user—especially those in marketing, in order to discover the influencers who matter to their market instead of trying to perform some generic form of influencer measurement across the entire Web. The former has immense value, while the latter has little if any value.

"The premise is still the same: which of these voices are the opinion leaders (a.k.a., the influencers) listening to, and in turn, which are influencing my market? And as good marketers, it's critical to identify both of these voices: the people writing the original material being used to influence your market, and the influencers who are helping with that influence by passing the message along.

"It's not a new concept, but it is increasingly difficult to do effectively, because we have to sort through millions of potential conversations daily across traditional online and social media and heuristically derive influencer models that allow us to determine who really matters among the chatter. What was once a relatively simple, manual task—where all you had to do was pay attention—has now become a daunting, fire-hose-like stream of data being published or posted 24/7/364. m-PACT also puts a huge amount into content extraction and page processing. We are very good at cleaning data, extracting data, algorithmically finding information, and so on."

The Right Tools for This Work?

Lee continues, "To effectively manage this deluge of information, you need tools that allow you to determine who is talking about topics that matter the most to your market, so you can identify who among those voices actually have real authority and influence. This can be done by hand, but it is a time-consuming process—so time-consuming in some markets that there's no real way to reach conclusions before the very data you're evaluating has changed!

"Many new tools are on the market now that take a mixed approach to how and where to measure influence. Most of them just look at social media. They attempt to determine who on Twitter and a few other social networks really matter, and who have the reach and audience to influence a market or idea.

"To identify influencers, the m-PACT engine utilizes patent-pending processes and algorithms based on authority, currency, relevancy, volume, and other key data points. The m-PACT engine is designed to provide actionable information via a customizable dashboard and a set of reports.

"m-PACT presents an easy-to-understand influence map, which allows users to dig deeper into each influence to see what is actually being said in blogs, articles, and social media. It also offers contact details to assist in further potential engagement with these influencers. Based on what it locates on the Web, m-PACT reports what the influencers are saying and helps contact them.

"We believe there are some limitations with the first-generation tool sets in the market today—specifically, that many of the developers promote the idea that the tools help 'enable everyone to understand and leverage their influence.' While we think this is an interesting model—and, let's face it, everyone loves to check out scoring machines that attempt to measure how popular, influential, and 'beautiful' we are compared with others—the value of this type of tool for the marketing or analytics professional is extremely small.

"Measuring influence from a pool of Twitter IDs of people that I already know (including myself) is myopic: I am likely going to miss someone else. And measuring my score against another's, especially generic influence scores based across all topics, is of little value to someone trying to find the particular influencers who can really move their market.

"It is wise to be reticent with regard to making long-term predictions about the pricing or the technology powering these new tools, because the market and thirst for these burgeoning platforms are so dynamic and ever-changing.

"Analytic tools must have valid and logical output to be put to use by marketing and measurement professionals. Influencer measurement tools are no exception. That's why next-generation tools from mBLAST and other companies are focusing on measuring influence around defined topical areas and then allowing the analytics professional to dig deeper into the data to understand who is influential and why. Measuring influence is not about some arbitrary score; it's about following rules and best practices for how the measuring of influence has been approached for over 100 years."

Using Backlinks to Determine Influence

As mentioned earlier, using backlinks to determine influence is a carryover from search engines. There are both positive and negative points to the Web site or Web page backlinks approach to influence; let's take a look at both:

Positive: Easy to employ; information available from various public source APIs; free or inexpensive to collect

Negative: Proliferation of spam and noise on the Web makes it much harder to get anything useful from backlinks categorization as a basis of influencer selection

Authority Lists

Sysomos is a popular social monitoring platform that uses a combination of signals to define authority level. This is often used as another proxy for influence; although the correlation is far from perfect, it's still one of the better examples of the backlinks approach to influence measurement using public APIs to services such as Compete.com, Google, and Alexa, to name a few.

Each Web site has its own authority level, but it is not granular down to the page level, nor is it based on topic. What we really need—which no platform appears to provide as yet—is the authority level of a piece of content, such as text on a page and who it influences, as well as who influences the content; this is still an evolving field, and there will be many new developments even by the time this book goes to press.

All the factors or "signals" discussed above can be mixed in different ways to define influencer listing orders. And registering in any major Web directory is still a good practice, because categorizing pages in major directories provides a useful signal for topical influence when combined with other, more relevant signals.

Event Attendance

Another way to gauge topical influence is to actually participate in activities, events, conferences, and meet-up groups that correlate with interest in a particular topic. For example, I attend many search engine marketing and social media monitoring conferences; my conference schedule is online and can be crawled and categorized by social listening platforms.

There are plenty of other signals that can be used to find influencers as well:

- **Speaking at any conference** is an automatic influencer ranking (point score)
- Even simply **attending a conference** demonstrates interest (categorization) but may carry a lesser score than presenting at the same conference. Press coverage is a ranking factor for influence, as **being mentioned in any way by the press** or connected to an event or as part of a story can also be a signal.
- **Authoring book(s), paper(s), podcasts, and vidcasts** are ways of both categorizing a person's influence and ranking it.
- **Check-ins to locations** (often public and crawlable by search engines and social monitoring platforms) show interest and participation, especially if they happen frequently; they can be a ranking signal for influence.
- **Being a member of a group, organization, or meet-up group** is an influencer-ranking signal, as it shows interest in the organization.
- **Subscriptions to publications, magazines, and newspapers**— depending on how the data are gathered and categorized—can be an influencer signal. For example, people who subscribe to *The Economist*, a magazine that many in financial services and politics read, may be a matter for intelligence, which has a strong association with influence, in my opinion.
- **Comments to online publications such as the *Huffington Post*, the *New York Times*, or any online publication** can be data mined if they can be tied back to an individual's identity. In fact, services such as PeekYou have been able to aggre-

gate online personas and link them back to individuals making it easier for social media analytics platforms to gauge influencers on a subject.

▪ **Participation in forums and message boards** is a signal of interest and participation in the subject of the message board and the thread. When posting activity is added, a powerful signal is created that can be an important part of an influence algorithm. Platforms such as Integrasco can aggregate forum activity of a user across all the forums they post on when the user employs the same handle.

▪ **Facebook likes and shares**, to the extent this information is publically available, can be used as a signal for participation, interest, and influence (if what is shared is then shared by several others). In fact, a new breed of social media analytics platform is evolving around data-mining of Facebook brand fan pages. While there are no examples in this book, the author has seen strong activity in this area of analytics, and it is likely we will see several analytic platforms of this type in the next year or two.

▪ **Twitter retweets**, often rolled up into other influence metrics, can be a powerful signal if they happen frequently

▪ **Virtual followers and friends** are clearly influencer signals: anyone who follows an individual is in some way acknowledging, if not direct influence, the willingness to be reached and thereby the possibility of being influenced.

The more one searches for signals, the more information there is to categorize and match up, and the sky (or your data warehouse) is the limit.

Influencers as Experts

In 2010, Altimeter Group and Web Analytics Demystified came out with a set of 12 social marketing analytics framework metrics[11] that could be used for ROI and perhaps be used for influencer identification as well.

How Much of an Expert Are You?

People know me to be an expert in Web analytics, search, social media, and perhaps art, but how many more ways would someone want to categorize me—or anyone else, for that matter? Putting the world into predefined buckets allows us to change chaos into order and to take a million details and place them into a few themes or categories, which conserves our energy and attention for the things that really matter to us. Emotionally, it is much easier to see the world as black and white or a few shades of gray rather than see myriad colors surrounding us. By playing it safe, our blinders and prejudices about reality are confirmed, and we see much of what we want to see because of how we categorize situations and the people we encounter, and this can have both positive and negative implications.

Things are either good or bad, hot or cold, satisfying or unsatisfying, colorful or monochromatic, intelligent or dumb, and so on. Perhaps, we can handle only a few dimensions at a time, in order to remember and categorize a situation as well as to describe it to others. But what if there were several ways (or dimensions) to describe anyone or anything? Most likely situations and people would end up being categorized in two or three dimensions anway; most of the rest would be lost in translation. And so, while simplifying our choices makes it easier to choose, we might be tuning out information (or data) that we actually need to lead us to better decisions.

In summary, in categorizing individuals by their interests and activities, it is important to make sure our selections actually move us forward instead of limiting what we experience.

How to Find an Expert on Anything

Fresh Networks did an excellent report on finding influencers using 10 of the most commonly used social media monitoring platforms, including Alterian, Attensity 360, Brandwatch, PeerIndex, Radian6, Scoutlabs, Social Radar, Synthesio, Sysomos, and Visible Technologies.[12] With the exception of Visible Technologies, I have used all these platforms and reviewed most of them. From the standpoint of a brand, you would want to find out where your audience is in order to reach out to them.

Finding Your Audience

There are several online research and benchmarking tools that can focus on target audiences by demographics (age, gender, location, and race). Quantcast defines audiences by income, education, and behavioral characteristics (such as frequent visitors versus passersby). Some platforms, including ComScore and Quantcast, allow data collection using a JavaScript tag for much greater accuracy. Once you define your audiences with the type of information the aforementioned tools provide, you can reverse the filtering to find out, for instance, which online locations your target audiences go to.

Social media monitoring platforms such as Sysomos Map and Radian6 have been used to find audiences online, but with a limited degree of success. Imagine entering a crowded room at a party and eavesdropping on the conversations of several strangers. You are able to listen to only snippets of their exchanges and do not directly interact (you're not asking what they do for a living or what they believe, for instance). Trying to figure out who they are and what they believe is extremely difficult, because you are getting only fragments of information, certainly not enough to make positive determinations of anything you'd like to know. But thankfully, to find out those things, there are alternative methods.

For example, it is much easier to classify people by how they describe themselves through their user profiles (such as occupation, interests, activities, and Web sites), which can often be ascertained using their Twitter profile information, which is easy to gather by using free tools such as Follower Wonk, allowing a user to search profiles for influencers on a particular subject or location.

Follower Wonk

With the Follower Wonk platform, you can pull up a remarkable amount of information that is fairly accurate in a short period of time (a few hours on average).

Follower Wonk works well for finding influencers by geolocation, and it is easy to export the list it generates into a spreadsheet.

Figure 6-5 shows what Follower Wonk results look like.

Although Follower Wonk is a free tool, the quality and certainty of the information provided are pretty good, and it is a fine choice to use in lieu of a paid platform or service providing a higher quality of data and reliability.

Figure 6-5 Follower Wonk search results

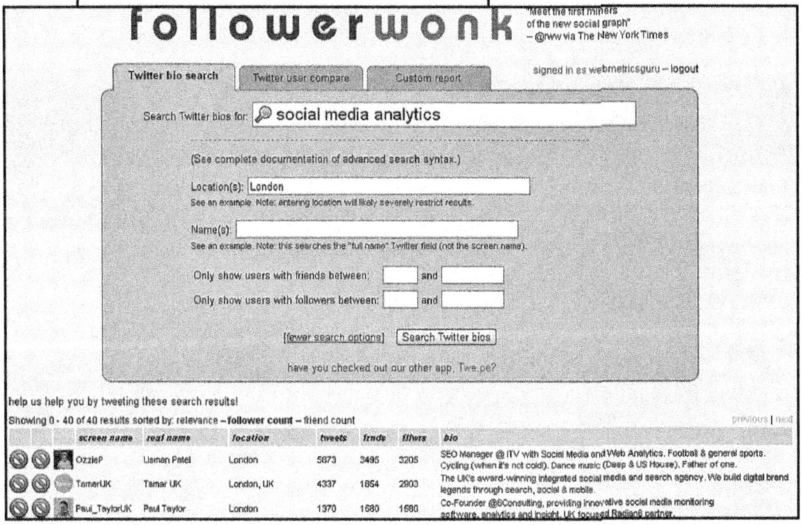

Source: Followerwonk.com

Klout

Klout.net is another way you can find influentials on Twitter by using a set of 11 metrics that the platform defines. Because each audience has influentials within it, reaching out to influencers is a way of connecting with people who follow the influencers. A Klout search is shown in Figure 6-6.

Klout continues to innovate and improve its methods of calculating influence, using a Klout score, which is frequently updated. Klout's information is derived from data on Twitter and Facebook. Klout, however, still serves mainly as entertainment and is unable to provide serious influencer lists that businesses would be willing to pay for, because the degree of certainty behind the data is too low. However, Klout has been improving its platform, and the information it provides is becoming increasingly more relevant.

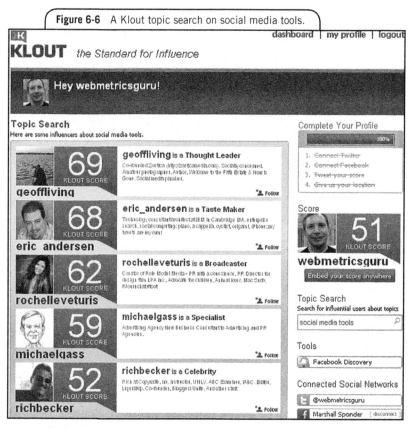

Figure 6-6 A Klout topic search on social media tools.

Source: Klout.com

Time is money, and Klout's focus on Twitter makes it good for finding influencers based on relatively short-term, topical online behavior (recent posting activity and history), but not at measuring influence that spans over months or years of activity.

TRAACKR

Traackr is as far from Klout as any two influencer platforms can be, although both offer similar end products for the users. Traackr is a paid service; it costs a few hundred dollars a month to produce a short list of 25 influencers, expandable to longer lists (which are updated on a weekly basis) for an additional fee. The usability of the lists and the certainty that they can be used for what they were intended is very high. Traackr offers an online authority list or "A-List," a collection of individuals that steer online conversations about a specific market or topic. The quality of Traackr's lists is next to impossible to replicate within monitoring platforms that are available at press time though m-PACT (which incorporates monitoring in its platform does a pretty good job at matching Traackr on quality). See Figure 6-7.

The influencer list or A-List takes about a week to generate; it is 70 percent automated, and the remainder is manual work to fill in gaps. Traackr's methodology includes iterative keyword crawling of social media platforms to search for the

Figure 6-7 A-List search of PR 2.0 influencers powered by Traacker

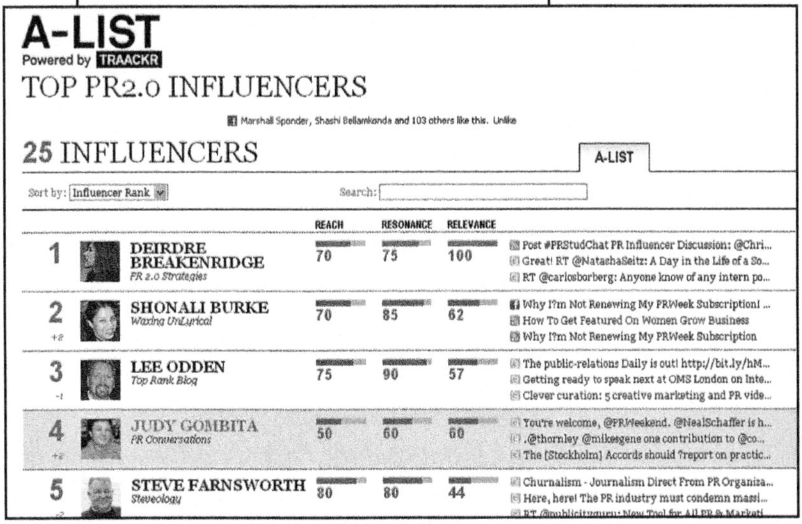

Source: Traacker

most active users and profile aggregation across multiple channels and accounts.

Traackr's Metrics

Traackr measures influence by the following metrics:

Reach: The ability to generate views
Resonance: The ability to spark conversations
Relevance: The ability to cover specific topics/markets

Ecairn

Another variant of the active-listening approach is using the Ecairn platform to create influencer lists of bloggers. It is a newer entrant in the influencer category, but it has actually been around for a few years, allowing for distributed list building along with machine-learning algorithms. Ecairn allows for an additional segmentation by category that can be built in; for example: "find social media ROI influencers in the dentistry segment of community and blogs." The most attractive feature of Ecairn is its ability to have remotely built lists maintained by different parts of an organization that can be continually leveraged. Ecairn is great for a company seeking to build lists and annotate them (for instance, with contact information), blending elements of a CRM into list building.

PeekYou

Note: The author is a member of the PeekYou Advisory Board.
PeekYou is an online aggregation service that collects publicly available information about individuals along with

their online accounts, which it makes available for free. Peek You.com has done a few interesting case studies, and I have published them on my WebMetricsGuru blog.[13] PeekYou is capable of doing a reverse lookup against URLs to verify the authors. In 2011, PeekYou will supply select social media vendors such as Radian6, via the Radian6 Insights Platform, with its data, and that will improve the quality and usefulness of various influencer searches performed on those platforms. An example of PeekYou search results is shown in Figure 6-8.

Currently, PeekYou fully resolves about a third of all the names in the United States with identification at the level above, and another third partially. While not all information is fully updated, PeekYou is a significant advance in identity information aggregation over most other platforms' products.

Figure 6-8 PeekYou search results for Brett M. Petersel

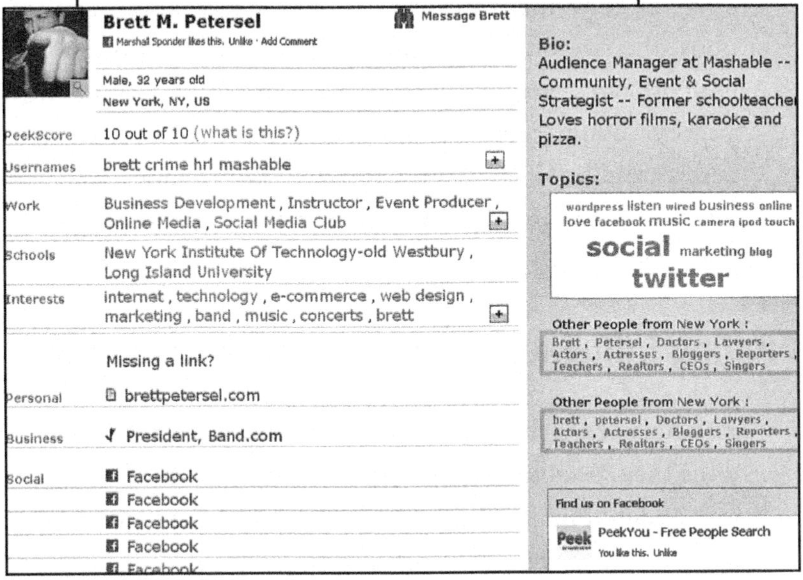

Source: PeekYou.com

m-Pact

Among the most interesting new influencer platforms is m-Pact,[14] which helps brands and agencies engage with the influencers who matter most to their target markets. m-Pact's Topic and Web-based platform constantly indexes millions of data streams from 700,000 publications and other media sources.

Pushkart

Yet another type of influence uses mobile customers in order to measure the social net worth[15] of their network of friends.[16] As of press time, Pushkart is a mobile app mainly for the iPhone, and is available only in New York City. The company plans to offer the service on the national and international stages.

Pushkart's proprietary algorithm determines the interest levels in consumer categories among mobile users' connections, the size of their social networks, and how often they use Pushkart. Each user is treated as a broadcast channel with a specific audience, reach, and demographic. As a result, businesses are able, via Pushkart's Social Networth index, to determine the value of customers who redeem "deals" entered with Pushkart.

Finding Influencers through Active Listening

Although many businesses perceive influencer lists as something they specifically buy or play with for free, there is another way of defining and finding influencers and the communities in which they interact: by employing active listening via social media analytics. In my analytics work, clients often request regular monitoring and insight (using some of the monitoring platforms we cover in this book).

Each of the social listening platforms offers methods to sort and filter online data, but there is no way to monitor well without actually reading and interacting with the online content being monitored. While listening for important trends and information, one finds individuals who stand out for a variety of reasons. When the name of a person sticks out in a listening report (an examination of trends and news that happens around a brand, subject, person, or whatever is being monitored), it makes sense to make note of it, along with the context of what is being said by that individual; an additional metric to collect is how many people subscribe to a blog via an RSS aggregator such as Feedburner.

Once a list is collected through active listening, it can be further examined for relevance and outreach if stakeholders agree over time that the entries are influential and remain so.

Investing in the listening process can create excellent lists of influencers, but these tend to reflect the keyword queries used in listening reports or profiles. Businesses and other users of social media analytics need to invest in social media listening to the extent that they are willing to build awareness and presence online. Similar to the benefits of regular exercise and having routine checkups, the case for online listening reports grows as social media awareness increases within the enterprise: the more you practice it, the more results you'll see.

Does Influence Add Up to a Score?

There are no universal metrics that work in every situation. Influence is relative and contextual. A few years ago, the Edelman Company published a distributed influence paper that attracted a lot of attention, but it was also widely debunked.[17]

In my WebMetricsGuru blog as well, I wrote a post about influence scoring a few years ago where I examined the formulas that I knew about at the time.[18] As we have seen in this chapter, there are several hard metrics and many soft ones that are most often subjective valuations depending on what is known as scoring and evaluation.

Engagement

Most of the time, content being analyzed for influence does not lend itself to deep analysis for engagement. Also, message recall and retention data, such as those used in a questionnaire, are qualitative and usually are not measured by site analytics platforms.

Influence

One thing is clear: scoring influence will hinge on the approach of the person doing the measurement, as there is no absolute right or wrong, and most often only a fraction of the information needed to calculate influence may be available.

Summary

No matter how comprehensive this chapter aims to be, it remains incomplete. An entire book could treat this emerging subject of influence in greater depth and might still barely cover the subject. I can say with conviction, however, that for the purpose of this book, influence is the ability of an individual to influence others to take some action. Influence can be intentional or unintentional, which probably should be taken into account.

Online social monitoring platforms such as those we discuss in this book have a window into measurement of digital signals, but as we have seen, most of the important attributes of influence only incompletely correlate with actual influence as we understand it. Social media commentator Stowe Boyd has a different take on how influence can be determined by finding the amount of "betweenness" and "high eigen values" in a list of influentials. He goes on to say, "Influence doesn't seem directly linked to how many people you are connected to. It's a function of being connected to others who have short chains to many other people with high betweenness. Or, looked at differently, betweenness is a measure of how many social circles, or social scenes, a person is connected to."[19]

It is not who you know, according to Boyd; it's *where* you know. Social network placement may have more of a role in true influence mapping than one's number of friends or connections. In fact, according to *Technology Review*,[20] a person who is strategically placed in certain locations within the social graph might be far more influential, ultimately, than more well-known social celebrities.

As Boyd says, "A less connected person who is strategically placed in the core of the network will have a significant effect that leads to dissemination through a large fraction of the population."[21]

Nevertheless, it is my belief that influence can be measured with properly developed formulas that are put into effect after the requisite data are captured.

chapter 7

Scorecarding: Collecting and Understanding Social Media Data*

Just what is a "social media scorecard"? Until there is a generally agreed-upon definition for what a social media scorecard
is and what it contains, everyone in the media, marketing, and
advertising industries must understand exactly how the term
is being used, whenever it is cited. This goes for research vendors and buyers, and for trade associations and reporters who
cover the space, among others. Providing case-by-case definitions is as important as explaining research methodology.

I think social media scorecards should offer more information beyond the normal buzz monitoring reports that social
media monitoring platforms provide. Information to add to
the scorecard includes Web site analytics (for example, Google
Analytics data) and organic search queries, because social
media marketing and search marketing are rapidly converging.
In fact, Facebook and Twitter messaging appear in the search
results of many search engines; it is necessary to keep both in

---

* Many of the ideas in Chapters 7 and 8 are derived from the work of Gary Angel
of Semphonic.

mind and therefore measure both in one place. I also think that scorecards should measure the progress of any campaign being run with social media of the brand being measured.

Too often data are being left out of scorecards that should have been included, such as the traffic to a Web site that was driven by quick response codes, mobile check-ins (such as on Foursquare and Facebook Places), or any house data (internal database information) on which social media has an impact. As usual, the more customized a scorecard or report, the more actionable it's likely to be, as the devil is usually in the details. Also, as scorecards become more complex, they begin to look more similar to the enterprise scorecards that medium and large corporations produce for marketing development or market research. Then again, getting access to site analytics house data and so on is not always possible, further limiting the end results.

I think actionable scorecards that use a two-tiered seg-mentation, as put forth by CTO Gary Angel of Semphonic. com, is the best approach for organizations in order to make scorecards actionable (for example, Gary gives an example of segmenting Web site metrics by Visitor Type/Online Customer, Offline Customer, both Online and Offline as shown in the Semphonic case study in Chapter 8). In addition, Angel points out that choosing the wrong metrics or key performance indica-tors around a site can set an organization backwards.[1]

Scorecards can become too difficult to maintain when they include information that is too hard and time-consum-ing to gather, such as behavioral data that have to be scored or coded by humans, customer response information, survey results, or content categorization that is not able to be auto-mated. I think an organization must define how important getting all the metrics in one dashboard is, as the integration work can be considerable. While there are continual improvements in automated machine-learning algorithms to categorize and score online content, the programs are not yet sophisticated enough to handle many of the expressions people use within their posts or their behavior online. Content that is accurately categorized is generally scored, or coded, by people, and it is expensive and time-consuming to compile this work on a regular basis. Typically, international monitoring projects such as those examined in Chapter 3 require a lot of manual work, and there are many other cases, such as in brand scoring, where a strong manual component of compiling a scorecard can make it unmaintainable.

Forums and Influencers

The technology to crawl forums deeply and pick out influencers (for instance, thread and topic administrators) is present in Integrasco's social media platform, which is discussed in Chapter 2 and elsewhere in this book. Integrasco's platform can collect minuscule pieces of information and construct profiles of every participant in a forum plus their interrelationships with other forums in which they've posted (which is fairly unique based on the platforms I have worked with).

Although Integrasco is having more success crawling forums and message boards than the rest of the platforms I researched, tested, and examined, much of the information needed for a scorecard ends up being subjective. It is necessary to go into a forum and spend considerable time looking at threads and observing who is interacting, and whether those people may be influential beyond a particular post in a thread; this brings into question how much time can be allotted for this level of subjective data-mining and whether it's worth it.

Approaches to Social Media Scorecards

According to the blog Gossamer, the new marketing skill set needed to analyze and create actionable social media scorecards is sounding more and more like database management, Web analytics, or statistical analysis. This is interesting, because, up until recently, social media was dominated by marketing professionals who had a limited interest in or understanding of the uses of online social data, including "cleansed data." But the new skill set is increasingly becoming an indispensible part of social media analytics today (as witnessed by this book), including:

▪ **Data gathering** Data are everywhere, but finding the exact data in question is similar to trying to find the proverbial needle in a haystack. Marketing managers need to know where to look and which automation tools to use to generate the data. Perhaps a mashup of data from various sources is also needed. Having an ability to fluently work with spreadsheet programs, sort, filter, and manipulate data are becoming core requirements of some jobs.

▪ **Data analysis** This is the most important part of the entire data-management process. Which correlations matter? Which trends are significant? For example, a Web site bounce rate of 45 percent can be excellent or terrible, depending on the specifics of your Web site. Successful data analysis requires both marketing and technical skills to know what the numbers mean and which numbers are important.

▪ **Data reporting** Ultimately, the marketing analytics process leads to recommendations for improvements, new programs, and new budgets. To convince various stakeholders of the importance of a marketing program utilizing social media, marketing managers must be able to make their case as vividly and quickly as possible, to make the numbers sing. Reporting skills and the ability to condense complex data into simple dashboards, scorecards, and other management reports are crucial to getting support from the rest of the organization. Translated into career-speak: know how to report and thus elevate your chances for a promotion and/or big raise.

Recommended Social Media Scorecards

In 2009 a post by Nathan Gilliatt, author of the popular blog Net-Savvy Executive, highlighted various PR agency approaches to measuring social media,[2] including Conversation Impact (Ogilvy PR), Fluent (Razorfish with TNS Cymfony and Keller Fay Group), and the Digital Footprint Index (Zócalo Group with DePaul University). Gilliatt was quick to point out that all three scorecards measure different things, like marketing effectiveness (Conversation Impact), perception (Fluent), and PR effectiveness (Digital Footprint Index). There is no golden metric that covers everything a stakeholder or client needs or wants to know.

Let's take a closer look at these three approaches to building agency social media scorecards.

Ogilvy Conversation Impact

The data used to populate the Ogilvy Conversation Impact scorecard[3] are listed below. Measures that are in **boldface** are ones that are often difficult to obtain and/or highly prone to error, meaning they are easily skewed.

- Reach and positioning
- Unique monthly visits

- Time on site
- Overall volume
- **Share of voice within category or brand family**
- Search visibility
- **Preference**
- **Sentiment index (percentage of positive mentions and percentage of negative mentions) in social media**
- **Share of positive voice in social media, *within category***
- Relative Net Promoter score, absolute or within category
- Action
- Registrations
- Sales
- **Advocacy**

Unique monthly visits, time on site, and overall volume for competitor sites can be obtained via third party-rating services such as Compete.com, Comscore, and Nielsen, but the main purpose is for benchmarking, not hard analytics. When used in lieu of site analytics, data are usually inaccurate and too often are not precise enough to actually be useful.

While not strictly accurate in their data, however, third-party rating services offer interested brands a way to compare themselves with one another in a nonthreatening way, using trending information (without compromising a company's internal company) that can be useful for marketing insights (which is the main function they serve).

Razorfish Fluent

The social influence marketing (SIM) score[4] measures two critical attributes:

1. The total share of consumer conversations a brand has online (reach)
2. The degree to which consumers like or dislike a brand when they talk to one another online (consumer sentiment, or likability). Consumer sentiment is akin to a Net Promoter score: likability can be a pretty fuzzy metric—fairly time-intensive to compute and, more likely than not, prone to manual errors, in the author's opinion.

Data are gathered via two sources, both very expensive and difficult to manipulate:

1. **The Keller Fey Group online survey for Consumer Share of Conversations** The sample is drawn from the largest online consumer panels and is demographically balanced for ages 13 to 69. Respondents are recruited to take notes on conversations in 15 marketing categories over the next 24 hours.
2. **TNS Cymfony social media** mentions data (Cymfony is similar to other platforms examined in this book, including Radian6, Sysomos MAP, Lithium Social Media, and Alterian SM2.) The data are scrubbed manually using a six-step process (which, because it is manual, is prone to error). The results are analyzed for tone or tonality (both by humans and by automated programs), and used for the consumer sentiment part of the SIM score. The formula for the SIM score is the net sentiment for the brand divided by the net sentiment for the industry. The components of the preceding formula are:
   - Net sentiment for the brand = (positive + neutral conversations − negative conversations)/Total conversations for the brand

▪ Net sentiment for the industry = (positive + neutral conversations − negative conversations)/Total conversations for the industry

Because the data for Fluent are scrubbed and analyzed for tonality, the process ends up being subjective, with results varying depending on who is doing the scoring. And, as I mentioned earlier, likability is of course difficult to measure objectively and in a repeatable way. For example, when others tabulate "likeability" with the same information, they should come up with the same exact score.

Zócalo Group's Digital Footprint Index

The DFI[5] quantitatively measures, scores, and tracks the progress of online engagement using three separate but interrelated components: height, width, and depth. These measures answer the central questions of a social media strategy and are almost entirely drawn from tools similar to Radian6, Sysomos, and BrandWatch, which makes it the only scorecard approach of the three being examined that is easy to replicate by other interested agencies with social media monitoring platforms such as Radian6. The Digital Footprint Index also lends itself to Web and social media analytics solutions such as Adobe Omniture SocialAnalytics, which merges Web analytics precision, segmentations, and analytics tagging with social media listening.

The DFI is the only published agency-type scorecard I have encountered so far that is vendor and platform neutral. Its use of the metaphors of height, width, and depth of conversations around a brand or subject make it more accessible to users than other scorecards, since the attributes are parallel to the three dimensions we human beings live in:

- **Height** How much is the brand talked about, and where are the conversations occurring? This measures the sum of all blog posts, forum threads, videos, photos, social networking groups, and Web pages. Excluded are Google's organic and paid searches that yield an absolute number. An example of this would be a brand working to promote itself through online video, uploading 10 to a video-sharing site such as YouTube. A simple method for calculating height in this instance would be to count the number of videos online: 10.

- **Width** How is the brand shared online, and how do people interact with it? How active are the communities within which conversations take place? Width is the sum of engagement metrics for each channel analyzed in height. Comments, thread replies, video views, and Twitter followers each contribute to this value. Width answers the question, "How widely is your brand conversation being engaged with and shared?" A brand that sends its message through the 10 videos referenced above would look to the total number of views, favorites, and comments to measure the width of its footprint. An understanding of these metrics provides the brand with an understanding of the effectiveness of its videos: 10 videos, each with 100 views, could arguably equate to 1 video with 1,000 views.

- **Depth** Is the brand understood and talked about in the way its marketers intended? Depth looks at whether the message was on target with marketing objectives and whether the message sentiment was positive, neutral, or negative. The DFI scorecard lends itself to automation, as most of the scorecard data can be gathered from the data being collected by measurement platforms today making it simpler to build in automation. However, multi-coder hand sampling remains the most dependable method for evaluating conversation when it comes to correctly identifying complexities of irony, sarcasm, and context. (Note to be fair that the DFI scorecard will probably require some manual scoring of information being tabulated for depth, or sentiment, as do the other approaches for likability, advocacy, and share of voice in a highly focused category; the scorecards should not be entirely automated if accuracy and actionability of the information is the main purpose of the scorecard.)

An example of this would be that of the 10 videos on YouTube in the previous two dimensions: not all may be a benefit for the brand. An analysis will probably need to read the commentary on the videos and manually score them as positive or negative to the brand.

All three scorecards and numerous social media tasks—including audits, keyword lists, landscape analysis, influencer lists, and deep dive dashboarding reports—suggest that the agency model requires a new type of marketing data analyst.[6] Clearly, the data being gathered are often entirely unstructured and often need much manual work, coding, and customizations to make them useful and actionable to the stakeholders who will use the scorecards to make marketing decisions.

Building Social Media Scorecards

One approach to building a simple social media scorecard requires manually grading different interactions (such as a tweet versus a blog post). Digital measurement frameworks such as Conversation Impact, Fluent, and DFI use many of the same operations as the digital brand management frameworks we will cover in this section. For example, digital brand management also lends itself to a model of how to collect and score information, as shown in Figure 7-1.

Table 7-1 is an example of how to organize various free and paid social monitoring tools to collect data on digital brand management campaigns. When an agency or brand uses a model for social media data, it is useful to have a list of tools to populate the information gathered in reporting.

Also notable among the tools and platforms in the figure are several useful free programs that are often used in an agency or brand environment, but that might not provide fully accurate information for campaign measurement. Whichever tools and platforms are chosen, they should be locked in at the beginning of a campaign, because the information for each tool often conflicts, and it's important to be consistent when mixing hybrid sources of free and paid data for reporting frameworks.

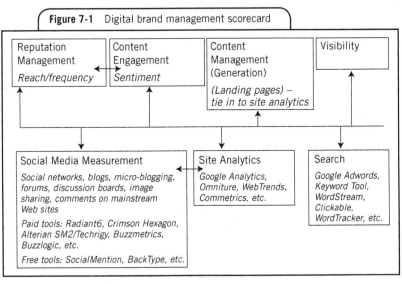

Figure 7-1 Digital brand management scorecard

Source: Marshall Sponder

		Content		
Reputation Management	**Content Engagement**	**Management Generation**	**Campaign Visibility**	**Search**
Various social media monitoring platforms, free and paid	Various social media monitoring platforms, free and paid	Google Analytics	Bit.ly	Google Keyword tool
Nielsen Threat Tracker	Alterian SM2/ Techrigy	Adobe Site Catalyst	BackType	Google Trends
Trackur	Sentiment Metrics	Coremetrics	BackTweet	Google Insights for Search
Reputation Defender	Twendz	WebTrends	Retweets	Compete Search Analytics
Scout Labs	Collective Intellect CI Listen	Compete	Site Analytics— visits to and page and unique views of campaign pages	WordStream
Google Alerts	Lithium	Alexa	Video Views	WordTracker
	Spiril16	ComScore MyMetrix	No. of tweets	Yahoo! Keyword tool
	Jodange (30-day trial)	Nielsen NetView	No. of followers	
		Quantcast	No. of comments	

Table 7-1 Organizing Free and Paid Social Monitoring Tools to Collect Data on Digital Brand Management Campaigns

Source: Webmetricsguru.com

Social Media Multiplier Scale

Once we collect and code online social media data (as mentioned in this chapter), we also need to rank (score) the information so we can tabulate it within a scorecard. Below is an example of a scoring system I used for a client in a recent campaign-measurement project.

- Blog content = 0.5
- News event = 0.4

▪ Video = 0.5

▪ Influencer rank = 1 to 100 (depends on celebrity factor)

▪ Tweet = 0.1

▪ Tweet with bit.ly = 0.4

▪ Message board = 0.3

▪ Qualified blog comment = 0.3

▪ New inbound link = 0.3

▪ Podcast = 0.4

▪ Widget = 0.4

Once information is collected and counted, we apply the multipliers shown above and come up with a score. Table 7-2 is provided just for illustration purposes; it does not measure a specific campaign.

Table 7-2 Sample Social Media Scores

Campaign Metrics Since Launch	Items	Social Media Multipler	Estimated Views	Twitter Followers	Social Media Score
Flickr	24	0.4	240		2,304
YouTube	16	0.4	606		3,878.4
Blinkx	8	0.4	20		64
Twitter	313	0.1	250	115,044	7,825
Other	24		10		0
Blogs	16	0.3	400		1,920
Facebook	5	0.3	150		225
Wikipedia	3	0.4	34		40.8
Message boards	2	0.3	3		1.8
Direct views (SM2)		0.4	1,396		0
Influencer views (Radian6)	328	0.1	23		754.4
Total					17,013.4

Source: Webmetricsguru.com

Gathering Information for a Scorecard

The Internet Advertising Bureau (IAB) is doing promising work in the U.K. to create a set of standards to score social media activities. It is attempting to create a social media framework to accommodate several types of scorecards that are categorized by media channel, including social networks, blogs, YouTube, Flickr, and Twitter.

More and more often, I hear of clients who want to know something "different," but they can't articulate what they want in a way that many approaches I discuss in this book can answer without a great deal of extra work, which they also are not always willing to pay for. One example would be to know the impact of online mentions and campaigns within a business-management-industry framework in the detail of those that McKinsey produces.

The online researcher or analyst runs the risk of literally following what is being asked for by the client and ending up providing something it doesn't actually need. In these cases, the client will often push back the report, and it may have to be redone. I wrote this book partly to solve the problem: presenting a list of questions will help eliminate some of the gap between what stakeholders want and what an analyst can actually provide, given the platforms, tools, methodologies, and time available.

The importance of having the right questions answered before any reporting or scorecarding begins was highlighted by an analyst I recently spoke with at Integrasco's offices in Grimstad, Norway: the analyst noted that when a client is vague about what it wants to know, reporting and insights can take up to three times longer to produce. Conversely, when a client's question is very specific, but there is not much relevant data to be found in online social mentions, reporting can also take two to three times longer than the optimal time allotted. That got me to thinking that analysts need the right level of detailed information (not too little, not too much), along with the appropriate platforms to compile and assemble insights and reporting; insufficient consideration has been given to this subject in the current literature on social media analytics, which is another reason I wrote this book.

With those points in mind, below you will find a set of questions that can help you gather information for a scorecard or any deliverable and avoid having to rework your reporting.

As Gary Angel, CTO of Semphonic, discusses in his interview in Chapter 8, asking the questions below may still not help with certain clients: ones that are overly vague, that do not know what they want in the first place and therefore cannot supply the information beforehand needed to perform the analysis. As he puts it, "In the traditional BI world, there's a paradigm for building reports that says you go out and interview the stakeholders, learn what they need, and then translate that into the underlying data model."

As it happens, that BI model doesn't work in Web analytics, according to Angel, and it won't work in social media either: the stakeholders don't know what they need and don't understand the uses of the data. In Web analytics and social media reporting, the analyst has to be the subject matter expert. That isn't true in traditional BI, and the implications are profound (this is discussed further in Chapters 8 and 10).

It is critical that the stakeholders' and clients' vocabulary, along with the ability to articulate it, needs to enable clear communication so as to come up with a consensus for deliverables.

Here are the questions to ask stakeholders and clients while gathering information:

- What is the billing code for the project?
- When is the due date for the analysis?
- For which brand will the analysis be performed?
- What is the business goal for the client as it relates to this analysis?
- What are the business tactics under consideration?
- What is the target audience demographic: age, gender, location, and description?
- What do you want to learn? (This will be the title and lead slide of the presentation of the analysis.)
- Do you need to understand the brand performance relative to a particular industry category?
- What are the brand's competitors? What are the names of their products? Please include descriptions and names of at least two competitors.

Here are more questions to ask, regarding specific requirements:

- What, if anything, should be *excluded* from this scope of work?
- Which channels or types of social media or SEO work are to be focused on?
- What time period is to be covered?
- Are we measuring ad- or coupon-related conversation, product- or brand-related conversations, or both types?
- Are there particular metrics that the brand has stipulated it would like to measure?
- Can you include an RFP, account plan, keyword lists, Web analytics data, strategy documents, or anything else relevant, accompanied by an explanation?

When the requirements are more detailed and cover search engine marketing as well as social media monitoring, the following questions related to keyword and volume analysis should be included:

- Do you have a list of keywords around the brand?
- What slang does the target use to refer to the brand or the target? (Chapter 3 mentions linguistic variants and slang words, which are used by influentials in a group more often than those outside a group.)
- What other keywords may be applicable?
- Can you provide common brand and product misspellings, and product names for each target brand and competitor brand?
- Are there any other related keywords, including names of product spokespeople, or other initiatives having unique keywords associated with them?
- Any there keywords that we should *exclude* in our analysis for your report or scorecard?

Finally, here are questions about additional refinements in reporting that might be occasionally required:

- Do you need to check Google for top results relevant to the brand and products: in a regular search, image search, or blog search?
- Is an SEO/SEM analysis required for your report or scorecard?
- Is a Google Trends analysis needed for relevant keywords for your report?
- Do you require a Facebook audit of owned Facebook destination(s)?

▪ Is a YouTube audit of brand content needed?

▪ Is a Twitter audit of your brand and competitors needed?

▪ How well is the brand or product site socially enabled? (This requires looking at all the features that your site and competitors provide, such as social sharing buttons, RSS feeds, frequency and quality of community management, and curation of brand content.)

Using the Right Platforms/Tools

Using the wrong tools to perform any analytics task will make it take much longer to perform, *if it ever gets done at all.* Conversely, when using the right tools and platforms, the tasks at hand may be much easier to do and can be partially or totally automated. I have gone around the world and seen this truth in action everywhere. Technology choices have a profound impact on pipeline flow, quality of what is delivered, and how long it takes to produce actionable insights.

Some platforms may be good for one purpose but not another, and too often not enough thought is given to the area of procurement of the right tools, technologies, procedures, and governance to enable successful reporting.

Share of voice tables and charts are fairly easy to generate (for example: Sysomos MAP is particularly good at comparing up to 8 competitors), but they are often diagnostic in nature, and thus no real insight comes from them. Clients require competitor analysis in reports, for clarity and perspective. An inherent problem with these types of charts is the query and the potential limitations of the monitoring tool or platform.

For example, in order to get the best results, it is often best to use a very long query with a lot of negative operators to filter out noise (if we want to monitor Orange, the European telecommunications conglomerate, we must filter out many other uses of the word *orange*—such as fruit, color, and chemical (Agent Orange)—while focusing only on telecommunications; this can produce a lengthy query string (perhaps 10,000 or so characters long) that most social media platforms cannot process: most platforms mentioned in this book can handle about 1,024 characters in a single query string. Therefore, at some point the queries become too large for the platform to handle. This is occurring much more frequently, particularly in industries such as pharmaceuticals, telecommunications, banking, automotive, and medical (to name a few), but it can be the case in almost any industry or category. The level of precision needed in writing and maintaining social media queries should not be overlooked; it is a time-consuming and difficult task, and its level of thoroughness will make or break the success of any report or analysis, depending on how it is performed.

Data Quality Depends on the Platform and the Analyst

According to Gary Angel, whom I interviewed for this book, there is an issue with data quality in social media analytics. Unlike Web analytics and even search data, social media monitoring mentions mined off the Web do not represent an entire view set of the data being analyzed. A different query (even a slight change in wording) and a different analyst performing it or the use of a different platform can bring up entirely different results. Angel adds, "With your Web site or your point of sale systems, the universe of data is pretty much fixed. That isn't true with social media."

The first step, and one of the most important steps in social media measurement, is carving off a relevant chunk of data from the vast river of news flowing out there. Ideally, you'd like to be able to carve out a really large set of data that covers everything in your industry that might be appropriate and then select a subset of it in ways that seem interesting to you.

Unfortunately, it doesn't usually work that way.

To begin with, most social media tools charge you according to the volume of news you listen to: the more liberal you are in your initial cut, the more expensive the tool. That's not the only problem, though. Many social media listening tools don't make it easy to pull a subset of the data from a large pool. If you collect, for example, both competitor and brand mentions in the same big pool, you often can't make a subset to isolate either. And even when you can make a subset of the data, specific reports (such as influencers) often can't be sliced in a similar fashion.

Gary Angel continues, "This puts a big burden on the analyst to set up the tool to match the way the data will be used. For example, you can't just create and use ad hoc classifications of the data as you decide you need them. Instead, you have to collect the data and put it into the categories and buckets you want to report on."

Analytics clients (which should be divided into marketing, PR/communications, market research, and enterprise reporting) have diverse needs and constituencies that require entirely different sets of reporting requirements. They are beginning to push back to analysts, asking more difficult questions—getting smart and realizing that the quality of data they are consuming is entirely dependent on the platform and the analyst who assembled the information.

This suggests a need for an enlightened approach to data quality and the analysts who shape it. In my opinion, it is the analysts who are the real stars within organizations, the ones that give social data meaning and context, positioning the marketing and communications departments to be productive by the correct use of analytics.

Building Scorecards for Online Brand Visibility

People engaged in social media generate events and information that can be tracked and tabulated.

With a little bit of spreadsheet work, it is possible to create a clear scorecard of online brand visibility using a popular free monitoring platform called HowSociable.com. Figure 7-2 shows a marketing chart derived from the platform's information and created using Excel. As with any tool, it's only as good as the analyst behind it, and much depends on using the best terms for a brand before starting an analysis for them.

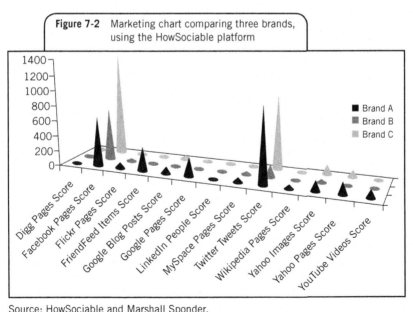

Figure 7-2   Marketing chart comparing three brands, using the HowSociable platform

Source: HowSociable and Marshall Sponder.

Level of Reporting and Analysis for Your Organization's Needs

There is no consensus on which platforms and reporting an organization should have, but some ideas are contained in various conversational threads. According to Chris Karnes, community development manager at ListenLogic:

It all depends on WHAT you're looking to get out of listening. If your goal is a dashboard w/ buzz and tracking how well you're doing for the clients, then something like Tracckr, Radian6, ViralHeat, etc. may be the best way to go.

If you're looking to get more out of the data and understand it more from a market research perspective or are interested in benchmark reports, then you should look into some of the other solutions out there.[7]

Listening and measurement are two different use cases for social media monitoring, according to Meg Sinclair, manager of corporate marketing and communications at Syncapse.com.[8] Listening (or monitoring) platforms provide a way to learn what is being said about your company/brand/product: measurement provides actionable insights that can improve performance moving forward. Gary Angel's interview in Chapter 8 echoes Sinclair's sentiments and provides more explanation of how different listening and measuring are from a monitoring and governance perspective, requiring entirely separate social media query sets and reporting methodologies.

Then again, a company or individual starting out will probably want to use free tools in order to work out what he is looking for first, access his needs, and then move on to paid services and platforms.[9] According to Giles Palmer, CEO at

Brandwatch, whom we will learn more about in Chapter 10, the progression from free tools to paid platforms depends on a user's need and sophistication.

Case Study: The Complex Media Network and Infinigraph

The Complex Media Network delivers information about every element of life that young, stylish men need to maintain their position at the top of the style food chain. The 47-publisher network provides consumers with an ultra-authentic deep dive into their core passions: fashion, music, sneakers, style, gaming, sports, and art and entertainment. Its mission was to determine which content is most relevant to the audience across the social graph, other brands the demographic is interacting around, which content is being shared, and distribution path and autofeed to the Facebook and Twitter sites to increase overall click-through and consumer engagement with its content.

The company, whose home page is shown in Figure 7-3, approached Infinigraph with a desire to get more out of the social presence by content optimization and at the same time grow the presence with the top 1 percent that is active across similar content sites. Its two stated goals:

- Build up social intelligence on content consumption and interaction on Complex consumers, and leverage that information to drive great quality traffic back to the publishers' sites.
- Drive target influencers to connect to Complex and increate the overall content shares, click-through rate, and distribution to increase reach.

Figure 7-3 *Complex Magazine* home page

Source: Infinigraph.com

Beginning of the Campaign

Infinigraph saw a large gap in how brands and publishers (publishers' networks) were using the social graph (Facebook and Twitter) to engage consumers and measure it to improve the overall performance through data intelligence. The ability to track where content is picked up and who shares it is based on crowd-source social intelligence and shown in the Content Consumption Graph.

There are two objectives here, as follows:

■ **Objective 1** Find out what Complex.com readers do on social networks and what type of content they like to read and share. Leverage that research information to drive great-quality traffic to publisher sites.

■ **Objective 2** Find and engage influencers connecting with Complex, and increase overall content sharing to increase reach.

Results

The numbers InfiniGraph produced speak for themselves:

■ Complex Web site traffic increased by 30 percent
■ Twitter followers increased by 25 percent
■ Facebook fans increased by 30 percent

Following is an example of how Complex's audience interacts with other brands and publishers, which social media analysts call "the affinity map."

1. An affinity map of the brands/products/services that consumers interact with the most is shown in Figure 7-4.
2. Complex used the Infinigraph control panel to gain social intelligence to boost content interaction between *T Magazine* and *Complex Magazine*'s own associated properties, such as Highsnobiety, with the online audience who visited *Complex Magazine*'s home page portal, where content from all its sister publications was selectively aggregated.

Figure 7-4 Affinity map

Brand / Page Affinity			Category	Followers	Affinity Score
		T Magazine	Products	9757	53
		Supreme	Products	62593	51
		Highsnobiety	Websites	36432	41
		DUB Magazine	Products	8438	38
		Undrcrwn Footwear & Apparel	Products	3269	33
		The FADER	Products	7810	27
		KARMALOOP.com	Services	95268	24

Source: Infinigraph.com

3. Trending content based on a brand's affinity drives greater social interaction and activation. (This is based on the point above; when visitors are presented with content from the Complex Network that Infinigraph finds they have more brand affinity for, it is highlighted, and that drives greater interaction rates, as seen by Figure 7-5.)

Consumers rely on friends and business associates to determine relevant content to share. This discovery process is propelled by social connections and influence. When Complex content trends, it gives the opportunity to expose its published content to a wider audience while improving social interaction.

To Aleksey Baksheyev, director of technology of Complex Media, the results were self-evident: "Infinigraph increased Complex page views by 30 percent and its Facebook following by 30

Figure 7-5 Trending content on *Complex Magazine* Web site

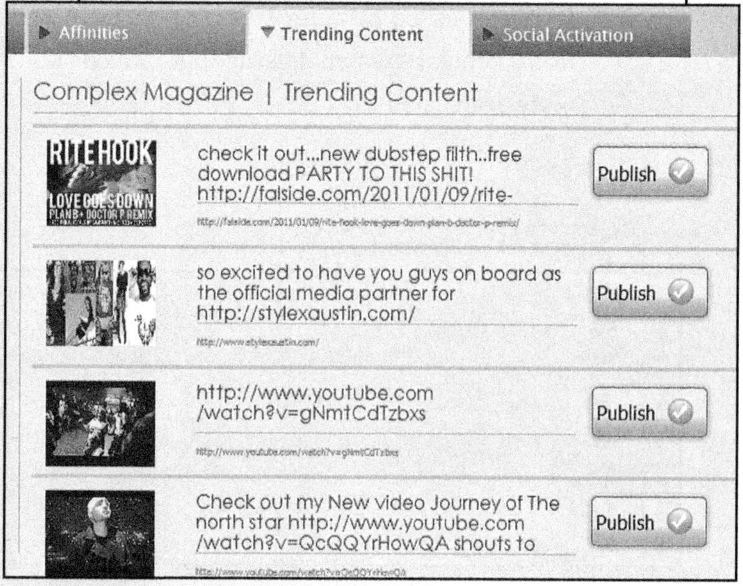

Source: Infinigraph.com

percent."[10] The New York–based company used Infinigraph's insights to expand its content distribution through the network, driving overall click volume and social interaction.

Infinigraph contributions were welcome because Complex's staff had been unable to keep up with content and posting demands 24/7. Infinigraph provided a clear way of managing this content stream, including measuring what was truly relevant to cross-post and repost.

Another welcome change was Infinigraph's simplified interface for tracking clicks, viewing well-performing content, and gaining insights into the social graph. The Infinigraph control panel allows content publishers to easily manage content feeds from many sources, with simple visuals that reveal trending brands around a company's social presence, while providing the transparent ability to curate overlapping Facebook and Twitter presences.

Details of the Infinigraph Case Study with *Complex Magazine*

The prime mover for this project was *Complex Magazine*'s director of technology, Aleksey Baksheyev, who managed all Web site operations. As a result of this project, quality interaction increased and was delivered to a new audience that helped bring in a greater social and content interaction (see Figures 7-6 and 7-7). As a result of working with Infinigraph, *Complex Magazine* was able to autopost high performers on weekends and thereby to provide greater click-through as well as on the same content item (which is shown in Figure 7-7).

InfiniGraph was able to provide content feed automation and optimization while identifying influencers in and out of network that increased traffic by 30 percent from Twitter, alone.

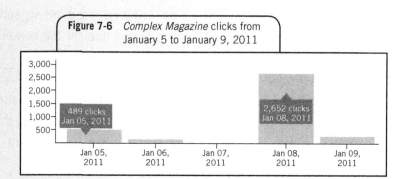

Figure 7-6 *Complex Magazine* clicks from January 5 to January 9, 2011

Source: Infinigraph.com

Figure 7-7 *Complex Magazine* most clicked-on content

Complex Magazine Odd Twitter: Tyler, The Creator's Craziest Recent
Tweets http://bit.ly/fK9Szr @OddFuture @ofwgkta   ×

Odd Twitter: Tyler, The Creator's Craziest Recent Tweets | Complex Blog
bit.ly
The Odd Future frontman has the wildest updates. We compiled some from the last month alone.

Post Insights not yet available, please check back later.
January 4 at 1:53pm · Like · Comment · Share · Promote   **970 Clicks**

Jacob Morales likes this.

Write a comment...

Complex Magazine http://bit.ly/fIEOHV   ×

Odd Twitter: Tyler, The Creator's Craziest Recent Tweets
www.complex.com
The Odd Future frontman has the wildest updates. We compiled some from the last month alone.

Post Insights not yet available, please check back later.
January 4 at 4:00pm via InfiniGraph · Like · Comment   **584 Clicks**

2 people like this.

Write a comment...

Source: Infinigraph.com

Overall Campaign Results

Ultimately, these were the results achieved:

■ Social activating influencers around their content (30 percent increase in Facebook)

- Increased influencer reach on Twitter by 25 percent
- Increased site traffic by 30 percent
- Reduced staff off hours and holiday workload through automation
- Simplified and automated finding relevant content for approval cross network posting

Summary

In this chapter, I discussed the various scorecards to use for social media analytics and the pros and cons of data collection to populate scorecards. This chapter also touched on defining requirements for monitoring social media, gathering information for analysis, and choosing the right platforms for the client or organization. In the next chapter, I will discuss advanced social analytics, and how to monitor these scorecards.

chapter <u>8</u>

Advanced Social Analytics: Implementation and Monitoring Scorecards

According to Simon McDermott, CEO of Attentio,[1] the increase in social media listening is directly tied to the growth of online social media. With more buzz, there are more applications to monitor buzz and more stories to track that have arisen to meet the need. In 2004, when the first listening platforms began to form, they were tiny niche companies, lacking critical mass. Few were using social media, and the companies involved were often funded by venture capital.

Business applications have evolved to include influencer spotting, campaign impact, and reputation monitoring. These applications have since been followed by agencies that get requests for trial projects focusing on social media listening, monitoring, and measurement. The U.S. market for social media monitoring has grown exponentially, with several "market research" projects being requested by clients. During the same period, the cost of collecting real-time data and storing them has also increased exponentially.

The information needed to collect social data and turn-
them it into insight can be thought of as a six-step process, as
you'll see in Figure 8-1, which was designed by Gaurav Mishra,
director of digital and social media for MSLGROUP Asia.[2]
This version of the process puts emphasis on aspects of data
collection (developing keyword lists while removing spam and
duplication) and tag data (often done with source filters in platforms such as Radian6). Most of the work for the social media
analyst seems to be in stage 3 (data analysis) and possibly stage 4
(consulting). The data collection and data-mining (steps 1 and
2) can determine whether the work will present fruitful results.

Social media scorecards that are intended to create meaningful insight for brands require more than basic monitoring
of mentions. The key to interesting social media research and
monitoring is the classification of information into meaning-

Figure 8-1 Six-step social media delivery process

(1) Listen		(2) Understand		(3) Engage	
Data Collection	**Data Mining**	**Data Analysis**	**Insight Delivery**	**Consulting**	**Solution Delivery**
• Develop keyword list based on industry drivers. • Set up crawler to pull data from relevant sources, geographies, and languages. • Remove spam/duplication.	• Tag data with content and source identifiers. • Identify tone and context by Bayesian filtering, machine learning, and natural language processing, plus human intervention.	• Aggregate data into useful information. • Identify trends, associations, shares, benchmarks, linkages, and momentum.	• Present insights to clients in the form of decks and periodic summary reports. • Enable clients to monitor realtime information via web-based dashboards/alerts.	• Identify strengths, weaknesses, opportunities, and threats for clients. • Develop social media strategy for clients based on SWOT.	• Identify social media tools best suited for clients' media strategy. • Develop and deploy social media tools. • Perform community manager role, if required.

Source: © Gaurav Mishra, gauravonomics.com

ful categories. To get the necessary reporting, analysts seek solutions from companies such as Attensity, Brandwatch, Radian6, and Sysomos at step 1.

Case Study: Semphonic Analytics

Semphonic is the largest independent Web analytics consultancy in the United States. The company was a pioneer in the field of Web analytics, and its enterprise clientele now includes many of the most important and largest brands in the world. Semphonic's full-service practice includes the creation of online measurement infrastructure, advanced-management and executive dashboards and scorecards, and advanced analytics based on online behavior using both Web analytics and advanced statistical and data-warehousing tools. The company is partners with all the leading enterprise Web analytics vendors and solution providers.

The increasing focus on social media campaigns and outreach has dramatically raised the profile of social media measurement data in large corporations. For instance, a large software company (that shall not be named here) wanted to understand how its marketing efforts were having an impact not just in its community, but also in the competitive camp. It wanted to find ways to target neutral and competitive influencers. Traditional methods of Web analytics were insufficient to complete the task, because the vast majority of site traffic was limited to the company's own community.

The goal of this effort was to create a complete picture of online marketing impacts by integrating Web analytics data with social data to show how marketing programs were driving both "own community" and "competitive community" interest and engagement. Explicitly, part of the goal was highlighting places where marketing efforts had become too focused on the company's own community and were not driving new adoption or sales.

Nearly 10 different data sources (including three Web analytics tools, two online panels, public search engine data, internal data sources, and two social monitoring tools) were used and integrated to provide information by product area about the size and intensity of the online owned and competitive communities. This funnel was narrowed to comparisons of similarly classified search terms in order to understand how social chatter was translating into early-stage finding behaviors. The online panel data were used to narrow the funnel to traffic at owned and competitive sites. Finally, Web analytics data were used to show how owned Web site traffic responded to these upstream influences and how successful the company was in engaging competitive traffic.

Aims and Objectives

This was a social media measurement project, not a social media campaign. Significantly, social media measurement tends to address one of two basic concerns: measuring the effectiveness of social media campaigns and using social media for market research. In a sense, this project was a hybrid: many uses of social media measurement were market-research oriented, but an explicit part of the goal was to create a complete view to provide better insight into the impact of the increasing number of social PR and marketing efforts.

The system was designed to support a fairly broad range of stakeholders. Key among these were online regional and product-line managers who made marketing-allocation decisions for the online world. Another significant audience was the senior marketing managers who sought to monitor regional and product performance and assess the overall state of the brand, as well as the effectiveness of new approaches to social marketing.

Details of Approach

The project began with a significant two- to three-month effort to establish an entirely new set of online marketing key performance indicators (KPIs), particularly around social media. The endeavor included the development of a new framework for Web site KPIs as well; this was based on a two-tiered segmentation of visitor type and visit type.

Because there had been very little social media reporting, there was little consensus about how the core metrics should be used or interpreted. Part of the KPI work was based on the capabilities of the existing tool set already in place at the enterprise. For some of the functional areas, however, particularly social listening and panel-based research, several new vendors were evaluated and interviewed. One of the most important, but problematic, requirements was the need for significant international support.

As is often the case, the core integration tool was Excel. Not only was Excel widely in use, but it provided convenient integration with some of the key data sources (such as Web analytics). Although the number of data sources was large, most of the data fit reasonably within Excel constraints.

One goal of the reporting systems was to provide as much automation as possible around monthly production. Because of the range of sources used, this proved to be a challenge.

For any large scorecard or dashboard effort, one of the biggest difficulties is generating consensus about how to measure success. This is particularly true when social media systems are included. Few organizations are really prepared to commit to fixed versions of social success—perhaps rightly so, given the fluid nature and immature state of the medium.

Semphonic's particular brand of online and social media reporting also faces challenges, because the company generally tries to introduce a completely new language framework on the data. The framework focuses on a two-tiered segmentation: audience type and touch point (or "visit," in the Web analytics lexicon) intent. For each type of visitor and for each activity he or she is trying to accomplish, a unique metric for success is established.

Surprisingly, in this project our client faced more resistance around the traditional Web analytics scorecards than around the social reporting. A number of Web properties and marketers had fairly entrenched ways of viewing their success, which were often focused on total traffic numbers. Changing the way these sites were measured raised significant concerns by their stakeholders.

On the other hand, marketers were less committed to their existing methods for measuring social media and had less organizational stake. Most marketers embraced the new language easily and preferred it to what little reporting they had previously done, much of it focused solely on mentions data.

A second significant challenge for this project was internationalization. For Web analytics data, sites generally capture locale and language. Unfortunately, most of Semphonic's other data sources did not support all regions particularly well. Panel data, in particular, was thin in many critical regions: using consumer panel data outside the U.S. and the EU is extremely challenging.

Listening data are almost equally affected. Not all listening sources extend across regions, and when they do, coverage can be spotty. In addition, the methods of reporting required significant classification exercises—meaning that it was difficult for the company to support any language other than English.

Internationalization is hugely difficult when it comes to social media analysis and reporting, and the software company considered this one of the hardest and least successful aspects of the project. Finally, automation of the reports was a significant challenge. The final report set was built in Excel and was fairly extensive. The full workbook contained eight major reporting sections, each of which contained multiple data sources and potential drill-downs; few of the company's data sources supported direct automation.

The most problematic issues were the panel data providers and the listening tools. In both cases, Semphonic often had to resort to very rudimentary levels of automation (in some cases, cut-and-paste) to extract the necessary data. Although the reporting system couldn't be fully automated, a great deal of automation logic was built into the Excel templates. This allowed most of the data to be extracted automatically and, where that wasn't possible, required no more than a manual insert of a fixed data block with all the classification, filtering, sorting, and presentation handled in Excel.

A final, and very common, challenge was resolving a significant internal debate over the use of sentiment data. Semphonic was reluctant to include sentiment data in its reporting; analysis suggested that it was not reliable, and Semphonic discouraged its use. However, there was strong demand for inclusion based on executive interest. This is a battle Semphonic lost, settling for a strong warning in the reports that the sentiment data were unreliable.

Details of Successes and Outcomes

Some of the most interesting data use took advantage of additional classifications to present panel and social listening data in new contexts.

Marketers were particularly interested in the use of panel data to identify shifts over time in visitors using competitive sites before or after using the clients' sites. When a visitor moves from a competitive site to a client site, Semphonic views this as a win; when a visitor moves from a client site to a competitive site, Semphonic regards it as a loss. By tracking these wins and losses over time, you have a unique metric for determining if your Web properties are more successful at holding visitors and keeping them out of competitors' sites.

Another important accomplishment of the panel-based reporting was the use of classifications to identify potential display and link marketing opportunities by looking for neutral sites with a high affinity to the client sites. These reports gave an actionable dimension to the panel-based data that had been lacking.

The use of social listening data, search impression data (both classified by brand and product terms), and Web site data to create a three-level marketing funnel also proved interesting. This three-level view made it easy to see where marketing efforts needed to be focused: upstream to build awareness, at search to capture traffic, or at site to retain and engage.

Finally, the classification of influencers by topics gave a different twist to a common social media listening report. The topic index for influencers made it much easier for marketers and PR staff to target messages based on theme and topic to the most appropriate outlets and people.

Results

Enterprise dashboards are growing ever more complex. The integration of multiple data sources is great for providing a much broader and richer view of the competitive landscape and marketing funnel to marketing executives. Using all these data sources comes with a significant price in terms of complexity, however, particularly around automation and internationalization.

Getting the most value from social listening and panel-based research tools generally requires additional levels of data classification. Simply reporting mentions data is not generally very interesting. As with most projects, the biggest challenges were organizational. Surprisingly, Semphonic found that the time was ripe for creating a better reporting framework around social listening and panel-based data. Because organizations haven't hardened into standards in these areas yet and there is little organizational stake in any particular metric or method, it proved easier to adjust the reporting framework than in the Web site space.

This suggests that measurement organizations should move aggressively to standardize on robust measurement and reporting around social media before uncontrolled and poorly thought out homegrown measurements become organizational norms and acquire institutional stakeholders committed to their preservation.

Tools Drive the Data

According to Gary Angel, while social media tools can help us answer the basic questions of whom, what, and where of online conversations, these programs deliver information with the assumption that someone is going to read a river of news and operate on the data. Social media reporting, in the context of the current generation of social media monitoring tools, presents several key challenges: it is hard to find time to read or use the river of news reporting for the purposes for which it was intended.

The top three actions of the most recent versions of social analytics platforms are:

1. **Culling** Capturing social mentions and exporting the data in them in a useful way
2. **Classifying** Trending posts into meaningful categories and handling sentiment analysis
3. **Contextualizing** How we frame much of the information being collected so that it is actionable

In one case study, less than one percent (0.2 percent) of all data pulled from product or brand mentions (Radian6) from a client's dashboard was actually useful for the clients' monitoring[3]; the rest, 99.8 percent of all mentions collected, were filtered out. This statement highlights the justifiable perception by seasoned analysts that social media monitoring and analytics are too difficult to implement for a company that does not understand the basic requirements and limitations for data analytics.

Classifying Social Media Data

The classifications available for social media data are created by the platform vendor and usually include the type of media (blog, message board, or Twitter) and sentiment (positive, negative, etc.), are mainly behavioral and usually need to be applied at the topic profile level to be effective.[4] Keyword groupings may need to be set up accordingly: by industry verticals, such as financial services, with sub-keyword groupings in product interest, life stage, and role, for example. Within each of the sub-keyword groups, it is possible to get more detailed with smaller groups, such as stocks, options, and bonds.

Topic
Sentiment
Source

Influencer

Impact

There is a significant amount of classification of social media data (usually by analysts, since it is currently too hard to automate) required to produce the sophisticated, relevant dashboards presented in this section.

Classification Key Points

It is best if the keyword group classifications are set up when a topic profile (in Radian6, for example) is set up and not later on, when pulling a report. Afterward, it is too labor-intensive and almost impossible to maintain; many platforms do not allow a full historical pull of data once the keyword groupings are changed without paying an additional fee, although a few do (such as Brandwatch and Sysomos MAP). Figure 8-2 shows an example of keyword group classifications for the financial industry.

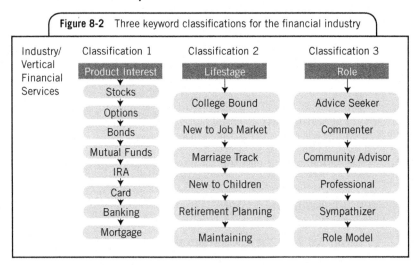

Figure 8-2 Three keyword classifications for the financial industry

Industry/ Vertical Financial Services	Classification 1	Classification 2	Classification 3
	Product Interest	Lifestage	Role
	Stocks	College Bound	Advice Seeker
	Options	New to Job Market	Commenter
	Bonds	Marriage Track	Community Advisor
	Mutual Funds	New to Children	Professional
	IRA	Retirement Planning	Sympathizer
	Card	Maintaining	Role Model
	Banking		
	Mortgage		

Source: Semphonic.com

Conversely, straightforward reports of mentions and mention trends, common in many social media reports, are among the least interesting aspects of social data, because little that is of real value can be learned from them without additional classifications and coding.

Like culling of data, classification of the river of news is not static and will need constant, ongoing maintenance. Also, manual sentiment analysis (via scoring) should be used, because automated sentiment analysis is too vulnerable to obvious errors to be useful for measurement or analysis.

Context Key Points

Gary Angel believes that putting metrics into a specific business context helps make the information much more usable.

Mentions

- Which products or conditions get the most feature mentions?
- How does the brand compare with competitors' in customer support mentions?

Influencers

- Have influencers' topics changed as a result of PR?
- Has a shift occurred in what influencers say about a brand's topics via PR?

Upstream/Downstream Sites

- Are we winning more than we are losing (mentions and market share) to competitors?

As well as planning for a more large-scale IT integration with marketing and analytics, we should ask the right questions and get answers from the right people in an organization.[5]

Relaying Data to Your Client

Social media analytics dashboards and reports are most often going to enterprise clients who are marketers and project managers with pieces of information that will eventually be discussed in the boardroom. So how do you relay data to a client? Start by ascertaining how sophisticated the client is insofar as what he needs to know and how well he can articulate it to the analyst and/or team.

Social Media Maturity of Clients

How comfortable is the client with technology? For example, does she understand mobile apps? In general, how much does the client/stakeholder grasp about the nature of the tools and methodologies that are used by analysts to generate their deliverables?

The best place to begin is to determine the level of social media maturity of the client.[6] I have adapted the following four maturity levels from Collective Intellect's presentation, "What Is Your Organization's Level of Social Media Maturity."[7]

First Level: Monitoring

Organizations who function at this level:

- Listen to what customers are saying.
- Typically use free keyword or paid tools such as Radian6 that require a lot of manual reading and annotation to gather insights.

▪ Struggle with volumes of data, unable to deliver much intelligence.

▪ Use topic profile setups and configuration with some insight.

▪ Utilize dimensions such as likes, followers, posts, on-topic links, and votes.

▪ Feed topic profile river of news into text-mining platforms for serious analysis.

Second Level: Online Research

Organizations who function at this level:

▪ Integrate social media insights into other aspects of their business.

▪ Make more sophisticated use of social media tools to turn data into insights.

▪ Make some attempt to blend qualitative data (such as survey data) with data being culled from online listening.

▪ Make use of semantic filtering (assigning gathered content into the right categories and making those categories fit into a larger research schema).

▪ Attempt to engage in team collaboration, using newer engagement platforms (such as Alterian or Radian6).

Third Level: Social Targeting and Data Management

Clients who function at this level:

▪ Integrate social CRM and analytics tracking.

▪ Capture and measure leads using social CRM.

■ Demonstrate an ability to respond in real time with issues management via social CRM.

■ Set up business processes that tie in with measurement goals, such as social outreach and influencer identification.

■ Target new and existing customers using listening systems and social CRM; provide unique, actionable insights and analytics that help drive business forward.

Fourth Level: Social Business Collaborations

Organizations who function at this level:

■ Surpass the first three maturity levels, following best practices to engage with customers, prospects, and influencers while measuring what is and is not working and changing what doesn't work into what does.

■ Build a data cube (commonly called a data warehouse) and append social media data into existing CRM data.

Are the Deliverables the Client Requests Achievable?

After you understand the client's requirements, it's time to determine whether the analysis you or your firm provides is capable of meeting those needs. Perhaps there are technology, time, manpower, cultural, and/or information constraints in place that will have an impact on your ability to deliver reports. If so, there is still the question of whether you're able to deal with the issue—or rather, if not, whether you should just admit that you can't deliver what is needed, given the current set of circumstances and capabilities. These are all important concerns.

Client or Stakeholder Framework

In my work within organizations, broadly speaking, I have come to see deliverables as having four primary stakeholders: marketers, PR/communications, and research- and enterprise-information systems as outlined in Figure 8-3.

Each of these stakeholder groups wants something different, and it's best to know with whom you're dealing when you provide reports: what you produce should fit the needs of the stakeholder. Identifying the type of stakeholder up front saves a lot of time and expense.

Let's take a closer look at this framework. It raises several key questions about the relationship between you and your clients within an organizational framework.

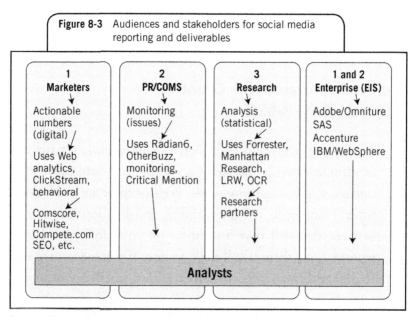

Figure 8-3 Audiences and stakeholders for social media reporting and deliverables

Source: Webmetricsguru.com and Marshall Sponder.

1. Is your analytics reporting oriented toward clients' marketers, PR/communications, researchers, or EIS (enterprise information systems)? Each category requires a different kind of monitoring, reporting, and dashboard, so it will affect the data you provide.

2. How sophisticated is the client's industry regarding social media?

    Certain industries (such as telecommunications, Internet marketing, and travel) are more sophisticated in the use of social media and, by extension, analytics.

    Other industries (such as pharmaceuticals, financial services, and government) have many regulatory restrictions and may be less proactive in their needs for analytics.

    Finally, industries such as retail, packaged goods, hotels, and restaurants may be relatively unsophisticated about social media use, including social media analytics.

3. How mature are the stakeholder's knowledge, needs, and expectations about social media analytics (of the marketers, PR/communications, and research types)? The ability to satisfy stakeholders will depend upon what type of reports they are used to and whether social media analytics platforms can produce those reports, or not.

    Is the client a newbie, or is he or she a bit more sophisticated and knowledgeable? If the client is a newbie, then the deliverables will be totally different from those if he is knowledgeable. Further, the questions a stakeholder has will differ depending on his level of sophistication in social media.

4. What is the budget allotted for social media analytics and dashboards? Does the client expect results for free, low

cost (under $500 per month), moderate cost ($1,000 to $5,000 per month), or premium cost ($5,000 per month or more). These numbers are likely to vary in different situations.

5. How much time is allotted to deliver results? "Ad hoc" reports are one-time deliverables that are usually done with little notice. "Immediate" reports are often created to put out fires in an organization. The project work will often span weeks, months, or years.

6. How much integration with other data sources (such as e-mail lists, house data, search data, Web analytics data, demographic data, and psychographic data) is required? The Semphonic case study presented earlier in this chapter, with all its complexities and overlaying of data sources, is an example of data integration in the extreme. Generally speaking, any reporting that needs data integration will greatly increase the time and expense of a project, but it will also increase the likelihood the information derived will be actionable—which is why organizations undertake this type of project in the first place.

7. Is there a multinational or multicultural requirement for listening and analytics?

   Is listening only in English (or another language), or is it in several languages?

   Is listening only in one region (country, state, or city), or in several regions?

There may be no set templates or best practices for social media analytics deliverables; the form and format of reports and analysis will vary depending on whom the reports are for and what their needs are.

Sample Advanced Scorecards

Assuming that you have some idea of the information your client will be looking for, here are examples of the kinds of advanced scorecards you would present to them. All scorecards in this section require significant categorization by analysts beforehand.

Semphonic provides the following sample scorecard (Figure 8-4) for IT security management; it layers specific category or product mentions of a brand against its competitors', along with the proportion of online comments related to features, pricing, and/or support. In addition, the main topics of discussion are presented in the word cloud labeled "Brand Characteristics" at the bottom of the dashboard. As mentioned earlier in this chapter, uncategorized online social data are rarely interesting by themselves, but once the data are layered with other information, the combined data become far more actionable.

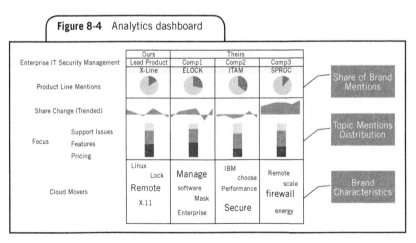

Figure 8-4 Analytics dashboard

Source: Semphonic.com

The information provided in the dashboard (such as Ajax, Browser, Open Source, and ASP; see Figure 8-5) shows lead influencers by subjects on which they have an effect. In the Semphonic case study mentioned earlier, lead influencer identification by subject was one of the more interesting and actionable aspects of the deliverable for the client. To produce this scorecard, each influencer was ranked in topic areas, which is another aspect of data integration and categorization. This example further reinforces the notion that actionable information often requires customized data overlays, and simple influencer identification without this layering of information will probably not be actionable.

The dashboard shown in Figure 8-6 is another composite, created by overlaying third-party audience duplication data from ComScore MyMetrix (a panel-based competitive-analysis platform for advertisers and publishers) for downstream sites (sites to which visitors go after leaving the client's) with the shift in activity on those sites from the past

Figure 8-5 Influencer dashboard

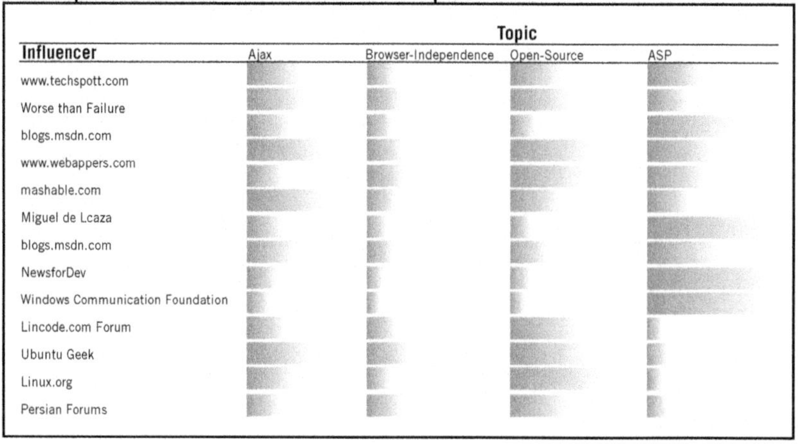

Influencer	Topic			
	Ajax	Browser-Independence	Open-Source	ASP
www.techspott.com				
Worse than Failure				
blogs.msdn.com				
www.webappers.com				
mashable.com				
Miguel de Lcaza				
blogs.msdn.com				
NewsforDev				
Windows Communication Foundation				
Lincode.com Forum				
Ubuntu Geek				
Linux.org				
Persian Forums				

Source: Semphonic.com

Figure 8-6 Brand affinity dashboard

Key Pubs	Affinity	Brand (Us v. Them)	Shift	Top Topics	
www.silverlight.net	8.7		=	Silverlight	Flash
www.webmonkey.com	11.7		+++	Chrome	Mobile
www.lc-tech.com	10.9		+	Data Recovery	Security
learnonline.nku.edu	8.6		--	Classes	Programming
ajaxcontroltoolkit.codeplex.com	5.7		+	AJAX	Windows
idealprogrammer.com	9.2		++++	.NET	PHP
www.cyberdefender.com	2.2		---	Security	Browser
www.webnewswire.com	5.7		+	Software	Systems
www.epxerts-exchange.com	4.1		++	Programmer	Analyst
www.dotnetnuke.com	15.2		=	CMS	.NET

Source: Semphonic.com

reporting period (generally the month preceding the current one). The two top topics on those sites are also noted. In this case, overlaying three layers of information provides the best level of actionable information. Depending on how well the data are prepared and cleansed, this level of dashboarding is easily manageable.

The dashboard shown in Figure 8-7 layers three different sources of information: Web referrals; the likelihood of a visitor's being an exisiting customer or a new prospect, based on where he was directed from (such as direct traffic or social media traffic); and which of five categories the visitor falls into (based on predefined segmentation). This dashboard, in particular, required an advanced implemenation of tagging that Semphonic is expert at helping to implement.

Once the necessary data segmentations were set up, creating this level of dashboarding was not complex. However, it does take a fair amount of scripting to automate. Once again, by overlaying three layers of information seamlessly, Semphonic has made data that are ordinarily only diagnostic (such as site visitors by type) into actionable data. This

Figure 8-7 Visitor referral dashboard

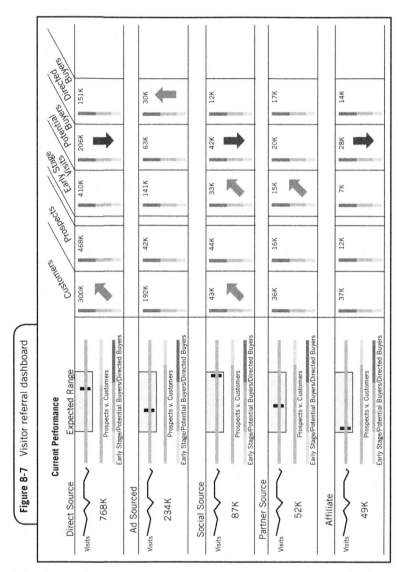

Source: Semphonic.com

transformation is a well-known feature of Semphonic's work in the analytics industry.

The Semphonic traffic modeling dashboard in Figure 8-8 is my favorite, and I have written about it on my WebMetricsGuru blog several times. The dashboard shows attribution probabilities for increases and decreases in site traffic. The same approach that drove the creation of this dashboard can be adapted to show social media traffic; and, with a fair amount of programming, it can include any dimension or classification mentioned in this chapter. In addition, by automating attribution, analysts can provide more insight while the reporting template answers first- and second-level questions, such as "I see a spike in X; what is the cause?" or "There is an increase in followers; can you calculate the probabilities against a series of known events?"

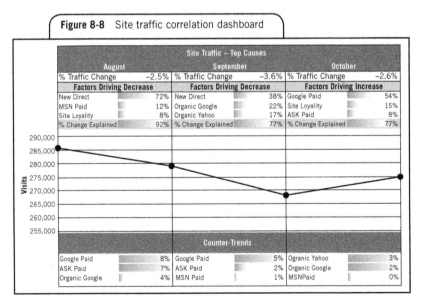

Figure 8-8   Site traffic correlation dashboard

Site Traffic – Top Causes								
August			**September**			**October**		
% Traffic Change		−2.5%	% Traffic Change		−3.6%	% Traffic Change		−2.6%
Factors Driving Decrease			**Factors Driving Decrease**			**Factors Driving Increase**		
New Direct		72%	New Direct		38%	Google Paid		54%
MSN Paid		12%	Organic Google		22%	Site Loyality		15%
Site Loyality		8%	Organic Yahoo		17%	ASK Paid		8%
% Change Explained		92%	% Change Explained		77%	% Change Explained		77%

Counter-Trends								
Google Paid		8%	Google Paid		5%	Ogranic Yahoo		3%
ASK Paid		7%	ASK Paid		2%	Organic Google		2%
Organic Google		4%	MSN Paid		1%	MSNPaid		0%

Source: Semphonic.com

According to Semphonic's Gary Angel, the originator of the modeling chart shown in Figure 8-8, the essential idea is to build an analytic model of a concept such as traffic (or conversion, satisfaction, efficiency, or engagement), and then embody that model in a report. Furthermore, Angel explains the programming used to create this chart:

"To do this, we dump all the relevant data for the model into a working spreadsheet. Then, we create a (fairly complicated) Excel macro that processes the data using the analytic model. It then populates the report spreadsheet with the core numbers being tracked, along with the analysis of the key causal factors and countertrends.

"The beauty of this approach is twofold. First, a good deal of analytic complexity and intelligence can be built into the model. This can prevent a decision-maker from misunderstanding or missing the contribution of key factors (like visitor loyalty) on traffic. Second, it allows the report to encapsulate all the key information in one simple presentation that provides actual immediate and well thought-out answers to the inevitable questions."[8]

To go even deeper into these and other social media monitoring issues, I asked Angel to participate in an interview.

Profile: Gary Angel, CTO of Semphonic.com

Gary Angel, whom you have met in various passages of this book, is president and CTO of Semphonic. Angel cofounded Semphonic and has developed the company's industry-leading online measurement practice. Since Semphonic was founded, he has led the consulting teams for its largest enterprise clients. His groundbreaking work in hands-on Web analytics includes the development of functionalism (the public-domain methodology for tactical Web analysis), pioneering work in the creation of SEM analytics as a discipline, and numerous methodological improvements to the field of Web analytics and the study of online behavior.

Angel's background in CRM, survey analysis, database marketing, large-scale data-mining, and business-intelligence have helped keep Semphonic at the leading edge of online measurement. He has spoken at many conferences and is also a regular on the Beyond Web Analytics podcast. The X-Change Web Analytics Conference is also Angel's original concept and idea.

The Reasons for Conducting a Social Media Listening Report

Gary Angel begins by saying: "With the growth in social media as a marketing channel, there's been tremendous interest in moving marketing programs into social settings and, quite naturally, tracking them. If the analysis of social campaigns is your focus, you're probably concerned with the same general set of questions and metrics that exist when you study any other type of marketing campaign, such as who you're trying to reach, how many of those people did you reach, and whether your message had any impact.

"That's important stuff, and there's no doubt that social campaigns present some fairly serious challenges when it comes to measurement and analysis. In many ways, though, I think a second use of social media, as a pure research channel, is actually more interesting. Taking away the whole question of campaign measurement, social media presents unique opportunities for tackling a range of classic business research projects, such as competitive landscaping, brand perception, and product and feature discovery. These types of analysis projects use fundamentally different techniques and ask quite different questions than social media campaign measurement."

Mobile and Social Media Strategy

Regarding strategy for mobile and social media, Angel says, "Every business will need the right infrastructure to take on mobile and social media efforts. What should businesses invest in now, to stay ahead in monitoring?

"I'd start by saying that there's an immediate governance issue here that organizations really should address. If you're leaving the choice and setup of a social media monitoring tool to your PR folks, you're effectively forfeiting social media analytics. As I've said, if you start by thinking of these tools as research and measurement tools, you'll at least be putting them in the right place in the organization and having the right people making decisions about the choice of tool and the necessary configuration and governance."

Conducting a Social Media Listening Report

Angel continues, "Much of how you conduct the report depends on the size and scope of your enterprise. Naturally, part of this difference is institutional: If you have more stakeholders in a large organization, more meetings, more approvals, and more politics, then navigating all of that to produce a report takes time. It isn't just institutional issues that make size and scope so important. I've seen midsized businesses with complex Web sites that are more difficult to measure than ones used by much larger enterprises.

"In social media, however, size often introduces significant additional complexities. The more product lines you have, the more you need to track. The more things you're involved in, the wider the social listening pool. Large brands tend to attract more mentions, have larger competitors, and just in general put more demands on listening tools.

"In our experience, there are two significant steps when it comes to producing a social media listening report. The first is deciding on the universe of topics that are of concern. Since we push hard to get organizations to do more with social media than brand tracking, this can take some significant effort. Every product area and every business line will have its own lexicon, its distinct competitive set, and its own unique challenges when it comes to social listening. If you aren't spending weeks setting up your social media listening tools and profiles, you almost certainly aren't doing it right.

"The second big job is figuring out how to translate the basic listening metrics into reports that make sense and are useful. We're starting to have a stronger point of view on how to do this. That makes it easier, because one of the big challenges in social media has been that it's so new, there really aren't standard best practices around reporting. For the most part, I think this is an easier job than the first step. If you've done a good job deciding what you are interested in and then configuring your tools to collect it, translating the raw data into the reports isn't going to be as challenging. At the large enterprise level, I think any serious reporting effort is going to take months. That's just a fact of life and a direct result of the complexity of those organizations, particularly when it comes to social media."

What a Social Media Listening Report Should Contain

"Before I answer the real question," Angel says, "I want to give a completely serious nonanswer. A social media listening report should contain clean data. One of the biggest problems with most social media listening reports I see is that they are based on data streams that are poorly set up initially and aren't regularly cleaned or vetted for data quality. Social listening data can be incredibly muddy and turn bad almost instantly. The most important and difficult step in getting a social media report is getting clean data to report on. Beyond that, I think any good social media listening report should track your brand, your key competitive brands, and your overall industry. Having all three levels provides essential context around almost any social media metric.

"Second, I think a good social media report will drill down underneath brand mentions to product or interest areas and specific business lines. So much of the real data is down at this level, particularly when it comes to broader industry reporting and analysis.

"Finally, a really good social media report will encapsulate some of the key areas of traditional enterprise research: PR effectiveness, trends in new interests or products, brand strength, product kudos or complaints, and the competitive position between your brand position and your competitors."

What Is More Important, Good Data or Good Visualization?

Angel continues, "Good visualizations are a lot harder than most people think, and, frankly, I'm not sure we'd claim to be truly proficient at them either. I've always been a believer that it's more important to have the right information than the right visualization. I've seen decision makers work with really, really ugly and difficult reports and be successful because they believed the data inside was important.

"Having both good data and good visualizations is, clearly, the best situation you can look for. But if you have to pick one, I'd still suggest concentrating on the quality of the data. That being said, there are tools like Tableau and Spotfire that make delivering interesting visualizations much easier. Let me put it this way: having a good visualization or tool won't make up for a poor approach to the data or its bad quality. If you're convinced your data is good and meaningful, you should be thinking about tools that will really let you maximize the information. If you're not convinced of that, then your focus shouldn't be on visualization."

The Unique Nature of Social Media Data

"With your Web site or your point of sale systems," Angel says, "the universe of data is pretty much fixed. That isn't true with social media. The first and one of the most important steps in social media measurement is carving off a relevant chunk of data from the vast river of news that's out there. Ideally, you'd like to be able to carve out a really large set of data that covers everything that might be of interest in your industry and then select a subset of the data in ways that seem interesting to you.

"Unfortunately, it doesn't usually work that way. First, most social media tools charge you according to the volume of news you listen to. So the more liberal you are in your initial cut, the more expensive the tool. That's not the only problem, though. Many of the social media listening tools don't make it easy to make a subset of the data from a large pool. For example, if you collect both competitor and brand mentions in the same big pool, you often can't pull a subset of the data to isolate either.

"And even when you can make a subset, often specific reports (such as influencer reports) can't be sliced in a similar fashion. This puts a big burden on the analyst to set up the tool to match the way the data is going to be used. For example, you can't just create and use ad hoc classifications of the data when and as you decide you need them. Instead, you have to collect the data and put the data into the categories and buckets you want to report on."

Differences between Monitoring and Measuring Social Media

Angel continues: "When you set up profiles for listening, you can generally live with quite a bit of slop, because you're counting on having human eyeballs quickly scan the listings and a person can and will easily filter out the noise. So if you're setting up a social media monitoring tool and your focus is on listening and responding, you're not likely to care much about filtering out noise or categorizing the data; you want to be as inclusive as possible and let the human reader do the filtering.

"For reporting measurement, that isn't going to work. Nobody is reading the actual posts and filtering them, because they are being aggregated up into mentions and sentiment numbers. And if there is noise, that noise goes directly into the numbers. When you set up a profile for measurement, you're going to have to iteratively eyeball the listings and try to exclude types of posts you don't want, or use a machine learning tool to do that. In addition, you have to constantly monitor the data stream to ensure new types of conversations that you *don't* want haven't snuck into it.

"One of the main points I try to make to people about social media profile setup is that if you are doing it for reporting, maintaining it never really stops, and you will have an ongoing governance and maintenance task. But for pure listening and responding, that isn't true. Once you've set up a profile, you may never really need to tune it."

Setup for Monitoring Solutions

Angel continues: "Any really good social media classification system is going to provide all the basic classifications [as shown in Figure 8-9 on the next page]."

The Costs Involved with Setup

There are costs involved with setup, as Angel notes: "Many social media monitoring platforms charge the client by the number of profiles and volume of mentions collected. Setting up two sets of profiles for every customer or report, when each profile tends to cost thousands of dollars a month to maintain—not to mention keeping it clean and relevant—makes this a real problem. I have yet to find a client who doesn't care about cost, and there is a legitimate cost-of-measurement issue here.

"Not every measurement you can do is worth doing. I tend to believe there's a lot of value in social media measurement. Semphonic's clients spend a lot of money on traditional research techniques, such as focus groups and tracking surveys, that can potentially be replaced or improved on. In a

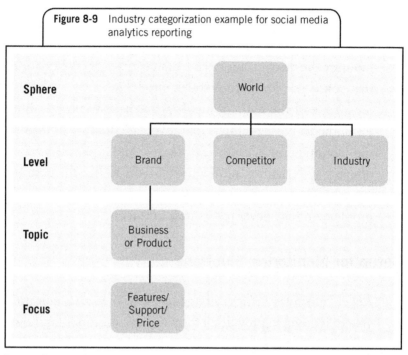

Figure 8-9 Industry categorization example for social media analytics reporting

Source: Semphonic.com

perfect world, though, tools wouldn't need to charge you a premium to measure the things you think are important."

Setting Up Effective Topic Profiles for Various Reports

Angel continues: "There really is a substantial difference in what you're going to report. It's probably a truism that reporting needs to be tailored to audience, but social media reporting and analysis is a very broad book. If you are targeting PR stakeholders, they need to understand influencers and how influencers are trending. They still need the topic, competitor, and business classifications the marketing guys need, but they are going to be looking at how those cuts play out in the world of influencers.

"Strategy guys don't care so much about influencers, because they are more focused on what the trends in social conversation can tell them about product and marketing opportunities. And, of course, you have the social marketers whose primary interest is in classic campaign reporting translated into the social sphere. However, these differences tend to play out more in the types of metrics and reports stakeholders consume, and less in the actual configuration of the profiles.

"I don't care who you are in an organization, you still care about your brand versus your competition's, product line A versus product line B, and how your business tracks versus your industry's.

"Most reporting gets reworked over and over again before it is approved and presented to a client because of differences in how stakeholders and clients describe information versus how an analyst sets up profiles and pulls data to create reports and insight. And a lot of freshness and insight gets lost in the process back and forth.

"In order to make everyone's life easier and cut down on the reworking of reports, here is how you improve the situation. In the traditional business intelligence world, there's a paradigm for building reports that says you go out and interview the stakeholders, learn what they need, and then translate that into the underlying data model. As it happens, that BI model doesn't work in Web analytics, and it won't work in social media analytics either, because the stakeholders don't know what they need and don't yet understand the uses of the data.

"In Web analytics and social media reporting, the analyst has to be the subject matter expert. That isn't true in traditional BI, and the implications are profound. Much of the conventional wisdom in Web analytics and social media are borrowed from more mature BI disciplines, and that's why you often see requirements-gathering exercises producing meaningless reports."

Differences between Keyword Groups for Social Media Listening and for Online Search

Angel continues: "Social media keywords and phrases are similar to and different from search phases. I suspect that a large search program has many useful and interesting keywords that should be explored from a listening perspective, but I certainly wouldn't expect a direct relationship. Even between internal search and external search we often see very different keyword patterns.

"I'm sure that the frequency of use between search words and social words isn't going to match well, but search programs are often quite exhaustive and I think they would be a good resource for keyword discovery. One thing to be aware of, though: not all search programs do much competitor brand keyword campaigns. There's a very good chance that even if you're buying a competitive brand word, you aren't buying a competitor's product words. But those words are worth studying from a social media analytics perspective."

Data Enrichment

Angel advises: "It is valuable to measure the social profile of visitors to a Web site through doing surveys. At this time, most monitoring doesn't involve site analytics. Tools like PeekYou aggregate social and public record data. I'm a big fan of data enrichment, both in aggregate and at the visitor level.

"At the visitor level, the key to good data enrichment is to have a valid key, such as an e-mail address, and make sure the necessary opt-ins or privacy protections are in place. One advantage to aggregate level integrations is that you generally don't have the same privacy considerations. When you put data together at the aggregate level, it's often more of a reporting-level task. It's often useful, for example, to show site satisfaction numbers in conjunction with conversion numbers, because aggressive conversion drives can lower brand or site satisfaction scores.

"You put the two together so that decision makers see a better, more realistic picture of the world. I think the same is probably true of social and site data. There are lots of interesting potential synergies in combining the two types of data into a single picture."

The Value of the Analytics Model as Applied to Social Media

Angel continues: "The model [illustrated in the type of dashboard shown in Figure 8-8] captures not just the trend in traffic; it immediately identifies the factors that drove the trend, the extent to which they contributed, and any countertrends that were also in place. To get the same intelligence from any non-model-based report set would take a big chunk of work and a fair amount of knowledge about Web analytics—the two things that a good report set is supposed to make unnecessary! The more I work on reporting, the more I think that the distinction between analysis and reporting is meaningless. Unless you embody good analysis in your reporting, you'll never deliver a good report set."

Summary

Social media analytics and measurement began from a rocky foundation of early-stage platforms and tools, some of which are just beginning to mature. The choice of tools and platforms a business uses for analysis and reporting ends up shaping the reports, and good analysis may be much harder if the wrong sets of tools are in place. Also, the choice of platforms and the methodology used have a profound effect on the deliverability and costs of reporting. Insights that provide better, more informed choices tend to deliver much more satisfying results.

Furthermore, the most interesting aspects of social media dashboards require significant data categorization and data layering (with up to three levels of data), which is time-consuming but leads to insights that clients ask for but rarely get. We introduced the notion of the maturity level of clients and organizations along with industry categorizations useful for social media monitoring and reporting.

Finally, we ended the chapter with a sampling of social analytics dashboards provided by Semphonic.com that embody combinations of several data sources in order to provide actionable insights.

chapter 9

Going beyond Monitoring: Content Creation and Content Tracking

It is one thing to create social media and quite another thing to measure it so as to optimize content creation. That's almost a requirement as platforms become more intelligent and people become serious about using social media as a marketing tool.

Some of the case studies in this book, such as the one on InfiniGraph (Chapter 4), discuss changes in online content that are detected by measurement and cycled back to improving content. It's best to think of the entire process as an ecosystem similar to the SEO organic search ecosystems I wrote about in late 2010,[1] however, in that social media (recent tweets, Facebook discussions, check-ins, etc.) become search content with the Google Search Engine indexing that often result in displaying the latest postings of an individual in search results. What is good for social media also tends to be good for search engine results.

According to John Battelle, founder and CEO of Federated Media, social media provides "branded content," while search engines provide information. "Branded content, however, is far more social [than content mills like Demand Media's] because branded content is written with a human voice and published by a branded entity [you, a friend, campaign, cause, company, brand, etc.]. Search drives a lot of traffic to branded content, of course, but once there, people are more likely to share branded content than content produced mainly for search results such as 'how to tie a tie.' The former is socially shareable ('hey, check this out, it's interesting'), and the latter is specific ('I need an answer, and I don't think my friends have the same need right now')," according to Battelle.[2]

Arguably, "branded content" is measureable using social media monitoring and Web analytics, and can be considered to be "more social" than nonbranded content (in that people will have more interest in sharing branded vs. unbranded content). But once social media content surfaces, it should fit into a longer-term strategy, where valuable content becomes evergreen. Setting up social media analytics with clear measurement goals will assist in achieving that strategy.

Looking at search keywords typed into Web sites (finding out what people are looking for using Web analytics site search reports) and mashing up that information with social media monitoring of content emerging from site search leads to more and better content for the brand, based on case studies tracking Old Spice and Delta Airlines.[3] Imagine if the content team could prioritize content based on not only this historical demand from search query volume, but also real-time input from social media monitoring.[4]

One way to harness social media in order to get your message out: use Google to find bloggers (who are influencers on a subject of the search query by appearing within the top 10 search results) while looking at relevant search queries.[5]

In addition, by using Google Webmaster tools, Web analytics, or a social media monitoring platform such as Radian6 (Radian6 can integrate with Web analytics platforms such as Adobe Omniture, WebTrends, and Google Analytics), a site owner will have the means to identify and write about what is engaging on its site.

Determining Your Social Media Analytics Readiness

Social media is a emergent communications medium that is considered to be free and available to everyone. Sometimes this incorrectly leads to an assumption by many on the content creation or on the agency side that measurement of social media can be set up as more of an afterthought. Tracking content can often require just as much enablement work as enterprise and large e-commerce sites have put in place to track their users and content using site analytics for many years.

The usual data on the radar are easy to capture: hits, followers, page views, and so on. Additional metrics, including knowing the results of efforts in terms of which were the most effective in bringing in sales, expanding the customer base, and increasing exposure of the brand, are also required. Information is available to show that social media outreach is effective in driving new business and revenue, although often those supporting data are difficult to capture.

This elusive quality is what I referred to earlier as "ultraviolet data," we can't see ultraviolet light, yet it's present all around us. The same holds true of much of the data a business or organization should capture; the data exist, but they are not being captured properly for use in site analytics or social media analytics.

Another common challenge for social media measurement is that most business processes are misaligned with the business's goals for measurement. The work I did with Cecilia Pineda Feret and Havana Central, which led to my white paper with Compete.com on spectrum analytics, mentioned in an earlier chapter, provided two examples of misaligned measurement processes.

1. Communications issues between marketing and community management leading to lost sales and analytics tracking.
2. Missed opportunities to engage with Havana Central's enthusiasts, who check in using Foursquare while having a meal.

The case of Havana Central involved individuals who were communicating (or not) while interacting in ineffective ways using incompatible business processes. These individuals were also using out-of-the-box analytics that had not been thoughtfully configured to track the results of their specific business processes. This often happens when using free platforms such as Google Analytics, and it often leads to lackluster business performance measurement. The insights analytics can deliver need careful setup, but it's not just about measurement; we also should consider tuning the business process itself.

Through my work with Havana Central, I came to see that business and measurement goals and tactics that are core to a business need to inform one another, need to be coupled and folded, so to speak, much as we fold our hands together. When we fold our hands, there is no room for misalignment, and that is true of any structure, such as a table, chair, or building. Misaligned table legs will cause the table to collapse. Misalign a building foundation, and the foundation cracks.

This same level of alignment is needed in social media measurement, *yet I find it is hardly given any thought*, and is often treated incidentally by content creators, agencies, and brands, which is one of the principal reasons I wrote this book.

To audit a business's readiness for full-spectrum analytics tracking, one should list all the sources of data the business has and which campaigns and marketing initiatives the business is running; the data sources should be listed vertically, and the marketing campaigns and initiatives should be listed horizontally. (I have written about how to merge these in my white paper on the subject, which you can view or download and read at http://www.scribd.com/doc/38176762/tracking -social-media-roi-using-spectrum-analytics. The information in the following section is based on that white paper.)

Enabling Data Collection

In some cases, enabling data collection in business is easy and straightforward. But often it is awkward and difficult to patch data holes, or blind spots, where needed information is missing, resulting in an inability to measure business effectiveness.

Enabling Ultraviolet Data

Taking a closer look at a specific campaign or marketing initiative against the sources of data available is the best way to find tracking solutions that address weaknesses in the campaign's current analytics. For example, an analytics enablement audit was set up to track online reservations at Havana Central that were made via its Facebook fan page using the OpenTable application on it.[6] Using additional codes suggested by the audit process, Havana Central was able to capture important reservation information within Google Analytics. This is a built-in function of analytics packages, but often it is not utilized. With that information, Havana Central was able to evaluate the marketing effectiveness of Facebook to drive customers to the restaurant.

Going through each campaign and finding ways to use analytics tracking, a business moves toward a 360-degree view of its data, where everything needed to show return on campaign investment is present and accessible, ultimately in a dashboard.

All that remains is to ensure that the collected data can be overlaid, that a common key (such as an e-mail address, Twitter handle, social security number, address, and so on) identifies all transactions—no mean feat in itself.

In more advanced cases, a data cube or data warehouse can be built to marshall a company's business data into a programming structure that allows deeper insights than conventional analytics software allows for.

Employing a data cube or data warehouse allows a company to perform "what if" and predictive analysis on a combined dataset containing all company data, leading to insights such as the number of times a customer visits a brick-and-mortar store or outlet to make a purchase, or how many times that same item was searched for online. Any information within a data cube can be correlated and analyzed using predictive analysis and regression statistics, leading businesses to save money and resources by optimizing their products, services, and offerings.

However, when a common key (such as common record locator for Google Analytics, OpenTable, SeamlessWeb, direct e-mail marketing, and so on, as was the case in many smaller businesses like Havana Central) is lacking, the information needed to populate the data cube will be spotty, noisy, or hard to translate to the right structure for it to be effective. In fact, most small and medium-sized business cannot afford to build a data cube today, and even if they could, they would not know how to use it. In the future this may change as businesses become more measurement savvy and platforms evolve to simplify and bundle data collection tasks in a way that makes it easier for businesses to implement tracking.

According to Gary Angel, the CTO of Semphonic, "When you integrate data into a data warehouse, you open up new questions, targeting opportunities, and analysis methods that otherwise don't exist."[7] In fact, business intelligence tools (of which a data warehouse is a part) allow business owners to see relationships in the data that ordinarily would be impossible to detect, and therefore open up new possibilities for analysis.

Enabling Business Goals, Strategy, and Tactics

Brian Solis, a well-known voice for PR 2.0, has stated that the case for new metrics can't be made until there is an intrinsic understanding of how social media engagement affects us at every level.[8]

In 2010 on the "MP Daily Fix" blog, Paul Williams shared a very well visualized image of what business goals, strategies, and tactics look like for a business campaign.[9] Many times, people fail to formulate their business goals in a clear way; this complicates the measurement of their goals and tactics.

Once the diagram or map of instructions is created and vetted, it should be used for enabling social media business strategy along with social media metrics (and other metrics, as needed). Filling in the gaps and correcting erroneous assumptions is much easier than trying to devise a program with no idea of how it is to be structured or flowed.

Creating a Tagging Strategy

Once a program outline is approved, it is time to put goals, strategies, and tactics into place, along with analytics tracking (such as Google Analytics, Adobe Site Catalyst, or WebTrends). This provides a significant part of the analytics tracking needed and is not difficult to implement provided that analyst understands how to create, assign, and add tagging to Web sites and URLs. Enabling social media measurement by using Google Analytics,[10] it is possible to capture key performance indicators such as traffic (quality and quantity), engagement level, goal conversions, e-commerce direct sales, and cost savings by comparing social media with other marketing channels.

Google Analytics tracks campaigns, advanced segmentation, goals, and custom reporting through structures built into the platform and enriched by using custom URLs and Google Analytics URL Builder.[11]

Creating Custom Tagging in Google Analytics

Generally speaking, a tagging strategy for analytics should include the following traffic definitions[12]:

Source: Web site sending traffic
Medium: Traffic type, such as social media or cost per click
Campaign: A campaign name determined by user
Context/Term: Unique identifier used for split testing purposes

The Econsultancy case study in Chapter 11 is an example of campaign tracking with social media in mind.

Using URL Shorteners to Capture Offsite Campaign Traffic

Bit.ly and similar URL shorteners provide another good way to track social media using truncated URLs. These can be used for campaigns that site analytics cannot track (such as marketing effort), but that do not register as a hit on the company's "landing page." Much of the content created for consumption does not result in direct visits to the brand Web sites; shortened URLs are one way the site analytics could track this content as it moves around the Web.

Setting Up Advanced Segmentation

Google Analytics has additional features, such as advanced segmentation, used to create custom segments such as "social media traffic" or "e-mail traffic" based on URL strings or other parameters. These can be very useful in supercharging reporting and insights by creating a custom segment within site analytics around the tagging, and correlating it with marketing efforts and social media mentions.

Setting Up Goals in Google Analytics

It is fairly easy to assign goals to campaigns in Google Analytics (although you need administrator privileges), which help track such goals as successful completion, goal value, channel value, and e-commerce transactions.

Custom Reporting

Using Google Analytics custom report generator, it is possible to build exactly the report you want, showing only which information is needed, presented directly to stakeholders and clients in a neat package.

Analytics Tracking Results for Enablement

With enablement in place, much of the information needed to track social media via Google Analytics will be evident, along with charts needed to demonstrate return on investment.

Compete.com Audience

When a site owner adds a Compete.com audience tag to its Web site or blog, Compete.com can collect audience profiles, and map demographic and psychographic information that may be of value to the business.

Alexa

Another free platform, Alexa provides audience data and can be useful when other sources of more reliable information about viewers are unavailable. Alexa data and Quantcast are similar as far as audience profiling goes, but the results are not an exact match.

Alterian SM2, Sysomos MAP, and Radian6 Insights

Alterian, Sysomos, and Radian6 Insights provide demographic information in monitoring profiles, although it is not particularly reliable and is based on a subset of online mentions of age and gender; in Sysomos Map, industry data are also available. These platforms, while providing some useful information on audiences, are not really designed as robust market research platforms. However, as social media analytics matures, and as more of the Web is tagged with metadata, the utility of social media analytics platforms for market research will increase.

Forrester Technographics Profiles

Forrester's Technographics profile[13] categorizes traffic based on participation in social media. Its focus is on behavior, and it could be a useful addition to other audience-profiling tools presented in this section as an overlay based on age, gender, and location.[14]

There are many other ways to slice and dice audiences, and this book does not aim to examine them all.

Finding Content to Map to Your Audience

Using Forrester's Technographics profile is one way to create content that is in alignment with the users of a Web site or a sales or marketing initiative. Once content is created, it is easy to track using any number of methods including site analytics and RSS metrics such as Feedburner.

There is another aspect to identifying audiences that needs consideration, however: members that move from one segmentation to another. Typically, movements of this nature are from new customer to regular customer to brand advocate, and so on.

As online audience members shift from one segment to another, the content they consume is also likely to change; this should be tracked using automated dashboards or, if that's too

206 Social Media Analytics

difficult, a spreadsheet (similar to the advanced dashboards we examined in Chapter 8).

Tracking Content across Multiple Channels

Newer analytics platforms such as LinksAlpha and Tynt provide a way to track content across marketing channels and tie it back to authors. But these tools are as yet not widely used. At the time of this writing there are few platforms available to track content as it is consumed across marketing channels, but that is likely to change as social media analytics matures as a marketing discipline.

Tracking Social Media Outreach Using Social CRM

With all the work going into creating and measuring the right content for the right audiences comes the need to engage viewers directly, when it makes sense. This engagement could be to build customer loyalty, address issues or concerns, or simply to build market share beyond the audiences you have now, including analytics tracking of audience-building efforts. While there are an abundance of Twitter tools that claim to facilitate contacts between individual Twitter accounts and aggregation of information and responses in any number of platforms, there is no point in going over them all here, because this is social media analytics book. Yet it's also true that very few of the typical platforms are enabled for social CRM, where both tracking and the possibilities of social media ROI lie.

The time of social CRM and integration is here, according to the Altimeter Group.[15] While just about every social media listening platform can "monitor" the basis of social CRM—the conversation—it takes an entirely different approach to measure communications effectively. This brings into view a series of platforms not previously discussed: Cognos, Hyperion, SAP, and SAS. Social CRM, as an outgrowth of conversations now being tracked, is moving into the realm of the call center, with analytics and tracking more related to enterprise tracking and business intelligence than they are to social media. Platforms such as Bantam Live (acquired by e-mail subscription list platform Constant Contact in February 2011)[16] have approached social CRM in one way (as a single point of contact), while others, such as Lithium, have approached it in another, snapping up Scout Labs earlier in 2010, integrating social listening into social CRM. Salesforce.com's acquisition of Radian6 in March 2011 is a good indication of how crucial CRM is becoming in social media analytics. I discuss this in Chapter 12.

By the time this book is published, most of the early movers in social CRM will be available on the market, according to the Altimeter Group,[17] including social marketing insights, social sales insights, rapid response, and enterprise collaboration, while others, such as social campaign tracking, will become available in late 2011 or early 2012.

It would be premature to discuss social CRM metrics along with social CRM return on investment. Yet some platforms, such as Radian6 (Engagement Console), Alterian SM2 (Engagement Console), and Synthesio (Unity), are already providing a framework for engagement, suggesting that social CRM is needed to foster and track intimacy and influence through interactions with customers.

These are best followed through a customer relationship manager, in this case, social CRM. And engagement metrics suggest social CRM is needed.[18]

Case Study: The University of Texas M.D. Anderson Cancer Center

The University of Texas M.D. Anderson Cancer Center is a top authority on cancer treatment. As one of the larger cancer hospitals in North America, the center treats more than 90,000 patients a year. Having grown into one of the leading authorities in its field during the past 60 years, the hospital aims to become the world's premier cancer center, through programs that integrate patient care, research, and prevention. There is also an extensive education facility for students, trainees, professionals, employees, and the public.

Recognizing the Value of Listening

An early adopter of social media in the medical world, the hospital's external communications department had started using it back in 2007. Twitter, Facebook, and the blogosphere were the initial focus, as an increasing number of people were writing about their cancer experiences and treatment online. The hospital even set up a specific role to monitor what was being said about both the brand and cancer-related topics, in addition to the communications being created by the institution itself.

"About three years ago, we realized there were patients and prospective patients using social media to discuss their concerns or ask questions about treatment or find out about the hospital," explains Jennifer Texada, the center's communications program manager of digital and new media. "We were using free monitoring tools from Twitter and Google, plus Technorati and a few RSS feeds, and we could see some interesting conversations going on. But it took a lot of time to look at these manually."

The hospital also recognized that there had to be many more conversations that it wasn't aware of, and it was also about to expand its own social media programs. So it began looking for a better method of listening to the social media world.

"Our desire to get closer to patients and the general public online, and engage with those who were socially connected, meant we had to be able to monitor a much larger number of sources," Texada adds.

Aims and Objectives

Here are the objectives of the project:

1. Proper structuring for the social media monitoring process

2. Better method for listening to (and engaging with) the social media world; reduce time spent on monitoring

3. More comprehensive look at social media conversations; ability to dig deeper to identify key influencers and target audience

4. Measurement of the benefit of social media campaigns; ability to link ROI to social media efforts

"We decided to start using Alterian SM2 just over two years ago, as it gave us a proper structure to our whole monitoring process and let us measure the benefit of our campaigns," Texada says. "It's a lot more comprehensive than isolated tools, and we can now see everything in one place, dramatically reducing the time spent on monitoring. Even using the free evaluation version I could see the power and value it could bring to the hospital."

About Alterian

Alterian helps organizations to create relevant, effective, and engaging experiences with their customers and prospects through social, digital, and traditional marketing channels. Alterian's customer engagement solutions are focused in four main areas: social media, Web content management, e-mail and campaign management, and analytics.

Alterian uses its technology either to address a specific marketing challenge or as part of an integrated marketing platform, with analytics and customer engagement at the heart of everything. Working within a rich ecosystem of partners, Alterian delivers its software as an off-site service or on premise.

Approach, Challenges, Outcomes

A critical issue for M.D. Anderson was being able to search message boards, such as Planet Cancer, set up by patients and survivors of more than 100 cancers. "A lot of tools couldn't see deep enough into message boards, but we were able to with SM2, which helped identify which ones we should watch or join," Texada continues. "The number one reason we selected Alterian, however, was its amazing level of customer service, right from my first dealings with the company. Every time I tweet them with a question, I receive a call within minutes. Being a small department, this level of support is invaluable to us."

M.D. Anderson began using Alterian SM2 to monitor its brand and then moved to include awareness of its campaigns and particular topics, such as the results of one of its clinical trials or a new cancer drug that comes on the market.

Example 1: Electronic Medical Records

An initial business driver for using Alterian SM2 was to see how the center could link ROI to its social media efforts.

One such project was the hospital's monitoring of a set of keywords from a PR and social media campaign and then tracking clicks back into its site. The campaign had been designed to increase the number of physicians registered with the hospital's online electronic medical records (EMR) system, increasing the number of patients referred to the hospital. Using Alterian SM2 to track the campaign's spread, in addition to Web analytics, revealed that patients' social activity was responsible for a 9.5 percent increase in referrals in a three-month period.

"This was a real eye-opener, to see how social media could benefit the business," Texada says. "We could see which activity made most impact and which had spread fastest."

Example 2: Evaluating Public Education

M.D. Anderson's public education department, on the other hand, used Alterian SM2 to monitor mentions of topics not necessarily relating to the hospital, but to wider cancer-related issues, to measure if its own messaging was on track. The department's goal is to satisfy the public need for information rather than drive patients to the hospital. Monitoring has become core to its operations; its success is measured by how many individuals it is able to reach.

While planning its program for the year ahead, the team ran searches on keywords and topics to help inform its strategy. An example of the tactical outcome was the decision not to run the same Prostate Cancer Awareness month as the year before. With Alterian SM2 now in place, the team members could search historically and saw that social media traffic around the initiative had been low. As a result, the public education department ran a more straightforward communications program, focusing on men's health. It saw a significant increase in traffic.

"Comprehensive monitoring really helped us understand what type of content drives more conversations," Texada says. "In addition to some messaging on cancer prevention, the recent campaign centered on announcements and alerts about healthy eating, eating on a budget, and exercise—so more content of benefit to a broader audience."

Conclusion

The hospital now uses Alterian SM2 for general listening, social media campaigns, public relations, marketing, customer service improvements, and search engine optimization.

M.D. Anderson uses Alterian SM2 in a host of other ways, including:

1. Monitoring its blog to engage with individuals who react to posts and build new relationships with key influencers
2. Improving patient relations and customer service by identifying patients with an issue, or resolving complaints about concerns such as waiting times
3. Refining the hospital's SEO strategy by examining keyword performance and gaining ideas on what to change or expand to improve traffic

"By applying the output of SM2, we're able to respond to patients and those talking about the brand a lot more often and much faster than before," Texada says. "Over the past year, we've witnessed an increase in the number of mentions of M.D. Anderson, and word is spreading that we're listening via Twitter, Facebook, cancer blogs, and message boards, and that we're responding to our various audiences."

Overall, here are the results of the campaign:

1. More efficient and comprehensive monitoring of social media channels.

2. Enhanced listening, which builds stronger relationships through better patient relations and customer service.
3. Social media has become a more strategic tool for M.D. Anderson, driving more engagement with the public and health-care community.
4. ROI and the value of social media can be easily shared with management.

Internally, the reports from Alterian SM2 have helped achieve a greater understanding of the benefits social media bring to the institution. "The insight generated lets us see how we're influencing our different audiences on an individual level and the benefit of engaging through these channels," Texada says. "I train my colleagues about how great social media is, but what makes them really sit up and take notice are the statistics SM2 reveals. If I can show that 3,000 people mentioned our brand last month, for example, and this is where we featured, then people take notice. The data is the keystone of my internal training program."

Keeping the wider management team regularly up-to-date is easy too, because reports are quick to create in formats everyone can use. "Many people in health care can be very esoteric and don't focus on the ROI of social media. But VPs and directors want to see numbers. SM2 lets me analyze, display, and share findings very easily; it gives me the facts which show that activity X made Y impact. These are the ROI metrics executives want."

Future Plans

With some upcoming changes to its brand and a push to increase national awareness, as accountability becomes even more of a focus, M.D. Anderson expects to use Alterian SM2 much more for tracking improvements in activity.

Texada plans to increase the use of Alterian SM2's historical data back to 2007 in various benchmarking and reporting exercises, while SM2's geomapping ability will help monitor national efforts, as it shows the location of conversations and their intensity. "We've continued to broaden our use of the tool even further, not only to keep guiding our marketing communications strategy and social activity but also to uncover other ways it can help improve the business such as customer service.

"Measuring and reporting on the social space is evolving all the time for us. From simple beginnings, it's now becoming a key part of driving more effective engagement with the cancer community and wider public."

Summary

Tracking social media that is created to engage audiences is an emerging use of social media analytics, though the applications are still immature. I think content and channel metrics for social media will mature rapidly in the next two years, as content owners learn to work with these platforms and change content in real time to better engage with audiences that are on their Web site.

This chapter discussed some ways to track online content, such as analytics tagging and rudimentary audience measurement in order to get started; however, there are several newer approaches coming to market directed at publishing, travel, and enterprise markets that this chapter barely touched on.

One example is VisualRevenue LLC (www.visualrevenue .com), which uses real-time analytics to evaluate the profitability of front page and section page news stories on mainstream media newspapers such as the *Daily News,* creating greater engagement though the use of audience and channel analytics, along with the ability to curate content instantly (Visual Revenue has this capability, allowing editors to have the final decision on a recommendation produced by VisualRevenue's advanced channel intelligence).

Adaptive Semantics on the AOL *Huffington Post* use real-time automated intelligence and machine learning moderating 100,000+ comments per day, along with identifying and tracking influencers on the publication, is one more case of using technology, audience intelligence, and tracking to increase the value of online content. It is likely that Adaptive Semantics will be powering parts of the new AOL (*Huffington Post* was acquired by AOL in February 2011).

Finally, InfiniGraph's work with *Complex Magazine*, which we presented in an earlier chapter, where real-time feedback and curation from the social graph produces increased clickthroughs and time spent on site, and therefore more profitability for the publication. I have driven home the point that VisualRevenue, InfiniGraph, and Adaptive Semantics are examples of audience intelligence and tracking emerging now that are the real future of online publishing (newspapers and magazines) in my WebMetricsGuru blog.

chapter **10**

Monitoring Tools and Technologies: The Limits of What We Can Collect

In order to acquire and deliver accurate and actionable data, you should understand what to listen for, and when, while culling data from social listening platforms such as Radian6 and Sysomos, which we've discussed in previous chapters.

It is of the utmost importance to know the readiness of clients to engage in social media before making any decisions. Further, it is a good idea to grasp how a business operates (an understanding of the industry sector, along with key considerations and timelines, are also becoming necessary) in order to listen for main factors influencing the category, product, or service.

Acting on the data being collected from social analytics platforms is fast becoming a business intelligence application that requires an entirely different set of processes, discipline, and personnel from those used by uninformed or misguided clients who are just beginning to use social media as if it were only a marketing medium rather than business intelligence.

This need has fueled an interest in enterprise applications that require stringent controls and quite a bit of up-front software development, but organizational structure and the DNA of MarCom companies (PR, marketing, and communications, whose specialties are focused on communications and "spin") are incompatible with the skills, vocabulary, lexicon, disciplines, and budget that enterprise applications require. Hopefully the DNA of MarCom will adapt over time. I hope this book plays a role in helping to bring this most needed change in understanding but today (and for the foreseeable future) business intelligence is best found in market research firms rather than in PR or communications firms.

Most of the self-serve platforms used by marketing and communications, such as Brandwatch, Lithium, Radian6, and Sysomos, are able to provide actionable information, but only with a lot of manual work (the resources, methodologies, and budget needed to use self-serve platforms are not well understood within the MarCom environment, *but neither is the value of these results*, making it difficult to deliver on the full value these platforms are capable of providing).

On the other hand, machine learning systems such as Adaptive Semantics, Crimson Hexagon, and Glide Intelligence appear out of the budget or imagination of many marketing agencies, leaving those marketers in a bind when it comes to running social listening programs for their clients. CEOs, CFOs, and CMOs are finding social listening reports in their executive dashboards and questioning their validity, and the dissatisfaction regarding basic reports is increasing as the same executives adjust budgets to allot a larger share to social media while wondering if it's really worth it.

No doubt, online social listening platforms and reports lack the precision to produce the type of numerical data needed for financial predictions that decision makers are accustomed to seeing (For example, this was explained in the Chapter 8 "Semphonic Analytics" case study, where increasing focus on social media campaigns and outreach raised the profile of social media measurement in large corporations. However, in order to fully understand the impact of social media on an organization, a new marketing analytics framework and set of online marketing KPIs needed to be established.)

However, decision makers increasingly want to see online social listening data put into the larger perspective of their dashboards and reporting. This creates a bind for stakeholders and clients who are being asked to show progress against marketing and PR campaigns with imprecise "online social data" that are often slanted and modulated by the platforms and individuals who are preparing them. In summary, most self-serve online listening systems are simply not able to handle enterprise problems or to provide the enterprise solutions that are required today.

Learning how to take the results of online monitoring tools and craft them into a message or statement requires a bit of skill and intuition that is often not appreciated. It's like art, but with a bit of science mixed in, but it's not rocket science. One task you will have to learn is how to summarize all the relevant information online. Doing so is a challenge most analysts (social media, Web analytics, marketing intelligence, or otherwise) struggle with.

Attempts to summarize news range from Google's Living Stories (a discontinued collaborative experiment with the *New York Times* for presenting customized news) to Nielsen's BlogPulse Key Phrases (a listing of all the most-used phases of previous days with links to the stories and Web sites associated with them). The Sysomos MAP social media monitoring platform also utilizes text analytics to summarize online conversations into significant phrases.

Some platforms such as Crimson Hexagon allow users to apply their own labeling to a group of stories. Once sufficiently trained, Crimson's algorithm attempts to find similar stories. However, the analyst who builds the categories and structures the questions is the ultimate determiner of the meaning of what is applied; therefore, the analyst provides the true meaning to the data, while the platform is just a focusing method.

That is why I have posited in this book that the *social media analyst*, above all, should be treated as an expert and *the final decision maker* for most marketing intelligence and social listening deliverables; but, I admit, my viewpoint is squarely at odds with current staffing policies within the marketing communications industry today, policies that are still largely based on messaging context, delivery, and spin. Social media analytics are increasingly being used within MarCom agencies that are employed to measure online opinions around a subject or brand and its changes over time.

I often think about these issues in practical terms—typically, about how easy or difficult it may be, hypothetically, to quickly find an independent third-party market research or measurement service that would objectively measure the results of communications and spin to a client's satisfaction at an acceptable cost. It may be that the very structure and costs associated with business communications are at odds with accurate measurement.

However it may be, I have come to believe marketing and communications agencies are not the most appropriate entities to measure marketing or PR campaigns run on behalf of their clients, especially within social media. Too often there is an inherent conflict of interest, as MarCom firms measure their clients' online buzz, and data can be skewed, often unintentionally, to show the successful completion of agreed-upon campaign goals. As demonstrated in previous chapters, online social data are very easy to skew; the quality of data that is culled, classified, and interpreted varies by the platform employed and the analysts preparing the reports and insights. As a result, *the very last place* from which accurate measurement should be expected to emerge is from the source of the clients' messaging, spin, or influencer outreach.

Yet, because of the nature of how campaigns are pitched, agreed upon, set up, and run, MarCom agencies are increasingly landing significant measurement and governance tasks connected with their clients' campaigns, driving up agency revenues, while satisfying clients' more immediate goals of knowing just how well their campaigns are performing in search and social media.

A better use of social media monitoring in MarCom would be to test a concept, prepare a pitch, or perform some basic online research for a client, while leaving the actual measurement of a client's campaign, as well as more intensive research efforts, to an independent entity or third-party research firm.

Influencer identification and outreach is an area where marketing communications agencies add measurable value, but I am much more skeptical about entrusting measurement tasks to them.

Brandwatch Platform Case Study with Giles Palmer, CEO of Brandwatch.com

In 2005, the U.K. government put together a proposal for a local search engine for the city of Brighton, with a view of eventually rolling it out to the rest of England. The purpose of this project was to attract interest to the town and to help people living in Brighton understand what was going on there and help them access local resources such as library records and newspaper archives.

To accomplish this, the government needed a company to come up with a Web crawler, index, and user interface. Brandwatch competed with Autonomy, an enterprise search company with a $3 billon market cap at the time, and won, probably because Brandwatch put forward an approach and proposal more in line with what the government asked for.

It took a year to build the search engine, crawler, and indexing software; Brandwatch had the copyright to the code base, but at the time it wasn't clear which was the best application to build on top of it. Palmer said he had a lot of confidence in his new platform because he had put his best developers on the project and had built it from the ground up.

Sentiment Analysis

During Christmas 2005, Brandwatch was building public authority Web sites in the United Kingdom. By chance, a conversation with employees of Spannerworks led to an examination of how the new platform might help search engine optimization, with the idea that online sentiment could also enhance SEO work.

The idea of incorporating sentiment analysis was proposed to Brandwatch CTO Fabrice Retkowsky, who has a Ph.D. in artificial intelligence and machine learning, along with another member of the team who also had a Ph.D. in machine learning. (Brandwatch now has five people with doctorates in artificial intelligence and machine learning; it initially, in 2006, had two.)

Looking back to early 2006, as the social monitoring industry was in its infancy, Brandwatch looked for other organizations in the social listening space. Initially the company thought it was the first to come up with the idea, but it was evident that others already had, including Buzzmetrics and Cymfony (the two market leaders in social listening at the time).

Palmer brought the idea back to his engineers and asked them to analyze sentiment on the Web. They told him it was tricky, domain-specific, and not too accurate. However, initial feedback on the idea was positive from businesses and individuals, who were asked whether knowing what people said and felt about their businesses on the Web was useful; the need was clearly present with everyone he spoke to in the corporate area.

Given the market response, Brandwatch went forward with sentiment analysis despite the difficulties with doing it well or accurately.

In May 2006 Brandwatch raised the first of three rounds of financing: £600,000 from angel investors to develop one of the first true listening systems, which launched in August 2007. Back then, there were many things supporting the idea that this was a growing space and the social media revolution was in full swing. For one thing, Facebook was adding members exponentially, while Google's acquisition of YouTube amplified the reach of social media, not to mention that there were many smaller social media platforms popping up on an almost daily basis.

Initially, Brandwatch crawled and indexed 250,000 sites, mostly based in the U.K., but this number has grown quite a bit over the past three years—up to 20 million sources worldwide, by November 2010; it was at that point when I met with Giles Palmer in Brighton, U.K., to discuss Brandwatch's history and architecture while interviewing him for this book. As it turned out, demystifying data sources and sentiment analysis for social monitoring is a surprisingly complicated endeavor.

Active Sources of Information

Using a site called Netcraft.com, it is possible to discover how many registered sites exist (227 million as of September 2010).[1] When analysts say they are tracking 227 million sites, what does that mean? For instance, is Blogger.com considered to be one domain or source by a social media monitoring platform, or are vendors counting the blogs that are hosted on Blogger.com? What about Facebook?

According to Palmer, Technorati calculates there are 130 million blogs it has crawled. Yet of those, only 10 percent are updated once a month, and 1.3 million are updated once a week. Palmer thinks that there are probably fewer than one million forums that exist around the world.

However, Giles Palmer provides an interesting insight on the actual number of active domain names on the Web. He points out that there is so much misinformation and lack of any standard definitions around this issue. I hope his explanations will help to clear things up and produce a level playing field where listening platforms can be compared for procurement fairly.

When listening systems are considered for procurement, they are usually compared in terms of several features, including the number of active sites (sources or domains) that are crawled and processed. The task of choosing a platform is made confusing because of the inconsistent claims from various vendors on the features and capabilities of their offerings, including the number of active sources they crawl and store in their indexes.

For example, one platform might claim to crawl 20 million active sources, while another claims to crawl 200 million. The number of active sources a platform crawls is probably less important today than it was in the past, because many people have reduced the time they spend writing blogs while shifting their online activities to Facebook and Twitter, according to Palmer.

The rise of social media networks has simplified things somewhat, but the number of active sources is still a consideration when deciding on a platform; with so many differences in how sources are counted, it is a daunting task to choose the best system for your business or personal use.

Even a vendor that claims to cover 200 million active sources might end up covering those sources less well and have less data than another vendor or platform covering fewer sources but doing so more comprehensively. Logically speaking, with six billion people on Earth, almost 1 out of every 50 would have to be a content creator online with his or her own site in order for there to be 227 million active domains; Palmer believes that 227 million sources is an impossible number, and the real number of active sources is a bit smaller.

Demystifying Web Sources and Sentiment Analysis

As there are no standards in place for counting Web sources at the time of this writing, social monitoring platforms can count active sources any way they choose, and this causes further confusion when choosing among platforms.

Sentiment analysis is another feature that is evaluated for procurement; one vendor claims 75 percent accuracy; another, 85 percent accuracy; and yet another, 95 percent accuracy. Palmer thinks all these comparisons are meaningless, because platforms cannot be reliably compared when they use different definitions to quantify the benefits they claim to offer.

The procurement problem has arisen because buyers want the decision of choosing a platform to monitor or measure social media to be simple. Platform comparisons using checkboxes such as the number of sources covered, the number of languages included, and the number of real-time feeds allow buyers to compare apples with apples.

More likely, the author believes, checkbox-based procurement decisions made by organizations, companies, and agencies are actually *comparing apples to oranges*, not apples to apples or oranges to oranges, if everything Palmer says holds true. Since there are no standards for active crawling or sentiment analysis, nor any certifying organization to gauge compliance with those nonexistent standards, meaningful comparisons between the features and performance of the various social media monitoring platforms cannot be done just by looking at the marketing or technical specifications provided by a vendor and then comparing them with what other vendors claim to provide.

Perhaps the only measure that makes sense today, given the current environment, is to determine how well the features and workflow a platform provides will work in achieving the business goals in your organization, either by trying it out firsthand on a trial basis for a benchmark project or, better yet, by hiring a solutions design expert with enough experience to choose wisely (this is where specialists such as myself come into the picture, with enough experience in how these platforms actually work in a real-world environment, combined with an acute business acumen, to make better, more informed decisions on which platforms are truly best suited for an organization and how they should be set up and run. Using experts saves a lot of time and avoids all-too-typical scenarios where companies end up hiring 10 people to change a lightbulb, when only one was needed, if only a different set of choices had been made.)

Palmer won't comment on what other vendors claim, but he tries to keep Brandwatch's own claims real and transparent. At his firm, if he says that a feature's reliability is less than transparent, he can count on his techies to address the issue.

The main problem with demystifying Web sources and sentiment analysis as a basis for making a decision on procurement comes down to two factors:

1. It is very difficult to distill complex issues into simple numbers, and sentiment analysis is the best example of this.
2. Checkbox comparisons are not a good way to validate answers; instead, such comparisons lead to exaggerated claims (as already mentioned above).

Yet, because of the transparency of the decision-making process in most organizations, those in charge of purchasing desire an easy way to compare platforms. But the statements of features in each platform, necessary from a marketing standpoint, tend to be generic in nature and very hard to meaningfully compare to one another.

As a result of the overclaiming of features and benefits by vendors, there is a tendency for the social media analytics industry to be discredited in the eyes of industry experts and customers. I think this is just a sign of an early market lacking any accepted industrywide standards or regulation, and the situation is likely to improve over the coming years as industry associations step up to the plate, and release workable standards, protocols, and industry-accepted certification mechanisms, along with a maturing sophistication within customers and consumers about the true nature and capabilities of social media analytics services, in terms of both the limitations they have and the best uses of the medium.

In one case, during a proposal, a competitor of Brandwatch's made a claim that its sentiment analysis was 95 percent accurate, based on tests that it had run. What riled Palmer was that the vendor did not explain the test or state the size of the data set being used, nor did this vendor address the caveat that the accuracy of the sentiment analysis might differ in a larger data set, thus setting unrealistic expectations.

The Market Evolution over the Past Four Years

In its early days (2004–2006), Brandwatch looked at some of the research published by Nielsen's Buzzmetrics and was impressed by its sentiment analysis and linguistic analysis capabilities. It appeared that Buzzmetrics was ahead of the curve, that it had some really smart analysts and had acquired the Israeli search engine Intelliseek three years before. Brandwatch had its work cut out to catch up.

But four years later, newer entrants, including Brandwatch itself, Radian6, and Sysomos, have seemingly closed the gap between their platforms and Nielsen Buzzmetrics; Palmer's take on this is that small, focused teams can often move quickly and therefore be extremely effective.

The Social Media Monitoring and Data-Gathering Process

Search engines collect information on Web pages and sites using automated programs called crawlers. Information is downloaded from the Web and stored in an index. This is how Brandwatch's platform operates, but according to Palmer, it's not the way many other vendors acquire most of their data.[2]

In order to make a proper contrast between what Brandwatch does and what it believes its competition is attempting, to examine how data are collected it is necessary to take a look at both the positive and negative aspects of data acquisition.

RSS

Monitoring systems find different feeds on Web sites and use them to deliver data to their systems. RSS feeds are easy to work with because they contain only relevant content (that is, they have neither advertisements nor site-navigation elements, for example). The downsides to using RSS feeds are that they are often incomplete, they may not provide the full text of a page, and they also may not include other relevant information, such as images. Furthermore, RSS feeds often don't include comments on blogs or updates on blog content.

So, even if monitoring systems use RSS feeds, they may have to crawl pages directly to get these additional data. Also, sites that don't have RSS feeds, including forums, have to be crawled directly.

Federated Search

According to Wikipedia, federated search is the simultaneous search of multiple online databases or Web resources, and is an emerging feature of automated, Web-based library and information retrieval systems.[3] An example of a federated search is the site http://addictomatic.com. Type in a query and Addictomatic will do a real-time federated search of sites. The limitation of federated search is that the data are not usually stored by the federated search system, so historical analysis is not possible. Because there is no page processing, obtaining metadata (such as location, number of posts in a thread, sentiment, and recurring phrases) also is not possible. In addition, there is a risk that the source systems will stop playing ball and block the federated search queries, which would be fatal.

For a social media analytics platform, the issues with federated search will be historical in nature. Databases are populated with online mentions and posts over a period of time in order to be queried later, but data query using federated search cannot be used to acquire data from the past—say, a year ago—because the systems being queried do not have the data any longer.

Application Programming Interface

Searches using an API are similar in nature and limitations to federated search, but API searches are executed using an interface that is designed for the purpose. For a site such as Twitter, there is the Twitter Firehose, the entire collection of live tweets from all over the world, so companies can download the whole lot (an estimated 100 million tweets per day as of the end of 2010, and probably closer to 200 million tweets per day by the time this book is published in August 2011). But very few analytical companies have availed themselves of this vast data-flow opportunity because of the expense and storage requirements involved.

Typically, programs send several thousand queries per hour to the Twitter Firehose, Facebook, and other sources via GNIP (http://gnip.com/), which aggregates social media data from dozens of other social media sources for an economical monthly fee. Getting the results for current searches, GNIP customers include most of the monitoring platforms discussed in this book, such as Integrasco, Alterian, and Collective Intellect.

On the other hand, to Palmer's point about API and Federated Search, GNIP is not as effective at executing a search involving historical data from the Twitter Firehose several weeks or months in the past (such as a query against GNIP for a term the monitoring platform had not stored data on in the past); in order to gather results of a query of this nature, full access to the Twitter Firehose and a capacity to store all its historical data over time is needed, a massive investment of computing resources and storage (even in the Cloud) that few vendors can afford.[4]

However, at the time of this writing, Twitter is providing its own access to Firehose data, with additional information and metadata from text analytics and influencer platforms like Klout, PeerIndex, and Lexalytics, and at a far more economical price than it had in the past.[5] The data offerings from Twitter appear to work symbiotically with newer offerings from social media analytics platforms like the Radian6 Insights platform, which are offering additional data dimensions from Insights partners for a monthly fee.[6]

Regardless of where information originates, there is a clear intent from various platform providers such as Radian6 to mash up and overlay information from various data sources in order to satisfy ever more voracious customer appetites for better and more palatable data. We can expect this trend to accelerate as social media analytics platforms mature in the coming years.

Data Feed

There are services such as BoardReader and Moreover that aggregate news sites, blogs, and forums. Most, if not all, of the other providers in this space get a lot of data from aggregators, and that saves them the expense of building and maintaining their own search engine.[7] As Giles Palmer is quick to point out, using syndicated data feeds from aggregators comes with a cost; there is far less control of the content being acquired this way, including what it contains, which has profound implications for several types of projects where precision is needed.

As we saw with the Brandtology interview and the Synthesio case study of the Accor Hotel chain in Chapter 3, utilizing custom crawlers to extract project-specific online data and metadata are vital key elements in the underlying Brandtology and Synthesio offerings. Without the custom crawling of select data sources, neither would be able to deliver superior value to its customers and would be little different in their offerings or results from self-serve solutions such as Radian6, Sysomos, Lithium (formally Scout Labs), Alterian SM2, and so on.

In addition, as pointed out in the Integrasco interview in Chapter 2, between the highly complex terminologies inherited within the banking, pharmaceuticals, and telecommunications industries (to name a few) and the complex data-mining necessary to extract relevant meanings from the data, the aforementioned self-serve platforms, by nature of the way they pull, aggregate, and store data, are increasingly unable to satisfy the in-depth insights many clients now require.

Finally, as Gary Angel, the CTO of Semphonic, states in Chapter 8, projects undertaken in most (self-serve social media analytics) platforms have poorly set up data streams and "noisy data," often set up by people who have misunderstood or trivialized the underlying technologies. These people may lack the time, budget, or trained resources to attend to these data governance needs. I have found this kind of situation is found in some PR and communications agencies, but really it can exist anywhere.

Gary Angel has been a strong proponent of newer frameworks for Web site and social media KPIs. However, these are based upon two-tiered segmentations of data, which are next to impossible to realize in social media analytics without a customized data crawl as per what Integrasco performed for Vodafone U.K. and Synthesio delivered to the Accor Hotel chain. All of this drives Palmer's point home that the quality of the data feed is the underlying foundation of social media analytics; without it, the most valuable insights and actionable information will most likely not be achieved.[8]

Private Networks

In order to obtain data from private networks, systems need to provide a username and password; otherwise, it's mostly the same routine as the other methods, except for the legal aspect (For instance, can a deal be struck with the site owners to obtain access to their data? Will they enable access to the site for our crawlers?)

If social media analytics platforms are able to get access to private network data, what they are allowed to do with the data may come into question. For example, Brandwatch has an exclusive deal with www.doctors.net.uk, one of the exclusive closed professional communities in Europe, and that took a while to set up.

Palmer points out that for most organizations, there are not many important closed networks to access, other than Facebook (which is the largest closed network in the world). As a result, Palmer doesn't see private network access as much of a problem when compared with other issues discussed in this chapter.

Page Processing and Content Extraction

Upon acquisition of data, it is imperative to determine if the data contains spam (spam identification) or duplicated content, and to find out which language the data are written in. Then follows the thorny area known as "content extraction." Palmer thinks content extraction is the one area the industry hasn't talked about yet. This is why he opened up to me in an exclusive interview about data extraction.

Google is already crawling more of the open Web than any other company (although it has been noted that Google crawls and indexes less than 1 percent of the entire content that is on the Web).[9] There are millions of sites, many with their own unique structure. The task at hand is to figure out how to extract just the information desired for research purposes, while leaving out the noise (such as ads, headers, footers, and navigation aids).

Automated content extraction is critical, but some aggregators extract content manually, and it can take weeks to add a new source of data when programmers write custom content extraction software for each new data source. Getting content extraction right is absolutely critical for providing a useful listening service, but content extraction is a slow process to program and does not scale well, according to Palmer.

How Brandwatch Works

Although Brandwatch is a paid service, it has a leg up on the free options. The challenge for free tools is that processing and storage are expensive. Brandwatch has spent £500,000 (close to $850,000 at the time of this writing) on hardware from August 2010 to November 2010 alone. In order for the free tools to remain that way, they need to find an alternative business model or to rely on other services for most of their data processing and storage.

A user of Brandwatch writes a query, saves it under a name or label, and generates a call to the application that goes to the search indexes. The results come from the indexes and are processed for sentiment, paired phrases, linguistics, and machine learning. After chugging away for 5 to 10 minutes, the platform generates an e-mail to the user indicating that the query is ready to view.

At that point, the user types in any query the user wants, and the system generates the charts, graphs, and reports required. In Brandwatch, the query fetches all the data, but clients can refine the query once the results are displayed. A user of Brandwatch builds workspaces where he continues to refine the query and annotate it (with his own metadata). Palmer mentions that custom databases for annotation of social media data are a useful addition to Brandwatch's offering.

This is why Sysomos Heartbeat (a relational database that allows users to mark up data) and Sysomos MAP (with no relational database for user markup) are so different from each other on the backend, according to Palmer.

In a year or two there will be some consolidation of platforms, with perhaps three or four clear winners emerging [*author's note:* Giles Palmer's observations in November 2010 are prophetic, given the recent acquisition of Radian6 by Salesforce.com for 326 million dollars in March 2011]. Acquirers of these service-type platforms could be PR/communications agencies, other data providers who want to add social media monitoring and analysis, or integration partners such as CRM systems.

Palmer also harped on the scalability challenges surrounding social monitoring and data storage. This is one of the barriers to entry that Google's former CEO Eric Schmidt cites when he touts his company's competitive advantage. Will cloud services come to the rescue here? Only time will tell.

Figure 10-1 shows an example of machine learning algorithms employed by Google to semantically break down the most likely categories related to a search query.

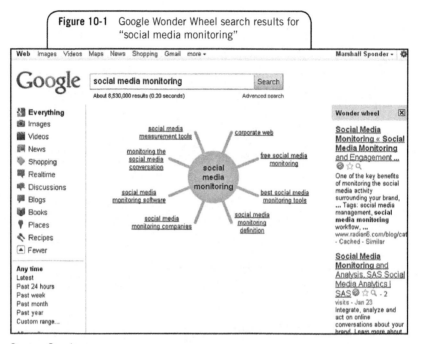

Figure 10-1 Google Wonder Wheel search results for "social media monitoring"

Source: Google.com

The Question Becomes the Answer

As the results of a query in social media depend on the query itself, the tools for getting "accurate" data reporting are open to interpretation. Social media monitoring platforms and search engines have a lot in common, as both are keyword based. That is a good thing if you know what you're looking for and a bad thing if you don't.

Social media monitoring platforms and search engines require keyword research, including slang words, misspellings, customer-centric and product-centric words and phrases, and sometimes foreign language translations of phases you are interested in. However, algorithms are now beginning to replace keywords for paid search advertising.[10]

No one is absolutely sure whether every possible keyword phrase being used for online conversations is being covered. For the very best results, search queries have to be constantly retuned (that is, the sales or product team should continually pick up more information to add to a specific search or topic profile), and there's so much noise on the Web that extensive filtering needs to be employed to get rid of it. In the process of my own analytics work for clients, I found that 90 percent of online mentions of pharmaceutical drugs are spam.

Filtering out "pharma spam" is becoming more and more difficult, due to the query-length limitations of most monitoring platforms, not to mention the governance work of continually refreshing filters to eliminate new spam that crops up. Search queries and noise filters need to become more specific in order to get clean data, and that usually means longer queries.

However, the more specific search queries become, and the bigger they get, the more time it takes to run them (to a point, sometimes, where the queries get so long they cannot be run at all). Here's an example:

---

http://map.sysomos.com/?sDy=14666&q=Excedrin+AND+NOT +(recall+OR+Viagra+OR+%22no+prescription%22+OR+%22 without+a+prescription%22+OR+coupon+OR+discount+OR+ orthopedic+OR+%22cgi-bin%22+OR+%22http://%22+OR+ atarax+OR+%22:-%22+OR+buy+OR+compare+OR+purchase +OR+buspar+OR+preview+OR+%22non+prescription%22+ OR+CVS+OR+limit+OR+ad)&eDy=14848&luc=true&viw=dash board_main_basic&sFl=&hrq=Excedrin&sco=DATE_ISOME&

If the preceding query is run in Sysomos MAP, most of the space is taken up with what to exclude (everything after the capitalized AND in the first line). This query is very small compared with how long it could be written for better accuracy.

There's so much work involved with setting up and running searches effectively that many users of listening systems have become disillusioned with them and are openly questioning their value. According to Asi Sharabi, at No Man's Blog:

> *Over the past 8 months I tried and tested practically all of the key players in "social media monitoring services": Radian6, BuzzMetrics, Brandwatch, Attentio, Techrigy (SM2), etc. And I have very few good words to say about them. The few good words will be in relation to the people who work at these companies—these are usually nice people. But the software and service is verging on epic fail—very problematic and clunky solutions wrapped in a big bold shiny (but rather hollow) promises. (OK, maybe I'm being a bit too harsh….but that's the result of two long nights sorting out monitoring dashboards.)[11]*

In the past, it was OK to be on the edge of producing a good report with pretty pie and trend charts that showed online mentions around a brand or subject, and present that to stakeholders. Stakeholders were generally happy to get any information on their social media efforts, because so many were unfamiliar with the capabilities of social listening platforms, to begin with. And while many stakeholders were suspicious and distrustful of the data collected this way, most of the time they had no benchmark against which to judge its quality.

As the field of social media analytics matures, the days of pretty charts and empty marketing promises are ending. Executives are getting serious about social media, and asking questions when reports do not make sense to them, bringing social media analytics reporting under intense scrutiny. The maturation process has taken the field from an afterthought to a critical business information function.

For certain types of businesses, such as pharmaceuticals, life sciences, and banking, it will be more problematic to find the best contextual information needed for an effective listening report, because the information needed may be industry- and context-specific, requiring an understanding of those subjects by the analysts who are preparing the listening report. As mentioned earlier in the chapter, a customized data crawl is often necessary to extract the needed information and metadata required for effective analysis, even when the best analysts in the world are on staff.

On the other hand, primary stakeholders may be unable to articulate what they want to know, and must turn to professionals who understand what listening systems can and can't do.

The limitations of listening platforms are certainly an issue in providing clients with the quality of listening reports they desire. But I found the main obstacle does not lie with the technology so much as with the various, often incompatible lexicons that individuals use to describe what they do and to determine what they need from social media analytics.

For example, I have found requests from stakeholders and clients that were difficult to execute because the platforms used (such as Radian6, Sysomos, Brandwatch, Alterian Techrigy/SM2, etc.) and the "ask" categories envisioned by clients (such as online reputation or situational analysis as a quick form of market research) were misaligned. In other words, the platforms could not deliver the marketing promises they were sold under without a significant human element, often unbudgeted or underbudgeted.

It may take a while before the data that social media analytics platforms are capable of providing and the expectations of customers fully intersect.

Problems with Self-Serve Systems

Many marketing firms have bought heavily into broader self-serve systems, such as those offered by Alterian Techrigy/SM2, Brandwatch, Radian6, and Sysomos, to name a few. Just to be clear and fair, any platform can be customized with individual data pulls on the backend (for an additional cost). But the issues with self-serve social media analytics platforms magnify and build up as time goes on, while customers push those systems to perform tasks they were never designed for. We've discussed the features and advantages of these systems in previous chapters, but now let's take a close look at their potential disadvantages and problems.

Here's my view of report generation: As the more advanced capabilities of a monitoring platform are leveraged by the analyst, the better and more actionable the reports become, and the less tiresome they are to read. Plus, from an analyst's standpoint, the more enjoyable reporting and analysis become as these advanced features are used. For example, using Brandwatch's advanced tagging and segmentation capabilities will reduce reporting time significantly while increasing the accuracy of the reporting. In every self-serve platform, features like this exist, but often they are not leveraged as well as they could be.

Data Consistency and Scaling Issues

While most self-serve platforms provide a historical database that goes back a few years, the quality of the earlier data may not be as comprehensive as that of the current data, and *it may or may not be normalized.* Normalization is the process of organizing data to minimize redundancy, according to Wikipedia.[12]

In 2010 I was invited by members of Infegy, the company behind Social Radar, to experiment with the platform and write about it.[13] While using Social Radar, I found the platform could generate trend charts that were normalized or un-normalized and wondered about the differences.

Infegy founder and CEO Justin Graves was quoted by Michael T. Chong, an international speaker and founder of the branded entertainment service Ubercool®, in a March 2011 blog post that explained Social Radar's normalization features. According to Graves, "Social Radar's database is much larger now and gets considerably more content each day compared to three years ago, so to make a trend over such a long time period useful, we need to normalize the data. Users can also switch to absolute counts if they need them."[14]

Clients changing platforms from Radian6 to another system, for example, will discover that none of their accumulated data will match up with any other system. In most cases, this means a fresh start is needed. Clients are becoming more curious and aware of the inconsistencies of their data and are asking the agencies who are preparing reports to fix the problems.

But agencies can't fix the problems, because the data belong to the platform vendor, not to the agency. Agencies and companies have a limited amount of control over the data they are purchasing from those platforms.

Another issue with self-serve platforms is the lack of interoperability of those platforms. Web sites can use two or even three Web analytics platforms for their unique features, yet track the same Web content and get similar numbers. The same cannot be said for social media analytics. The output of different monitoring platforms is, more often than not, entirely different even for the exact same searches.

In addition, customers often lack the necessary lexicon and vocabulary to articulate choices between platforms they might want use. As Giles Palmer mentioned earlier in this chapter, people are (usually) not interested in the details of how a social media platform works; rather, they just want to know if the platform is good for their purposes or not.

Specialized Platform Issues and Advantages

Specific platforms, such as Revinate (for the hotel industry), do solve one common self-service platform problem: namely, the inclusion of review site information, like TripAdvisor and Yelp. While not all review sites are covered, the most important ones for hotels are using Revinate. This is not unlike many of the specialized platforms that cater to a particular industry, in which customer opinion information is crawled and organized around a specific taxonomy or classification system,[15] such as a hotel address, room, hotel bed, hotel table, hotel chair, and so on. The service to create a much more detailed record and mashup of customers' experiences with a brand in a specific location requires a specialized approach.

Custom crawling of Web sites and organizing the search results into taxonomies is another example of what was covered earlier in this chapter. Synthesio, Integrasco, and Semphonic classified data in custom relationships and segmentations, which ultimately led to making the information actionable while placing the results in dashboards. Culled data is a commodity, but the organization of data into taxonomies and classification systems gives that information value and structure, ultimately leading to actionable insights for the recipients.

On the other hand, self-serve systems require a lot of human labor when used to create, essentially, unscalable taxonomies and work processes, sometimes for a single report (leading to situations where 10 people are needed, meta-phorically, to change a lightbulb). When this kind of work is undertaken, it is often not properly budgeted for or is severely underbudgeted, particularly within MarCom agencies where the right "DNA" is usually missing. This is yet another reason to move social media analytics out of MarCom and into an independent third-party service that can handle the rigor.

Inclusion of review sites is no small feat. Amazon peer reviews, for example, are notoriously difficult to get into mon-itoring systems, and manually adding URLs to social media analytics platforms often doesn't work, as vendors need to per-form custom programming to capture review site information in their platforms.

Specialized platforms with such needs will focus on bringing in these data, while self-serve platforms have more issues with accessing the data.

Some specialized systems offer white-labeling oppor-tunities, but considerable thought needs to be put into the customizations required for an agency's clients before using them. While Altimer Group Web strategist Jeremiah Owy-ang claims specialized platforms usually won't scale,[16] I find scaling to be less of an issue with specialized platforms than with self-service platforms. Specialized platforms can always add infrastructure in the Cloud, and scale up, while self-serve platforms that outgrow their capabilities are usually unable to scale without degrading performance.

Do It Yourself?

Good examples of DIY internally built social media analytics platforms are difficult to find. They are usually created for internal use within a company or institution. More likely, DIY tools will be confused with "free tools" that allow monitoring by using free platforms such Google Reader. Read my e-book "How to Build Your Own Social Influence Monitoring Platform on a Shoestring," which was presented in London at the Monitoring Social Media Bootcamp in March 2010 to get an idea of what free services provide.[17]

The real problems of building a monitoring platform internally are covered by Andrew Grill in his London Calling blog[18] and can be summarized thus: to capture the full Twitter Firehose (say, 100 million tweets per day, which will only increase as time goes on), plus all the other data from social media forums such as Facebook and blogs, would take terabytes of data per day. Most platforms, though, do not capture the full Twitter Firehose.

When you don't build or own the platform or collect the data, at least you don't have to worry about data duplication and spam (except the spam you already get from the monitoring provider). In the author's opinion, building a monitoring platform from scratch should be done only if it is impossible to get the needed data any other way.

Language and Multinational Issues

As discussed in Chapter 3, more and more companies are getting into monitoring operations across several different regions and languages. Most of the self-serve platforms are capable of monitoring several languages and countries. In some cases, sentiment can be monitored too, but usually it is not performed on each language.

Taking a long-term view, setting up monitoring is the easiest part, providing one can translate keywords properly to the other languages being monitored. To provide meaningful interpretations and insights is far more difficult, as the need to understand the language and context monitored online lies in their idiomatic or colloquial meanings.

Case Study: Synthesio and Accor

Synthesio is a global, multilingual social media monitoring and research company, utilizing a powerful hybrid of tech and human monitoring services to help brands and agencies collect and analyze consumer conversations online. The result is actionable analytics and insights that provide an accurate snapshot of a brand and help answer the ultimate questions: how are we really doing right now, and how can we make it better?

Founded in 2006, Synthesio has grown to include analysts who provide native-language monitoring and analytic services in over 30 languages worldwide. As well as Accor's, brands such as Toyota, Microsoft, Sanofi, and Orange turn to Synthesio for the data they need to engage their markets, anticipate crises, and prepare for new product and campaign launches.

The Client

Accor is present in 90 countries and has more than 145,000 affiliates. With 4,100 hotels and close to 500,000 rooms, the group's brands offer options to suit guests staying with them for either business or pleasure. Over 5,000 comments are posted each month about Accor's different brands (such as Novotel, Sofitel, and Ibis) on such sites as Booking.com and TripAdvisor. The company approached Synthesio with a proposal to take a closer look at satisfaction-related comments for both Accor's and competitors' hotels, a total of around 12,000 hotels worldwide.

When Accor first approached Synthesio, in 2008, it performed an audit of the brand's reputation. Synthesio concluded that 75 percent of comments posted about Accor's brand online were of positive sentiment. Topics discussed by Web users are similar to customer comments collected through other channels (such as on-site questionnaires and customer satisfaction surveys). Customers will use review Web sites to give objective comments on their stay. Online reviews could give a hotel representative an understanding of the reputation of the brand for a certain population of customers (for instance, tourism trips rather than business trips).

For Yves Lecret, Novotel's marketing director in France, "Synthesio's analysis of unstructured data offers a more global view of the brand's online reputation." The Novotel brand decided to put an ongoing monitoring service in place to complement its regular customer satisfaction data and raise brand awareness on social media.

Drivers for Change

There were three drivers:

1. Getting the Whole Company Involved

Synthesio created customized approaches geared toward different levels of clients. For the corporate marketing group, Synthesio created one global dashboard with the data on its entire hotel brand and subbrands as well as the brands of competitors globally. For brand marketing groups in each country where Accor operates, Synthesio created a country dashboard of all its hotels and competitors in that country (40 dashboards in all). Finally, for each Accor hotel, a specialized dashboard was created for the hotel and its nearby competitors (4,000 dashboards).

2. Cross-Analyzing Social Media Results with Internal Data

Synthesio worked with Novotel's corporate marketing team (Novotel is one of Accor's brands) to define a tool that analyzes Internet user satisfaction throughout all stages of a guest's stay in real time. Synthesio's results are systematically cross-analyzed with other internal indicators of quality, such as online customer satisfaction surveys and field tests.

3. Incentivizing Hoteliers

Accor is a top global hotel chain, a leader in Europe with no previous initiative in social media. Accor has set up a rewards system and training program for responding to online conversations that complement Synthesio dashboards for its teams in order to respond to online conversations that Synthesio's dashboards report.

Tracking Online Information about the Accor Hotel Chain

Synthesio tracked the online reputation for several hotel brands for Accor and competitors across different booking and review sites in Dutch, Chinese, English, French, Italian, Portuguese, and Spanish.

Synthesio's proprietary technology pulls in mentions of the brands into its index, automatically analyzes the data for keyword tags, and then classifies them into its corpus. Afterward, the information is crawled by Synthesio's crawlers, using highly specific queries to detect conversations on topics that are important for hotels and their online reputation, meaning everything from a customer's searching for a hotel to his checking out. [*Author's note:* As pointed out earlier, without the customized crawl mentioned above, Synthesio could not deliver the dashboard Accor needed.]

For this case, topics include all stages of a guest's stay, including prearrival, arrival, guest room, food and beverage, activities, and departure, and the subtopics including booking reservations, parking access, check-in, lobby, hotel services and cleanliness, Internet access, price, and payment.

Accor Hotels' goals for tracking guests were twofold:

1. Learn what customers are saying about the brand and competitors' hotels, and combine these results with their internal data.
2. Provide hoteliers with a monitoring tool and guidelines to take action around social media content.

Monitoring Online Mentions

In a period of economic recession, Accor (including its Novotel division) was more focused than ever on customer satisfaction and quality of service. According to Novotel France's Yves Lecret, the firm wanted to be able to "identify the root of a problem at its source, in order to be able to fix it as quickly as possible."

Social media data provided by Synthesio provide metrics to measure customer satisfaction and the efficiency of customer satisfaction programs. Synthesio and Accor worked together to define the scope of the monitoring dashboard project and came up with three goals (short-term, medium-term, and long-term) or milestones:

1. **Short-term goal: To raise awareness and measure customer satisfaction**. To accomplish this, they ran a pilot on a few hotels and raised brand managers' and hoteliers' awareness of the importance of social media data. They also built custom KPIs (see below) to measure customer satisfaction.

2. **Mid-term goal: To identify best practices.** Using the information obtained, they sought to identify which hotels were faring better than others and to compare the hotels among themselves, implementing social media data in Accor's internal monitoring system.

3. **Long-term goal: To improve customer satisfaction.** This was accomplished by identifying problems and improving Accor's online image and reputation, and by giving hoteliers guidelines on how to respond online and how to increase customer satisfaction and brand awareness.

Details of Approach

The project was global, and it unfolded in three phases:

Phase 1: Set-Up (three months)

- Agree with stakeholders on identification of hotels (Accor's and its competitors') to monitor for each country
- Define custom KPIs and dashboards for each level of hierarchy
- Detect 30 topics and subtopics to monitor and analyze in partnership with the customer service department

Phase 2: Pilot (one year)

A pilot was run on two or three hotel brands to test and optimize the service for brand managers and hoteliers. Corporate marketing went on "a social media tour" to present the service to each country and raise awareness of the importance of social media data.

- 1,000 hotels worldwide
- Three languages: English, French, German

Phase 3: Large Implementation (ongoing)

Accor decided to implement this service on a larger scale in order to:

- Have a homogeneous set of data for each brand and country
- Let each hotelier manage the hotel's online reputation

All Accor hotels are now monitored, and the results are integrated into the company's internal market research system. Accor worked on defining guidelines for hoteliers and worked with content providers (such as TripAdvisor) to provide more customer reviews on their own Web sites; see http://usat.ly/fOv8Q6.

- 4,000 hotels worldwide
- Eight languages: Dutch, Chinese, English, French, Italian, Portuguese, and Spanish

Success Factors

The company identified three success factors for the program.

Factor 1: Start Small, Think Big

Synthesio started Accor's project on a small set of hotels with the idea of proof testing how to implement the monitoring and dashboards globally. Meanwhile, the necessary back-and-forth with the Accor team during the first months of the project made it possible to build a powerful tool, suitable for all types of social media needs.

Factor 2: Get Commitment from Internal Teams

The corporate team at Accor worked closely with Synthesio to define the service and customize it to their needs. They largely promoted the service internally, meeting with each brand director globally and presenting the results.

Factor 3: Keep It Simple

Synthesio spent a lot of time working to understand Accor's needs as well as the different uses of the product in order to build user-friendly platforms that are easy to set up and to maintain.

Data Extraction Methodology

For Accor's project, as for any other, Synthesio used a combination of technologies and human analysis to provide the clients with exhaustive and qualitative data.

Data Extraction

This was the main challenge for this project. Synthesio had to put into place a system that can:

- Identify reviews on a specific hotel, even when the hotel's name is not mentioned
- Group reviews mentioning the same hotel on different Web sites
- Identify hotels' scores on review Web sites

Data Analysis Methodology

Some information can be detected automatically, such as which hotel is being talked about, main topics, and sentiment. The data were analyzed by Synthesio first for language and sentiment. Synthesio then provided Accor with an accurate understanding of the 30 topics monitored as part of the project. Finally, human analysts conversant in each language covered were used to filter the data and provide the level of exactness in cleansing and coding the data that Synthesio provides its clients.

Problems on the Project

On Synthesio's side, the main challenge was data extraction (see above, under "Data Extraction Methodology").

Semantic tools can be used only for a very top-line analysis. But, as there were 30 topics analyzed in eight languages, humans were required to make the necessary distinctions and classify data. As a result of taking on the Accor project, Synthesio had to staff to scale up quickly to handle the interpretation of online postings in 30 languages.

Synthesio also handled the data extraction challenge with three months of R&D and setup. At the same time, Accor installed rewards and training programs to complement online reputation monitoring of its hotels so as to motivate employees and train them on how to better respond to online comments and posts.

Finally, Synthesio learned for the future, to put in place from day one a shared road map with Accor that would clarify the timing for each new development in the process.

Variables

The main variables were exhaustiveness and the quality of the analysis.

Exhaustiveness

Accor's hoteliers who subscribed to the service needed to find every single comment published on their hotel integrated into their tool.

Quality of the Analysis

Because hoteliers have incentives based on their online reputation results, they need to pay strong attention to each comment's classification. Any wrong classification (bad sentiment instead of good) is immediately reported to Synthesio and is corrected very quickly.

Synthesio was able to aggregate data from multiple hotel reservation sites and synthesize them into a user-friendly dashboard, allowing hoteliers to quickly identify problem areas along with areas in which the client is faring better than others, and ultimately to compare one hotel with another on any number of topics.

Insights

Using both internal data and Synthesio's crawled data, Accor discovered that guests' room keys were being demagnetized by their smartphones. Accor alerted its suppliers, and they were able to fix the problem. Detecting the source of the problem quickly allowed Accor to prevent further costs and damages to its image.

Negative comments can be immediately pulled out from the data, as well as what they pertain to and exactly to which hotel. Each hotelier now uses social media as a new channel for customer satisfaction measurement.

Results of the Case Study

Within the Accor group, the Novotel brand has seen the volume of positive feedback increase by 55 percent in just one year, while the number of negative comments has stayed more or less the same. This has played an important role in the double-digit growth in online sales.

Rather than sift through sites that are far different from one another, the Accor marketing departments can now compare information directly. The company can now get an overview of its online reputation in just a few clicks.

The benefits of this program will have a broader effect, because Accor decided to include customer reviews from TripAdvisor on its own booking Web sites.

Accor was able to compare unstructured data with internal data and integrate both into its marketing mix. Synthesio developed a strong expertise on the ability to monitor data coming from multiple units and deal with local data. This approach could be relevant for restaurant chains or any other business involving a local service.

Summary

This chapter dug into the limitations of social listening analytics platforms and ways to surmount them. It is becoming increasingly evident that social listening is turning into a business intelligence set of applications that require data quality, data cleansing, multilanguage support, large query support, and creative, talented analysts to engage with analytics reports and insights, and turn social listening into market research.

In particular, we paid attention to custom crawling of specific data sources as a necessary prerequisite for effective and actionable social media analytics.

chapter <u>11</u>

Convergence: Mashing Up Data from Disparate Sources

With more open frameworks on the Web, applications, programming frameworks, and interfaces are also appearing. They are evolving to facilitate applications through "connecting Lego block" modules[1] with the audience, to engage with, listen to, or view and exchange ideas and information. There is so much data available to collect and process, with much "ultraviolet" or unseen, yet ever-present. Moreover, the rate of data creation is dwarfing the ability of organizations to listen to it, process it, and act on it. A data renaissance has arrived, but what does that mean for social media analytics in particular? In the following two case studies, we will see how social media analytics improved customer satisfaction.

Case Study: Integrasco and Vodafone U.K.

Integrasco is the world's preeminent provider of data-mining technology and analytical services for the telecommunications industry.

255

Integrasco provides global clients such as Nokia, Sony Ericsson, and Vodafone with the real-time distillation of consumer and business feedback from social media, CRM systems, and other key sources that guide their business decision making in the fields of R&D, design, application development, early issue detection for products and services, communications and customer service.

Integrasco AS was founded in 2004, with the head office based in Norway. The company has since grown to a workforce of almost 30 employees based in China, Norway, and the United Kingdom.

Integrasco utilizes proprietary, state-of-the-art technology and high-end analytical expertise tuned to the telecommunications industry to provide handset manufacturers, airtime operators, developers, and retailers with actionable insights that help businesses succeed. The firm's source-independent data structure, advanced AI-based software crawlers, and commitment to high-end analytics deliver an offering that is superior to the commoditized search-and-retrieve arena. [*Author's note:* Integrasco refers to the self-serve platforms covered in Chapter 10, although, to be fair, self-serve platforms evolved for quick snapshots of an area or subject, not the very precise, deep dive approach this case study is an example of.]

Clients benefit additionally from genuinely tailored solutions, face-to-face consulting support on demand, and industry category expertise.

The Client

Integrasco is Vodafone U.K.'s online buzz monitoring, analytics, and strategic consultancy. Integrasco has been working with the mobile carrier for over two years (*at the time of this writing*). Vodafone's long-term social media vision is "To empower our customers to interact with us and others in the way that they want, to get more from their telecoms experience."

Vodafone U.K. started its social media journey by asking Integrasco to map out the social media landscape within the mobile industry, analyze the findings, and formulate an appropriate strategy for competitive advantage. In addition, Vodafone made the decision to prioritize the identification and resolution of consumer queries and complaints, as well as engage with key influencers (customers and noncustomers) in real time, and has done so with considerable success.

To help Vodafone achieve its goals, Integrasco needed to design and deliver a powerful, sector-specific Web portal, and to train and assist Vodafone's Web relations team, now composed of over 15 full-time employees, to set up complex searches and algorithms. This allowed the team to run real-time searches across defined sources and engage with target audiences in real time. Since 2009, Integrasco services have expanded, and they now permeate almost every department in Vodafone U.K. See Figure 11-1.

Origins of the Campaign

The project was inspired by a realization that the U.K. mobile industry (along with a number of other categories, such as banking and utilities) is notorious for low standards of customer service, leading to high levels of customer churn, a major drag on profitability. Vodafone saw an opportunity to leverage a renewed commitment to consumer service as a significant brand attribute in a highly competitive, but almost entirely undifferentiated, category.

Jakub Hrabovsky, head of Web relations at Vodafone U.K., says:

Measurement and monitoring reflects the need for us to listen to what is being said across the myriad of social media channels and to understand what patterns, trends, and emerging issues are being discussed. Effective monitoring and appropriate response can help us pre-empt potential issues before they become major problems, can help guide our broader marketing efforts, and can even help us develop new products and services.

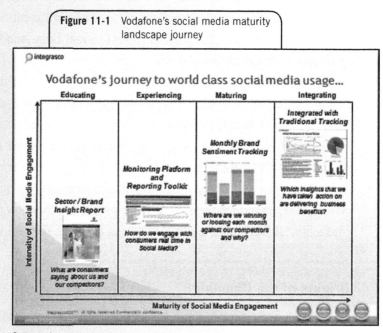

Figure 11-1 Vodafone's social media maturity landscape journey

Source: Integrasco.com

The key objectives for the project were to:

- Identify key influencers and engage with them around brand and campaign topics
- Generate positive sentiment and humanize the brand
- Reverse negative sentiment online

- Gather intelligence on the competition and gain customer insights to lead the market in innovation and customer service
- Identify and incorporate best practices for engagement
- Deliver a high customer query resolution rate and a satisfaction rate in excess of 85 percent

However, there were also some more specific goals of the campaign, and these were to:

- Surpass the nearest competitor in buzz volumes and sentiment impact
- Dominate the mobile handset discussion and be perceived as the mobile authority online
- Set up branded presences across the major social networks (Facebook, Foursquare, Twitter, and YouTube) and be present in more than 95 percent of all Vodafone-related online conversations in the U.K.

Details of the Approach

The methodology adopted for the project was based around four key principles:

Listening

Before embarking on the journey of social media engagement, Vodafone started by listening to find the relevant online consumer discussions about Vodafone, and then set up a process to continuously monitor the conversations.

Analyzing

In the U.K., buzz volumes and sentiment are measured across all social media channels in which users discuss not only airtime providers, but also general leisure activities (such as sports and music). The total percentage for each brand is calculated based on the total number of comments mentioning the brand, variations of the brand name, or any of the products or services for the brand, which are defined by a set of complex search queries that evolve over time and are qualitatively tested by Integrasco and the Vodafone team. At the core of the project was the goal of interpreting conversations and understanding the mindset of the consumer through analysis, to ultimately identify actionable insights.

Acting

A start-up Web relations team at Vodafone *(initially two employees)* was given access to and trained to use Integrasco's social media monitoring platform. Taxonomies or contextual searches were developed to ensure that the team could detect all relevant social media conversations and react with the online environment's need for speed and accuracy.

The team was given guidance about the nature of posts that merited engagement, and was consulted on topics that generate positive sentiment for the brand and drive brand association with products and services that would have otherwise been perceived as generic in the mobile telecommunications industry.

Achieving

The Vodafone U.K. Web relations team was extensively trained by Integrasco in the use of Integrasco's proprietary portal, regarding technical advice and complaints resolution. (This activity is undertaken in real time, 24/7.) Vodafone estimates that it identifies over 95 percent of all brand-related conversations online, typically within five minutes of the conversation's taking place.

Its own e-forum surveys demonstrate a resolution rate of 85.1 percent (exceeding the target of 75 percent) and a satisfaction rate of 86.3 percent (exceeding the target of 85 percent).

The project focused on U.K. social media conversations. A key requirement was to be able to identify over 95 percent of all brand-related conversations within social media and map all key influencers in U.K. social media related to telecommunications and mobile and airtime providers.

Stages of the Campaign

Integrasco divided the Vodafone campaign into five stages, numbered 0 to 4, as shown below.

Stage 0: Industry Landscaping and Influencer Audit

The objectives at this preliminary stage were:

■ To gain understanding of the brand reputation from a consumer standpoint (for example, what is actually recognized for the brand and what is not)
■ To identify and map out the influencers and platforms where relevant conversations are taking place
■ To gain understanding of customers' affiliation to a specific topic

Stage 1: Strategy Planning

Strategy planning included:

■ Workshops with key stakeholders
■ Sharing best practices
■ Developing goals and objectives

- Developing engagement strategies and engagement guidelines
- Developing a cross-functional team that worked with several areas of Vodefone's business operations in the U.K.

Stage 2: Implementation

The implementation stage involved:

- Setting up a monitoring platform for listening
- Developing search taxonomies
- Setting up social media presences and developing a credible online identity
- Training and workshops

Stage 3: Execution

The execution stage includes:

- Monitoring and early-issue detection
- Assessment and evaluation
- Recommendations and advisories
- Social media engagement
- Monitoring platform maintenance

Stage 4: Measurement and Evaluation

At this stage, the tasks at hand included:

- Measuring buzz and sentiment against goals and core KPIs (Net Promoter Score)
- Gaining actionable insights

The first three stages (0, 1, and 2) were put in place over the course of three months, starting in March 2009. Stages 3 and 4 are ongoing processes that were initiated fully in July 2009 after an initial pilot period in June 2009.

The Vodafone Web relations team is in constant contact with Integrasco to make sure that customer queries are resolved immediately, and the highest standards of customer service are achieved. Weekly status meetings ensure that best practice behavior is embedded. To inform engagement strategies and priorities, ongoing monitoring and analysis are done through a combination of the Integrasco proprietary technology platform and human analysis. Integrasco's methodology focuses on delivering qualitative, robust, analytical insights rather than purely quantitative data.

Data Collection

Accuracy starts with source data. Integrasco does not use third-party data [*author's note:* the subject of third-party or aggregator data was covered in Chapter 10] and legally collects all publicly available data, cleanses them, indexes them, and stores them on Integrasco's servers. While query taxonomy is not the most exciting topic for discussion, it is a very important one in the context of accuracy. Any user of search-oriented expressions (SOE), even through a desktop tool such as Google, will appreciate that a word search such as *orange* will deliver thousands of results, many having nothing to do with the mobile airtime provider.

Integrasco develops brand, product, and service taxonomies through a mixture of human and algorithmic processes and tools. This ensures an accurate mathematical distribution of buzz to brands and categories. Taxonomies are developed and tested to achieve the maximum possible containment and quality in output data sets.

Once fully quality-tested, brand taxonomies form the basis for providing accurate buzz volumes and sentiment measurement.

Measurement and Analysis

Integrasco measures buzz and sentiment at both a brand and a category level, defined according to Vodafone's requirements, in order to capture a complete competitive picture of consumer opinions in social media conversations. By drilling down into category peaks, the company's analysts identify emerging trends and fluctuations.

Knowing the issues that are the root cause of these fluctuations is critical to Vodafone's ability to address them. Early detection of issues that drive trends often provides valuable actionable insights for the client.

All major trends were analyzed and root cause analysis conducted to identify the buzz drivers, the issues driving the changes for the reporting period, in the context of:

- Overall period performance
- Changes to buzz volumes
- Changes to sentiment measurement
- Changes to product or category share
- Industry or sector versus brand issues
- Early detection of consumer issues
- Changes to the lead influencer and sentiment landscape
- Changes to platform volumes and penetration
- The addition of new blogs, forums, and platforms

Monitoring focuses not just on listening and reporting statistics, but also on identifying the trends and translating "what it means" and "who is influencing the discussion" in order to develop insights that are genuinely actionable by Vodafone. Integrasco tech-nology is language independent, and the analytics team is made up of multilingual analysts. The Integrasco team is globally scalable so as to meet its clients' requirements. The most important part of monitoring is to deliver actionable insights: who is winning, who is losing, why, and what Vodafone can do about it.

It is worth bearing in mind that the complexity of the mobile telecommunications industry, on the one hand, and the dynamic pace at which it is constantly evolving place additional pres-sures on the Integrasco analytics team to ensure that problems are accurately assessed and an appropriate strategic response is recommended.

Quality Control

Integrasco is an integrated part of the brand, PR, marketing, brand communications, customer service, and product quality teams, within its key retained clients, for providing social media monitoring services and tools. The company uses a collaborative approach with clients to develop reporting standards and mea-surement systems that are integrated into their core business sys-tems. Vodafone has access to a dedicated analytics team during its normal business hours.

Quarterly client satisfaction surveys ensure that Integrasco delivers according to the standards that Vodafone expects. Over the course of two years, Integrasco has consistently met its agreed reporting deadlines. One core requirement for Vodafone was that Integrasco must cover all relevant social media conversations in the U.K., and that is guaranteed on an ongoing basis, through inter-nal source discovery routines, client feedback, and data-delivery benchmarking. Apart from scheduled maintenance, Integrasco delivers 24/7 access to its service, allowing the Vodafone Web relations team to respond to customer queries in real time.

Challenges

To tailor the Integrasco platform to the evolving needs of Vodafone as the company became more experienced and efficient in its ways of engaging with its target audience was one focus of this project. An ongoing development process was constructed in which Vodafone and the R&D and analytics teams at Integrasco work together to define:

- Workflow requirements
- Source and data requirements
- Reporting requirements

The requirements were then mapped into milestone plans and developed according to the set priorities from Vodafone. As social media evolves with enormous speed, one of the biggest challenges is to continuously expand the source and data coverage to include the most relevant platforms and channels for online communications in the United Kingdom. This was done by dedicating resources from the Integrasco data management team to ensure quality through external tools and client reviews. Newer platforms have been included in the system as part of Integrasco's ongoing development plan. [*Author's note:* the newer systems referred to may be social media services such as Foursquare, Quora, and so on.]

The Results

Integrasco hadn't started with Vodafone U.K. as an online analytics provider, but rather as a social media consultancy focusing on online customer services and influencer engagement, as a word-of-mouth monitoring platform provider. The analytics and report delivery offerings developed as the client needs grew to integrate offline analytical reporting, along with buzz generated across social media channels.

Over the past two years, through active engagement across social media channels, Vodafone has been able to increase its online share of buzz [*Author's note:* "share of voice"] by more than 6 percent while the shares of all other brands have decreased. This makes Vodafone the second-most-talked-about operator in the United Kingdom.

After the first six months of engagement, Vodafone had successfully reduced negative sentiment, while at the same time steadily growing its overall buzz volumes in U.K. social media.

By tapping into the consumer mindset and dealing with customer issues in social media, Vodafone has successfully increased its customer satisfaction rates to over 80 percent in social media channels. Because of the success of the project, Vodafone expanded the team from two full-time employees to 15, and increased both buzz volumes and sentiment impact to regain the leading position in the market. Vodafone has also achieved the highest NPS (Net Promoter Score) for customer service in social media channels in the U.K. telecommunications market.

Conclusions

Vodafone successfully managed to build and maintain a strong online community through both branded channels on its own forum, Facebook page, Twitter, and YouTube channels, and also on external forums, discussion boards, and blogs. Data culled from the company's e-forums show that customer-problem-resolution and satisfaction rates exceeded their target.

The Net Promoter Score of this segment measured 35.1 percent, which is much higher than average, showing the true benefit of engaging with and supporting and assisting Vodafone customers.

Data Mashups

It's important to understand how to combine various sources of Web data effectively. The Vodafone case study is one example of information that, when combined or overlaid, provided greater value. Another example is the Havana Central restaurant chain, a typical small business that has close to 15 data streams to integrate, such as OpenTable, SeamlessWeb, GrubHub, Google Analytics, Radian6, and direct e-mail campaigns. Most of the data streams do not interoperate in any meaningful way, but eventually this interoperability problem will be solved. For the moment, using mashups, one can obtain results similar to using analytics platforms and tools available on the market or under development.

One solution to the interoperability issues may come from Facebook. If all data sources integrate with Facebook, it may be possible in the near future to provide interoperability, indirectly, via the Facebook API. However, this is pure speculation on the author's part.

The case for using Web analytics data, merged with social media listening data, is that they enable you to learn how much of the conversation being monitored online actually ends up arriving at a specific site (for example, a company Web site). This can be an integral part of social media return on investment, depending on how it is measured. The Radian6 platform, for example, integrates Google Analytics, Adobe Site Catalyst, and WebTrends Web Analytics.[2] Sentiment Metrics also integrates Google Analytics.[3] In general, site analytics data will be integrated into social listening platforms more often as time goes on. However, when measuring social media, we need to take a long-term view instead of regarding it as an immediate traffic generator (which is better suited for paid search, if the traffic is critically needed in the short run). Social media should be viewed as a long-term investment in building audiences of loyal fans.

Mashing Up Social Listening with Salesforce

When a customer representative provides information to a customer or prospect on Twitter or Facebook, how is the information stored, especially when another company rep might handle the conversation with the individual in the future?

The acquisition of Radian6 by Salesforce in March 2011 reinforced the likelihood that social media analytics platforms will include SocialCRM; Radian6 already had integration with Salesforce in place for over two years. Sysomos also has an integration with Salesforce, and many of the other listening platforms mentioned in this book interface with CRM systems. We can expect this trend of combining social listening with CRM to accelerate as we move into 2012.

Mashing Up Google Analytics and Social Media Monitoring

Google Analytics can track information from Google Places using custom URL tagging.[4] It should be possible to capture any mention of your brand or company and where it was generated with the listening process via the Google Analytics API. There is also a way to collect Google Analytics information (including social media traffic) and display it on Google Maps.[5]

However, a better way is simply to use custom segmentation for social media traffic in Google Analytics, and let the analytics chart it for you. Figure 11-2 shows the social media traffic segmentation of my blog, WebMetricsGuru.com, covering 2010.

Figure 11-2 Google Analytics country/territory visits to WebMetricsGuru.com

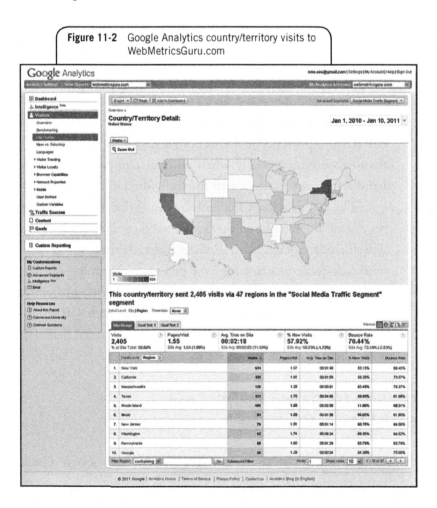

Mashing Up Social Media, Search, and Site Analytics Data

The same approach as used in the previous section can be applied with search engine visits. Figure 11-3 is a chart of the search traffic for the Havana Central restaurant chain in December 2010. In this chart, almost all search engine traffic to HavanaCentral.com originates in New York State [because the restaurants are located in New York City], so it is no surprise that most search traffic is generated by searchers who are living or visiting nearby.

Capturing Data from Product Locator Maps in Site Analytics

Merchandising and services Web sites contain product locator maps and, depending upon how Web sites are coded, information can be captured in site analytics that indicate the visitors interest in merchandise in a particular zip code or location.

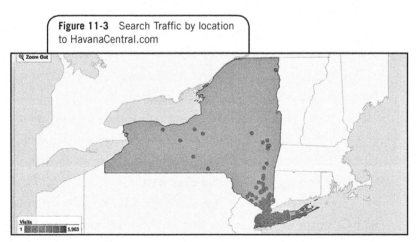

Figure 11-3 Search Traffic by location to HavanaCentral.com

Source: Google Analytics

While custom coding is often required to acquire information in Ajax, Flash, and JavaScript navigation pages, in many
other cases, the data are available and just need tweaking to collect them from site analytics and structure them into actionable
reporting [such as searches in a product locator by city, district,
or designated market area (DMA)]. Once the data are mashed
up, the brand can see which areas of cities have more demand
for its products and which areas have less, applying marketing
appropriately to meet short-term and long-term goals.

Mashing Up House Data with All of the Above

Often, a business has its own sales data or customer list data
that need to be merged with in-house site analytics data [such
as those from WebTrends, Google Analytics, and Adobe Site
Catalyst], including search engine visit data, site search data
for Web sites (internal search), and social media data. Most of
the time, custom programming and data repositories (such as
a data warehouse) are required, but there are some platforms
with the ability to mash up most data in one place.

Spreadfast's platform tracks and stores customer data
across several marketing channels (including Facebook, Flickr,
Hyves, LinkedIn, MySpace, SlideShare, Twitter, and You-
Tube) and blogging platforms (including Blogger, Drupal,
MoveableType, Lotus, WordPress, and any XML-RPC–based
blog.) With Tubemogul's professional and enterprise plans,
you can also publish videos to a wide variety of video sites.[6]
Custom integrations with social listening platforms such as
Crimson Hexagon are available, as well.

Spreadfast does not deal directly with "house" data, but
it does capture most of the rest of the information, including site analytics. It does not capture search engine traffic or

search rankings, although it might be able to derive them via site analytics. Geolocation data, produced by mobile devices, is only rarely mashed up, yet this seems a fertile area for business intelligence and analytics integration.

Other platforms such as SearchMetrics.com capture search engine rankings and site analytics data, but do not capture social listening information or house data. The ability to mash up data for social intelligence is quickly evolving. But the technology has still has not matured, and there is no single solution that makes it easy to capture the full spectrum of available Web data.

As a result of mashing large amounts of data together, it is possible to find the holy grail of data integration and business intelligence, depending on how intent the business is to collect and use the information.

Case Study: Econsultancy and LinkedIn

Econsultancy is an online community for digital and multichannel marketing professionals. The company shares advice and insight about digital marketing and e-commerce with its members. More than 95,000 Internet professionals use the site for help in making decisions, building businesses, and finding suppliers.

The Challenge

LinkedIn is currently the world's largest business-oriented social network, with more than 50 million registered users. Given Econsultancy's vast range of reports and marketing knowledge, LinkedIn represented an ideal place to position and increase brand awareness. The sheer size of the network and the range of Econsultancy's reports presented a challenge. The company had a challenge in terms of targeting its audience because of the sheer size of LinkedIn and the range of its own reports.

Initial ideas from Econsultancy on how to present itself on LinkedIn included making a branded group. A dedicated user group is the most common and straightforward method of communication by companies on the site. Econsultancy operates a unique business model, however, which made that approach complicated. In order to adequately promote its research products, Econsultancy required a large, multifaceted user base whose members would be unlikely to interact with one another on all subjects. In addition, Econsultancy.com currently hosts several busy forums, so the risk of migrating internal traffic to a third-party platform needed to be mitigated.

Econsultancy required a strategic, regular method of interaction across the entire network.

Details of Approach

The first step for Econsultancy was to identify areas where it could relevantly contribute. LinkedIn runs an "answers" forum, which is divided into categories that were parsed into suitable RSS feeds based on their compatibility with key research and best-practice areas: affiliate marketing, e-commerce, e-mail marketing, mobile marketing, online advertising and PR, project management, SEO and PPC, social media, strategy and planning, user experience, and Web analytics and measurement.

Econsultancy also added feeds from external business forums, open Q&A groups (such as those of Yahoo! and Wiki Answers), and several based on Twitter searches. Because it was an experimental campaign, Econsultancy decided to use free tools to correlate these feeds. Initially they were parsed through Google docs, but this was quickly discarded because of the time lag. The company also considered using Yahoo Pipes but eventually settled on NetVibes as a fast, free, and flexible solution.

In addition to basic metrics, Econsultancy decided to construct a specific analytics architecture in order to incentivize the campaign using the following main elements:

- Source = Staff
- Medium = Answers
- Campaign = Individual

By designating individual staff members as "campaigns," Econsultancy could then easily see who posted what, where they posted it, and whether the post resulted in traffic and conversions.

To ensure participation by staff, Econsultancy had two options. It could either make the answering process a part of all job descriptions or incentivize the campaign with a monthly rewards plan for staff driving the most traffic and/or generating the highest revenue. The first option was dismissed as impractical and an unfair additional demand on time and on staff members who were not directly related to the reports and editorial database.

The campaign analytics allowed Econsultancy to track this easily and make a small prize available [Econsultancy decided on Amazon vouchers] at the end of each monthly period.

Rollout

The rollout took place in two phases.

Phase 1

The editorial team carried out the initial testing. Analytics code was provided to be added to the end of any links posted. Problems encountered during testing included the fact that manually adding tracking code was too time-consuming and cumbersome.

The solution the team hit upon was adding a widget to the site for all staff members. When they signed in on-site, a small "Share This" link appeared. Each staff member could then generate a unique tracking code for any page on site, including reports, membership, and blog posts. Content was then easily shareable, and a custom bit.ly link (ec.ly) helped improve brand visibility when links were posted, as shown in Figure 11-4.

Phase 2

The campaign was then rolled out to include all staff members. Each day, the social media manager chose the best/most relevant questions from a variety of forums and forwarded them to a custom "Answers" e-mail address. All staff who wished to participate could subscribe to get mail from this address.

Figure 11-4 Using Share This widget to track Econsultancy posts

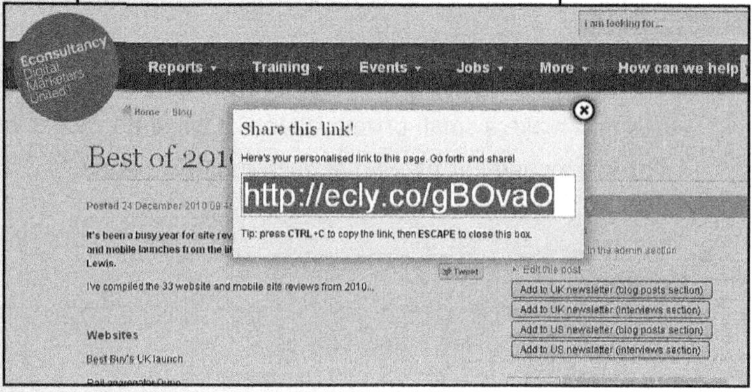

Source: Econsultancy

Significant Variables

The Econsultancy campaign's initial testing received a huge boost because of a viral article on the company blog. A link was shared by an Econsultancy staff person on LinkedIn that resulted in over 21,000 views. This early boost skewed the initial measurements, although it helped help Econsultancy prove the viability of the campaign. Over a three-month period, figures stabilized and the company started receiving new, valuable traffic.

Figure 11-5 shows the figures for the monthly period of November 23, 2010, to December 23, 2010.

Answers provided 6,937 visits, making it Econsultancy's eighth largest source of traffic.

Here are some further results:

- Bing provided 2,510 visits, while Facebook delivered 4,419 over the same period.
- Total revenue for this period was about £8,500.
- Per-visit value was in excess of £1.20.

Meanwhile, data generated from Answers has provided value in several core areas:

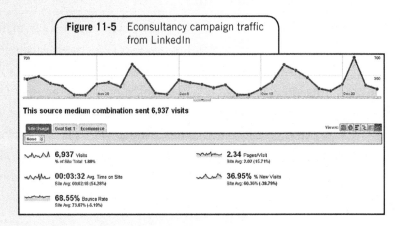

Figure 11-5 Econsultancy campaign traffic from LinkedIn

- Direct conversion to membership and purchase revenue
- Increased brand awareness and positioning across all forums
- Increased targeting of existing reports

Additionally, the ability to identify the trends in question has increased Econsultancy's ability to directly target future reports and guides to suit market demand.

What's Next?

Econsultancy will maintain continued engagement across LinkedIn and associated industry forums, including data gathering and awareness campaigns for branded groups. Links will target across relevant blogs in new markets.

Econsultancy will also expand into new markets, particularly in the U.S. and Asia, with relevant data and information in order to position the company as a leading source for digital marketers worldwide and increase its membership.

Case Study: Famecount

Famecount is a free service that gathers stats and rankings on the most popular profiles across the main social networks, including Facebook, Twitter, and YouTube.

The site ranks people and organizations based on their fan, follower, and subscriber numbers, and gives rankings based on country and category [categories include, for example, actors, food brands, and nonprofits]. The site also provides a Famecount ranking based on a person or brand's aggregated popularity across Facebook, Twitter, and YouTube.

The Challenge

Soccer is a matter of life and death for many people across the world. Its fans have an incredible competitive rivalry and sense of passion about their teams. And perhaps no nation is more passionate about soccer than Turkey. Meanwhile, Facebook penetration has grown significantly across many soccer-playing nations. Turkey has become the fourth-largest Facebook population in the world, with over 23 million people on the network as of November 2010.

These two phenomena together have led social networks, and Facebook in particular, to become a key medium through which soccer fans engage with and show support for their teams. This, in turn, has created a hunger from both fans and the teams themselves to understand how teams compare on the network and to see the key popularity trends.

By summer 2010, the leading Turkish team Galatasaray, based in Istanbul, was the most popular team on Facebook, of any sport, in any country. This was an extraordinary achievement, as the team outperformed such global superstars as Manchester United, Real Madrid, and the LA Lakers. Turkey's Facebook penetration, the passion of the team's fans, and its effective digital marketing were all factors explaining the Galatasaray team's popularity on Facebook. For the first time, Famecount's rankings enabled people to compare teams' popularity on social networks and view trends based on live data.

There was great interest in the rankings from soccer fans, the media, and the soccer teams in Turkey. Data were featured extensively in Turkish national press and in blogs and forums, and Famecount received a vast amount of Web traffic and e-mails from fans and stakeholders (including threatening e-mails from fans of lower-ranking teams). All these stakeholders wanted to answer the key questions, such as which team is the most popular, where does my team rank, and what is the trend and why?

Among the stakeholders interested in these data are the key clubs themselves, for whom relationships with fans are the core of their business. Social networks have become a key marketing vehicle for teams that use the networks to communicate key messages to their fans and to maintain engagement and support. Among the soccer teams whose social media managers use Famecount are Barcelona (the top sports team on Facebook as we go to press) as well as Turkish teams Fenerbahçe and Galatasaray.

The Solution

Galatasaray, led by social media manager Ebubekir Kaplan, used the Famecount data to put his team's performance into competitive context. Among other things, the data gave visibility to a large number of fake Galatasaray pages, some of which were taking fans away from the team's official channels.

Galatasaray was able to consolidate the fans of some of these unofficial pages to its own official page, giving a greater reach of its fan base. With the team's 4.7 million fans as of December 2010, Galatasaray is now nearing saturation of its Facebook connected fan base. Famecount also gave Kaplan a better idea of how U.S. teams, such as the LA Lakers, built significant communities around Twitter.

Galatasaray increased its focus on its Twitter communications, with the result that followers have increased more than tenfold within a year. Twitter became an important medium of dialogue with fans.

Conclusion

There is a need for organizations and for their customers [in this case, soccer fans] to understand social network data in a comparative context. Famecount met the need to answer the question "Which team is on top?" in the context of the world's major sports teams. Teams use the data to help benchmark themselves on the networks and to identify best practices across the sector. The competition induced by Famecount's public league table helps motivate teams' efforts to reach fans more effectively on Facebook and other networks.

Summary

While social media data are always interesting in themselves (*at least, for an analyst*), when business owners are able to combine data and layer them effectively, the information will become more useful and actionable.

chapter **12**

Where We're Going: The Future of Social Media Analytics and Monitoring

What will likely take place in the next few years in social media analytics and social listening? For starters, I believe we will be moving beyond keyword-based queries into machine-learning algorithms. Influencers whom I have spoken with echo similar ideas about the increasing use and refinement of latent semantic indexing (or some variant of it) and other machine-learning algorithms[1] in order to improve social listening, automatic categorization of content, and the ability to take action on the data.

In Chapter 4, we explored the use of ITA's Needlebase (now owned by Google), Glide Intelligence, Crimson Hexagon, and other applications of latent semantic indexing (LSI) employed by companies such as SAS, as better ways for extracting meaning from Web data. However, semantic information can also be gathered from sources that are not on the Web, such as internal house data, e-mail lists, or other internal databases.

The Crimson Hexagon Opinion Monitor, for example, provides several advantages over traditional keyword-based

searches, yet most of the benefit comes from proper training. Crimson Hexagon is just one example of future semantic analysis capabilities. Other machine-learning algorithms
will gradually mature and will largely replace keyword-based
searches (though it is difficult for me to envision a future
where keyword searches would be eliminated entirely).

Yet, replacing keyword-based searches has to happen, as it
has become too difficult to write effective queries. In addition,
those same queries need to be maintained. As we saw in Chapter 10, most listening platforms were initially modeled after
search engines (look at Giles Palmer's interview in Chapter 10
on the origins of Brandwatch.com), and they are running into
the same problems as Google[2] regarding the massive amounts of
online spam and content that is difficult to categorize well (as we
explored in Chapters 7, 8, and 10, categorization of online content is fundamental to providing actionable data and insights).

It appears that the earliest social media analytics platforms appeared in 2004, but the same could be said for social
media itself (according to the Merriam-Webster dictionary,
the first known use of the term "social media" occurred in
2004).[3] Following this line of thinking, social media analytics
began as an early stage of experimentation by entrepreneurs,
computer scientists, and some marketers to figure out how to
make sense of and capitalize on the growth of social media.

After seven years, we are in a position to evaluate social
media analytics platforms and to summarize what the industry has achieved and where it is going next.

As the future of social media analytics materializes before
us, analytics vendors appear to be even more directly focused
on improving the accuracy of their keyword-based queries,
while, more or less, ignoring machine learning. However, I
think the best solutions will incorporate both. I expect that as

more data are combined (Chapter 11) and further processed (using machine learning), we will see increases in the accuracy and usefulness of social media analytics platforms.

As the first-generation and second-generation platforms evolved from the use of keyword-based queries, keywords may still be our primary way of searching for information, but keywords have also limited how well we can define what we are searching for. Given all the linguistic variants (see Chapter 3), along with the limited query length (Chapter 10), keyword searching as a basis for gathering social media data is already showing its age.

One way to improve the accuracy of keyword search involves choosing sources of information carefully, performing custom crawls in order to gather the specific information a client wants, tuning keyword queries with a high degree of precision, and placing the results in a taxonomy or classification system that is meaningful for the project or client. (This is the approach that the Synthesio, Integrasco, and Brandtology platforms cited in this book appear to be using.) But as most self-serve platforms leave the user in charge of choosing sources of information and keywords and filtering the results; the results are becoming more disappointing as the Internet becomes more crowded with spam content. In addition, humans are needed to calibrate search queries and ensure their quality, often on an ongoing basis. Most of this is too expensive to set up and maintain.

That's why I predict the rise of machine-learning algorithms designed to make it simpler and more accurate for us to search and improve the quality of information we pull out of the social media.

Machine-learning algorithms can also be used to map content with the appropriate marketing goals, such as engagement. For example, according to Don Springer (a founder of the company Collective Intellect), Collective Intellect's CI:Insight[4] can run analysis on a data set at regular intervals to detect when individuals are ready to interact with a brand, thus facilitating humans' engaging respondents at the right time.

Another use of advanced intelligence is harvesting and targeting online profiles against specific demographic and geodemographic requirements, such as targeting people who want to go to Las Vegas and linking their online profiles to other aspects of their visit, such as choosing the right hotel, entertainment, or dining venue.

Case Study: Beehive

Beehive Strategy is a Hong Kong–based digital strategy consulting company established in 2010. Its goal is to help companies to transform their business in the new digital era by applying data-driven methodologies to open up a new dimension and approach to manage their business both offline and online.

In 2010, Beehive Strategy introduced Beehive Methodology, a management process that assists companies in using data to improve business strategy as well as in transforming their digital channel into an active business model that saves cost and increases return on investment.

Beehive Strategy provides advice and solutions on how to improve digital channels in order to increase traffic and reach potential customers. In addition, Beehive offers a complete digital strategy for businesses, with a detailed explanation and analysis of digital performance, such as Web site traffic and visitors' behavior patterns. The company also provides a monthly analytics service that helps monitor clients' digital channels to maximize their return on investment.

Beehive Strategy was founded by Kenneth Kwok, who has over 12 years of digital experience. Kwok started his career as a Web designer and later became a digital strategist. He spent most of his career with IBM, managing IBM.com and providing consulting services, which offered his blend of design, development, and management skills to IBM's clients globally.

A New Way to Track Offline Effectiveness

Many companies have become proficient at tracking online campaign and marketing efforts by using Web analytics software. On the other hand, in the new digital world, businesses also want to understand the influence or impact of offline media effectiveness. Therefore, Beehive's goal is to leverage QR code with Google Analytics, as well as a mobile device, to track the effectiveness of offline campaigns.

Beehive initiated a project to enable business to track the effectiveness of a marketing campaign both online and offline. This way, the business owner can identify which channel is the most effective.

In many cases, offline marketing is very hard to measure, but Beehive made the first attempt to measure online marketing via QR codes. The key driver for the project was developing a new way to gather data that business owners can use to measure offline campaign effectiveness, and to find how mobile devices can be leveraged.

In this project, the method being use to capture the data was a five-step process:

1. Add Google Analytics campaign tracking code to a URL.
2. Use the QR code being generated by bit.ly (the URL is shortened).

3. Print the QR code image and place it where people can scan it with their mobile devices, such as a storefront campaign (common in restaurants and other retail locations), or even on a menu or item of clothing. The possibilities as to how and where QR codes can be placed are endless.
4. Instruct the user to scan the QR code on a smartphone using a QR code reader or application on the mobile device.
5. Once the user captures the QR code, the user data will go to Google Analytics.

This method was introduced to the audience in Hong Kong at the Web Analytics Wednesday monthly analytics gathering. WAW was founded by Eric T. Peterson, who also founded the Web Analytics Demystified practice and blog, which focus on best practices around analytics. These meetings take place globally (usually on Wednesdays).

The purpose of this QR code project was to provide the option for marketing teams to track and measure multichannel campaigns involving online and offline marketing and to prove that the technology can be used successfully.

The key performance indicator was driving traffic to the event page, and the project implementation ran for a month and took four hours to set up.

Problems Encountered

The major problem Beehive encountered was that people were not familiar with QR codes or how to use them. Hong Kong users were still using e-mail more than social media or any other channel, and the users no longer needed to combine the offline data and online data for each individual campaign (as they did in the past using e-mail campaign results and merging them with Web analytics data).

In fact, using QR codes, they can easily leverage the tools they already have and get results quickly; the data will allow marketers to better plan their campaigns, whether they are online or offline. Users can also track offline media by using a mobile device.

The results of the case study showed that mobile users spend more time on a main Web page than other visitors [who did not find the Web site using a mobile device]. But the results also showed that the number of new visitors to the Web site resulting from the QR code campaign was very low, which was puzzling. It was not clear whether visitors first went to the Web site on their computers, and then afterward used a mobile device with a QR code reader. As the QR code was included in printed material, the company expected a higher rate of new-visitors than through other channels (such as search engines, e-mail links, or Web site referrals).

The only disadvantage of using QR codes is the lack of deep penetration of QR code into any given market space.

Social Business Is Born

Recently the term *social business* has come into use. *Social business* may gradually overshadow the term *social media* to some extent, but will likely never entirely replace it. Business is ready to be social, is ready to embrace social media analytics, and is on an upward learning curve of discovering how it should be measured.

The Future Is Materializing before Us

As this book goes to print, social customer relationship management, or sCRM, is rising in popularity. There is talk about sCRM's return on investment, in the same way that social media ROI has been a part of the conversation. According to Ray Stoeckict, vice president of professional services at Intelestream:

> *The landscape is changing as a result of sCRM companies looking to target the "social customer." Social CRM is still in its infancy at the moment, and it's difficult to know who is offering the best proposition. This is something that will become more apparent over the next 18 months or so, but it means it's not as simple as relying on the big CRM players, simply because they're the most well-known.*
>
> *Whether they can translate their previous success in CRM to sCRM (the one thing that most people on here will agree on is that sCRM is lighting the way forward) remains to be seen. There are a number of smaller players cropping up in the sCRM space, so they must feel that they have something that can challenge the big boys.*[5]

Merging Web Analytics Fully with Social Listening

As we move into 2012, many of the social media analytics platforms have been acquired, or will soon be.

I advocated having independent third-party analytics firms provide metrics around campaigns and market research, but at the rate social media analytics platforms are being acquired, it is unclear how many truly independent measurement firms will exist in a year or two to perform the analysis on the behalf of MarCom and client firms. I believe there is an opportunity to provide independent analysis, much as accounting firms do for their clients, but it is as yet unclear what form this will take. Whether or not a crop of new independent analytics consultancies will emerge, empowered to audit marketing initiatives (as I suggest in Chapter 10), is anyone's guess.

What remains to be decided is whether the single place to view all data ends up being a combined Salesforce/Radian6 repository or a conventional data warehouse (which is also Salesforce's expertise). Perhaps we'll end up seeing both types of platforms emerge from Salesforce and its competitors, one that is more database-oriented and another that is more social media listening based. We are also seeing strategy consulting firms such as McKinsey dipping their feet into social media analytics with larger enterprises grappling with how to understand and use this data. No doubt we will see much more of this kind of consulting in the years to come.

Profile: Bob Pearson, Chief Technology and Media Officer of WCG

WCG is a global communications consultancy. Its clients include Genentech, Pfizer, Medtronic, and Wyndham Hotels. Before taking the position as WCG's CTO, Bob Pearson was vice president of corporate group communications at Dell and head of communications at Novartis. He is a frequent lecturer and a blogger and columnist for HarvardBusiness.com, CIO.com, and Adweek.

Take Us Inside WCG Today

Bob Pearson begins, "I've had the opportunity to speak with leaders at hundreds of companies in the last five years about what they consider important when discussing analysis, metrics, and all forms of measurement. I've also spent my share of time client-side as VP of communities and conversations for Dell and head of global communications for Novartis.

"Remarkably, the majority of measurement firms and teams fail to address the concerns of corporate leaders. Too often, the consultants of the world become so fascinated with their technology or approach that they forget that all great innovation in this space will be client-driven. Data can only become an insight when a company decides it is valuable and worth acting on. Insights that don't lead to corporate buy-in are as useful as last week's newspaper.

"If I were to summarize what leaders are asking themselves about the future right now, I would use these five questions:

1. **How do I learn about B2B markets?** We know B2C is different from B2B, but how? Our experience shows that you have to track behavior as well as data to analyze a B2B audience, which is often less vocal. Basically, as audiences talk less, behavioral tracking's importance increases.

2. **How will I integrate with all research activities?** Leaders want to harness all related insights and build competitive advantage. Few firms come in with solutions that enable all research and all agencies to benefit today. It's important to take a Switzerland approach to analytics aggregation.

3. **What action do I take?** If leaders can determine which actions their team should take on a regular basis, then they are benefiting from insights. If they are not sure, they just have data. Insights are worth investment. Data is a waste of money. That's the corporate view, whether you like it or not.

4. **Are the analytics scalable?** When 10 languages reach greater than 90 percent of people online, it becomes important quickly to be able to analyze global trends and look across languages for a single brand. If you are not globally agile, you are very limited.

5. **How do I prioritize the incoming?** The amount of data that is available is staggering and increasing on a daily basis. When Google is processing 20 petabytes—20,000 terabytes—of data per day and Twitter generates more than 8 terabytes in the same time frame, it is fair to say that our data overload is growing rapidly. If a leader has a team of 100, and they can all do only two things each day to improve the business online, what are those 200 'things' in priority order?"

Pearson continues, "Overall, the trend for the analytics marketplace is quite clear, at least from the perspective of today's Fortune 500 leader. The field is wide open for those firms that can consistently provide insights that will lead to increased brand value, sales, and customer satisfaction. Those who cannot translate data into reliable insights that can be acted on in real time will be left at the roadside."

Summary

Much more could be said about the future of social media analytics and social media monitoring, but we will bring this discussion to a close here. As we move forward, all indications are that there will be some surprises, perhaps sort of an event horizon. Practitioners in the analytics field may be too close to see where the future lies and what is going to take place—a classic "can't see the forest for the trees" dilemma. We will all be partaking in it as it occurs.

Certainly in the Web analytics realm, there is a consolidation going on between site-centric Web analytics and social media analytics with the release of Adobe Omniture's SocialAnalytics, which should be available around the time this book goes to press. According to John Lovett at the Web Analytics Demystified blog, SocialAnalytics will solve many of the attribution issues around tracking social media and relating it to already established business and Web site metrics (see John Lovett's quote below, which I published on my blog early in 2011, about Adobe Omniture SocialAnalytics):

You could then trend the social data from campaigns and mentions against any metrics that you currently use within SiteCatalyst such as visitors or conversions. Thus, you could monitor the impact of your social marketing as a driver for website traffic and determine what percentage of that traffic actually purchased online as a result of the social campaign. The tool does this by making a correlation (versus actually pinning causation), but the statistical confidence will deliver assurance as to the validity of the correlation. This is magical. It actually enables users to quantify ROI from social marketing activities with a degree of statistical confidence. No one else has this that I'm aware of today.[6]

Beyond Adobe Omniture SocialAnalytics, we need to place social intelligence in the cash register or point of sale system to track transactions from social media to the money spent, thereby squaring the circle of social media return on investment, at least from the commerce perspective. I have posited this point of view several times in blogs recently, and it looks as though all the signs of a full convergence of analytics, marketing intelligence, and retail operations are before us.

In terms of the premise of this book, the fragmentation of technologies for social analytics and social listening, the gap between the providers or sellers of information and the buyers or clients of that information was not so apparent a few years ago. But now the gap between what clients or buyers want and what information the platforms and tools are capable of providing is so evident and so out of sync that few, if any, get the results they are expecting. That's why I wrote this book.

Today it is still true that the vocabulary of the average client, of these platforms and tools has not yet developed the ability to describe what they really want to know, while vendors still provide solutions that fail to deliver results that make any sense. But that situation is changing for the better.

My hope is that this book on social media analytics provides insight, clarity, and understanding, and is a part of a change for the better and of the improvement of the practice as a whole.

NOTES

CHAPTER 1

1. http://www.webmetricsguru.com/archives/2009/09/social-media-campaigns
-take-time-3-months-1-year-for-results/

2. I had been intrigued by the sharp increases in searches on the term *social media monitoring* and wrote about this at WebMetricsGuru.com at the end of 2009: http://www.webmetricsguru.com/archives/2009/12/400-rise-in
-social-media-traffic-due-to-search-engines-google/

3. http://www.webmetricsguru.com/archives/2010/08/facebook-places-web
-journal-august-15th-19th-2010/

4. http://blog.hubspot.com/blog/tabid/6307/bid/6450/Facebook-Places
-Launches-Allows-Businesses-To-Check-In.aspx

5. http://www.webmetricsguru.com/archives/2010/05/geo-local-social-media
-monitoring-and-missed-opportunties-of-social-media/

6. http://www.scribd.com/doc/38176762/Tracking-Social-Media-ROI-using
-Spectrum-Analytics

7. http://www.web-strategist.com/blog/2010/04/22/altimeter-report
-social-marketing-analytics-with-web-analytics-demystified/?utm_
source=feedburner&utm_medium=feed&utm_campaign=Feed:+Web
StrategyByJeremiah+%28Web+Strategy+by+Jeremiah%29&utm_
content=Google+Reader

8. http://www.webmetricsguru.com/archives/2010/04/social-marketing
-analytics-framework-review-share-of-voice-part-1-of-10/

9. http://social.venturebeat.com/2009/11/29/brightroll-says-video-ad-profits
-are-soaring/

10. http://www.slideshare.net/Ifonlyblog/iab-measurement-framework-for-
social-media-final4-3?from=ss_embed

11. Request for quotes should include Flash and Ajax tracking, but rarely do.
http://www.webmetricsguru.com/archives/2009/10/web-analytics-belongs
-in-rfps-and-pitch-proposals/

12. http://www.webmetricsguru.com/archives/2010/10/seo-enablement-for
-ajax-websites-and-social-media-monitoring/

13. John Lovett mentions Adobe Creative Suite 5 and the Omniture tracking enablement at http://john.webanalyticsdemystified.com/2010/06/22/
be-still-my-analytical-heart/

14. http://www.webmetricsguru.com/archives/2009/10/great-insights-about
-cookie-arbitrage-and-analytics-2010-at-sempo-ny-presents-the-great
-conversion/

15. Linden Labs made several improvements over the past two years, including the ability to address "in world" objects from outside the virtual world as per the announcement at https://blogs.secondlife.com/community/technology/blog/2009/07/07/http-in-and-lsl-communications

16. Eric T. Peterson is probably the most authoritative voice in Web analytics: http://blog.webanalyticsdemystified.com/weblog/2009/10/are-you-ready
-for-the-coming-revolution.html

17. http://www.webmetricsguru.com/archives/2009/08/more-on-using-radian6
-to-collect-video-views/

18. The DFI was first mentioned at http://www.zocalogroup.com/2009/07/
making-social-media-measurement-meaningful.html

19. http://blog.ogilvypr.com/2009/06/introducing-conversation-impact-social
-media-measurement-for-marketers/

20. http://fluent.razorfish.com/publication/?m=6540&l=1

21. My thoughts about three agency models for measuring the impact of social media are at http://www.webmetricsguru.com/archives/2009/09/on
-measuring-social-media-thoughts-and-a-scorecard/

CHAPTER 2

1. http://www.theharteofmarketing.com/2010/10/market-segmentation-with
-social-media.html

2. http://www.demographicsnow.com

3. http://marketing.about.com/od/demographics/a/generationmktg.htm

4. That there is no single demographic to follow this year: http://adage.com/
article?article_id=139592

5. The U.S. Bureau of Labor Statistics has a massive database of information that can help define the attributes of a target audience: http://www.bls.gov/

6. http://www.internetnews.com/stats/

7. http://www.claritas.com/MyBestSegments/Default.jsp

8. http://www.hitwise.com/us/:

9. ComScore Products are often used for media planning, and many other types of research are available at http://comscore.com/Products_Services/
Media_Planning_Analysis

10. Weeplaces.com is one of the newest audience research tools.
http://www.webmetricsguru.com/archives/2010/08/weepages-review
-foursquare-historical-visualization-platform/

11. Twitter Demographics was created over a weekend at the TechCrunch Disrupt Hackathon in May 2010: http://www.twitterdemographics.com/

12. DoubleClick Ad Planner view of DaniWeb.com: https://www.google.com/adplanner/#siteSearch?identifier=daniweb.com&geo=US&traittype=1&lp=false

13. Google Insights for Search for "TechCrunch": http://www.google.com/insights/search/#q=Techcrunch&date=today%2012-m&cmpt=q

14. http://advertising.microsoft.com/profile-matcher

15. www.Quantcast.com

16. Twitter is building a list of users' interests: http://www.telegraph.co.uk/technology/twitter/8016062/Twitter-building-interest-graph-to-target-users.html

17. http://blog.searchenginewatch.com/090311-094307

18. http://www.marketingpilgrim.com/2009/11/cup-of-joe-how-not-to-go-viral-and-look-like-an-idiot.html

19. Secrets of viral video creation: http://techcrunch.com/2007/11/22/the-secret-strategies-behind-many-viral-videos/

20. Tracking the viral spread of a video can often be done by looking at YouTube Insights (if the video lives mainly on YouTube): http://www.webmetricsguru.com/archives/2009/10/video-tracking-using-youtube-statistics/

21. ViralHeat provides several important monitoring features for a reasonable price; it also tracks the viral spread of your social media content: http://viralheat.com/home/features

CHAPTER 3

1. http://net-savvy.com/executive/companies/cic-data.html

2. http://www.socialmetrix.com/documents/SMXEcho-en.pdf

3. http://www.slideshare.net/lynneluvah/listening-to-multicultural-consumers

4. http://www.docstoc.com/docs/59408697/Linguistic-Challenges-Associated-with-Monitoring-Social-Media

5. http://en.wikipedia.org/wiki/Campbell-Ewald

6. http://www.criticism.com/linguistics/sociolinguistic-variable.php

7. http://blogs.forrester.com/nate_elliott/10-12-14-guest_post_james_mcdavid_on_how_smirnoffs_nightlife_exchange_brought_social_media_offline

CHAPTER 4

1. http://www.briansolis.com/2010/01/the-predictive-web
2. http://videos.webpronews.com/2009/11/13/matt-cutts-interview/
3. Ibid., www.briansolis.com
4. http://en.wikipedia.org/wiki/PageRank
5. www.needlebase.com
6. http://www.needlebase.com/videos
7. http://www.readwriteweb.com/archives/awesome_diy_data_tool_needlebase_now_available_to.php
8. Ibid., readwriteweb.com
9. http://www.sas.com/text-analytics/index.html
10. http://www.freepatentsonline.com/y2010/0145902.html
11. http://www.webanalyticsworld.net/2010/11/google-indexes-only-0004-of-all-data-on.html
12. http://theroxor.com/2010/10/28/the-awesome-size-of-the-internet-infographic/
13. http://www.readwriteweb.com/archives/theres_big_money_in_cyborg_mapping_apps_-_trapster.php
14. http://www.webmetricsguru.com/archives/2010/11/qr-codes-and-analytics-tracking/
15. http://www.revenews.com/barrysilverstein/rfid-hooks-up-with-social-media/

CHAPTER 5

1. http://www.forbes.com/2010/10/12/facebook-twitter-nike-followers-fans-social-media-marketing-zynga-cmo-network.html
2. http://www.syncapse.com/media/syncapse-value-of-a-facebook-fan.pdf
3. Ibid.
4. http://www.adweek.com/news/technology/value-fan-social-media-360-102063
5. http://www.allfacebook.com/how-we-got-to-40310-facebook-fans-in-4-days-2010-06
6. http://www.marketingpilgrim.com/2010/02/twitter-followers-worth-1-cent.html
7. http://kluriganalytics.com/2010/04/15/social-media-roi-value-of-a-twitter-follower/
8. http://seo.blogs.webucator.com/2010/04/01/total-twitter-follower-value/
9. http://www.bethkanter.org/24cents/

10. http://www.marketingcharts.com/direct/twitter-followers-seek-info-value-13770/
11. http://www.marketingcharts.com/direct/twitter-followers-most-brand-responsive-14186/
12. http://bits.blogs.nytimes.com/2009/01/09/are-facebook-friends-worth-their-weight-in-beef/
13. http://www.blogcalculator.com and http://www.tweetvalue.com
14. http://www.brasstackthinking.com/2010/06/analyzing-the-value-of-a-blog-post
15. http://altitudebranding.com/2010/05/13-truths-about-social-media-measurement/
16. http://www.scribd.com/doc/38176762/Tracking-Social-Media-ROI-using-Spectrum-Analytics

CHAPTER 6

1. http://en.wikipedia.org/wiki/Gabriel_Tarde
2. http://en.wikipedia.org/wiki/Paul_Lazarsfeld
3. http://www.mikearauz.com/2008/11/axis-of-influence-popularity-reputation.html
4. http://www.steverrobbins.com/the-book/
5. http://www.scribd.com/doc/38176762/Tracking-Social-Media-ROI-using-Spectrum-Analytics
6. www.mblast.com
7. http://www.mediabistro.com/prnewser/klout-helps-shankman-with-party-guest-list_b10832
8. http://klout.com/blog/2010/11/the-huffington-post-uses-klout-to-identify-top-influencers/
9. http://econsultancy.com/us/blog/6933-why-klout-doesn-t-count-putting-social-media-influence-in-context
10. http://www.web-strategist.com/blog/2010/04/22/altimeter-report-social-marketing-analytics-with-web-analytics-demystified/
11. http://www.freshnetworks.com/blog/2010/12/freshnetworks-social-media-influencers-2010-report-download/
12. http://www.webmetricsguru.com/archives/2010/09/peekyou-starbucks-case-study-using-peekdata-reverse-url-indentity-lookups-social-media-monitoring-platforms-will-improve-when-using-this-data/
13. http://www.mblast.com
14. http://pushkart.com/social_networth
15. http://pushkart.com/what-is-pushkart

16. http://technobabble2dot0.files.wordpress.com/2008/01/edelman-white
-paper-distributed-influence-quantifying-the-impact-of-social-media.pdf

17. http://www.webmetricsguru.com/archives/2010/01/social-media-influence
-formulas/

18. http://www.stoweboyd.com/post/2093344403/content-context-conduit-its
-not-who-you-know-but

19. http://www.technologyreview.com/blog/arxiv/24748/?ref=rss&a=f

20. http://www.stoweboyd.com/post/2093344403/content-context-conduit-its
-not-who-you-know-but

CHAPTER 7

1. http://semphonic.blogs.com/semangel/2011/05/more-examples-of
-semphonics-two-tiered-segmentation.html

2. http://net-savvy.com/executive/measurement/agency-approaches-to
-measuring-social-media.html

3. http://blog.ogilvypr.com/2009/06/introducing-conversation-impact-social
-media-measurement-for-marketers/

4. http://fluent.razorfish.com/publication/?m=6540&l=1

5. papers/Measuring%20Digital%20Word%20of%20Mouth.pdf

6. http://www.inbound-marketing-automation.ca/blog/2010/04/29/marketing
-analytics-and-marketing-management/

7. http://www.linkedin.com/answers/technology/blogging/TCH_BLG/
753731-58630600

8. http://www.syncapse.com/2010/11/syncapse-platform-gives-marketers
-ability-to-geo-target-content-on-brand-fan-pages-through-the-facebook
-platform-api/

9. http://www.web-strategist.com/blog/2011/03/16/the-state-and-future-of
-the-social-media-management-system-space/ (Note: See comment by
Meg@Syncapse.com in the blog.)

10. http://blog.infinigraph.com/social-intelligence-drives-improved-content-i

CHAPTER 8

1. http://www.slideshare.net/influencepeoples/attentio-simon-mcdermott

2. http://www.flickr.com/photos/gauravonomics/2323710051/

3. http://www.slideshare.net/influencepeoples/gary-angel-social-media
-dashboards

4. http://semphonic.blogs.com/semangel/2010/08/social-media-dashboarding -qa.html

5. http://www.toprankblog.com/2010/10/social-media-marketing-checklist/

6. http://www.collectiveintellect.com/blog/industry-specific-tips-for-using -social-media-analytics

7. http://www.collectiveintellect.com/blog/what-is-your-organizations-level-of -social-media-maturity

8. http://semphonic.blogs.com/semangel/2007/12/modeling_traffic.html

CHAPTER 9

1. http://www.webmetricsguru.com/archives/2010/11/the-social-media -organic-search-ecosystem-explained/

2. http://battellemedia.com/archives/2010/09/more_thoughts_on_demand_a_ referendum_of_sorts_on_google_and_social.php

3. Ibid., http://www.webmetricsguru.com/archives/2010/11/the-social-media -organic-search-ecosystem-explained/

4. Ibid.

5. Ibid.

6. http://www.facebook.com/havanacentral?v=app_4949752878

7. http://semphonic.blogs.com/semangel/2010/06/further-thoughts-on-data -warehousing.html

8. http://mashable.com/2010/01/26/maturation-social-media-roi

9. http://www.mpdailyfix.com/tactic-lust/

10. http://www.slideshare.net/ArtWilbur/social-media-measurement-using -google-analytics

11. http://www.google.com/support/googleanalytics/bin/answer.py?hl=en& answer=55578

12. http://www.slideshare.net/ArtWilbur/social-media-measurement-using -google-analytics

13. http://www.forrester.com/empowered/tool_consumer.html

14. http://www.forrester.com/empowered/tool_b2b.html

15. http://www.webmetricsguru.com/archives/2010/03/22k-and-altimeter -groups-social-crm-paper-plus-a-gap/

16. http://www.bantamlive.com/features/crm

17. http://www.slideshare.net/jeremiah_owyang/social-crm-the-new-rules-of -relationship-management

18. http://www.slideshare.net/martinwalsh/social-crm-definition-by-martin -walsh

CHAPTER 10

1. http://news.netcraft.com/archives/2010/09/17/september-2010-web-server-survey.html
2. http://net-savvy.com/executive/2010/06/
3. http://en.m.wikipedia.org/wiki/federated_search
4. http://www.webanalyticsworld.net/2010/11/google-indexes-only-0004-of-all-data-on.html
5. http://www.readwriteweb.com/archives/twitter_announces_fire_hose_marketplace_up_to_10k.php
6. http://www.webmetricsguru.com/archives/2011/04/radian6-summary-platform-and-other-radian6-improvements-recently-released/
7. http://net-savvy.com/executive/2010/06/
8. http://semphonic.blogs.com/semangel/2011/05/more-examples-of-semphonics-two-tiered-segmentation.html
9. http://www.webanalyticsworld.net/2010/11/google-indexes-only-0004-of-all-data-on.html
10. http://www.webmetricsguru.com/archives/2009/09/search-without-keywords-is-an-upcoming-trend-in-search-and-social-media/
11. http://no-mans-blog.com/2009/08/05/the-problems-with-social-media-monitoring-technologies/
12. http://en.wikipedia.org/wiki/Database_normalization
13. http://www.webmetricsguru.com/archives/2010/03/social-radar-update-and-romp-around-first-impressions/
14. http://www.ubercool.com/social-gui-future-of-control-panels/
15. http://en.wikipedia.org/wiki/Taxonomy
16. http://www.web-strategist.com/blog/2010/02/21/social-technology-buyers-matrix-broad-vs-specialized-vs-diy/
17. http://www.scribd.com/doc/29039169/How-to-Build-Your-Own-Social-Media-Monitoring-Service-Marshall-Sponder-Webmetricsguru-dot-com-3-31-2010-V2
18. http://londoncalling.co/2010/10/do-it-yourself-social-media-monitoring-not-for-the-faint-hearted-or-the-it-department/

CHAPTER 11

1. http://www.slideshare.net/webmeticsguru/the-future-of-social-media-monitoring-marshallsponder. (See slides 20 and 21.)
2. http://www.webmetricsguru.com/archives/2009/06/radian6-new-enhancements-plus-social-crm-webtrends-and-salesforce-intergration/

3. http://www.monitoringsocialmedia.com/page/Sentiment+Metrics+tool+info. See also http://www.sentimentmetrics.com/

4. http://www.seomoz.org/blog/tracking-traffic-from-google-places-in-google-analytics

5. http://freegeographytools.com/2008/plot-google-analytics-geographic-data-in-google-earthmaps

6. http://spredfast.com/info/features

CHAPTER 12

1. http://gking.harvard.edu/category/research-interests/applications/automated-text-analysis

2. http://techcrunch.com/2011/01/01/why-we-desperately-need-a-new-and-better-google-2/

3. http://www.merriam-webster.com/dictionary/social%2Bmedia

4. http://collectiveintellect.com/products/insight#page=insight

5. http://www.focus.com/questions/sales/what-are-best-cloud-based-crm-programs-virtual-companies/

6. http://www.webmetricsguru.com/archives/2011/03/socialcrm-scrm-and-web-journal-march-7-14th-2011/

INDEX

ABOUT THE AUTHOR

Marshall Sponder is an independent Web analytics and SEO/SEM specialist working in the field of market research, social media, networking, and PR. He provides digital data convergence generating ROI and develops data metrics, KPIs, and dashboards that drive businesses by setting and evaluating benchmarks.

For nearly a decade now, Marshall has been influencing the development of the industry, lately focusing on social media metrics. He also possesses considerable in-house corporate experience as a group leader at IBM and Monster, combined with contract work at Porter Novelli PR, and is currently a Senior Analytics Manager at WCG (Wiesscom Group); Marshall also has deep connections to the NYC start-up and development community and has his ear to the ground for any new developments and the next "new thing."

Marshall is Board Member Emeritus at the Web Analytics Association and Member of the Search Engine Marketing Professionals Organization (SEMPO) and WOMMA (the Word of Mouth Marketing Association). He holds an MA in Media Studies from the NY Institute of Technology and possesses a Certificate of Marketing Management from Baruch College.

CPSIA information can be obtained
at www.ICGtesting.com
Printed in the USA
BVOW08s1010130717
489169BV00006B/22/P